FUZZY-WUZZY

FUZZY-WUZZY

The campaigns in the
Eastern Sudan 1884–85

BRIAN ROBSON

Foreword by Field Marshal Sir John Chapple

'We fought with many men acrost the seas,
An' some of 'em was brave and some was not:
The Paythan an' the Zulu an' Burmese:
But the Fuzzy was the finest o' the lot.'

Rudyard Kipling

Spellmount Ltd
TUNBRIDGE WELLS

In the Spellmount/Nutshell Military list:

The Territorial Battalions – A pictorial history
The Yeomanry Regiments – A pictorial history
Over the Rhine – The Last Days of War in Europe
History of the Cambridge University OTC
Yeoman Service
The Fighting Troops of the Austro-Hungarian Army
Intelligence Officer in the Peninsula
The Scottish Regiments – A pictorial history
The Royal Marines – A pictorial history
The Royal Tank Regiment – A pictorial history
The Irish Regiments – A pictorial history
British Sieges of the Peninsular War
Victoria's Victories
Heaven and Hell – German paratroop war diary
Rorke's Drift
Came the Dawn – Fifty years an Army Officer
Kitchener's Army – A pictorial history
On the Word of Command – A pictorial history
  of the Regimental Sergeant Major
Marlborough – as Military Commander
The Art of Warfare in the Age of Marlborough
Epilogue in Burma 1945-48
Scandinavian Misadventure
The Fall of France
The First Victory – O'Connor's Desert Triumph
  Dec 1940-Feb 1941
Blitz Over Britain
Deceivers Ever – Memoirs of a Camouflage Officer
Indian Army of the Empress – 1861-1903
Waters of Oblivion – The British Invasion of the
  River Plate 1806-07
Heroes for Victoria 1837-1901
Commando Diary
Craufurd's Light Division
The French are Coming! 1803-05
The Glider Soldiers
Military Marching
Sons of John Company – The Indian & Pakistan
  Armies 1903-1991
A Guards Officer in the Peninsula 1812-14
Soldier On! The Testament of a Tom
Gentlemen's Sons

In the Military Machine list:

Napoleon's Military Machine
Falklands Military Machine
Wellington's Military Machine

In the Nautical list:

Sea of Memories
Evolution of Engineering in the Royal Navy
  Vol I 1827-1939
In Perilous Seas
Ordinary Naval Airmen
Haul, Taut & Belay – Memoirs of a Flying Sailor

In the Aviation list:

Diary of a Bomb Aimer
Operation 'Bograt' – From France to Burma
  – Memoirs of a Fighter Pilot
A Medal for Life – Capt Leefe Robinson VC
Three Decades a Pilot – The Third Generation
Bob Doe – Fighter Pilot
The Allied Bomber War 1939-45

© Brian Robson 1993

ISBN 1-873376-15-4

First published in the UK in 1993 by
SPELLMOUNT LTD
12 Dene Way, Speldhurst, Tunbridge Wells,
Kent TN3 0NX

British Library Cataloguing in Publication Data:
A catalogue record for this book is available from the British Library

Typeset by Vitaset, Paddock Wood, Kent
Printed in Great Britain by Biddles Ltd, Guildford, Surrey

This book is dedicated to Cynthia, Suzanne
and Vanessa, with love.

Contents

Illustrations

Maps

Foreword
Field Marshal Sir John Chapple GCB CBE

K IPLING'S poem from which this book takes its title was published
in the *Scots Observer* on 15 March 1890. It was subtitled 'Soudan
Expeditionary Force. Early Campaigns'. Thus it refers to the events of 1884
and 1885 covered by this narrative. There were two occasions in the two
Suakin expeditions when the British square was broken into, and both are
fully covered. There was also another dramatic setback during the parallel
campaign, at Abu Klea. All in all, the Sudanese proved to be a formidable
enemy and, as Kipling noted, they won the respect of the British soldier.

The Fuzzy-Wuzzy, as noted by the author, properly refers to the Hadendowa tribes of the Eastern Sudan, with their distinctive hair style of frizzed
hair matted with grease and coated with sandalwood – or as some authorities
say – bleached with lime.

Kipling, in the remarkable way that he had of absorbing the fine details,
had listened carefully to what the soldiers said about this first-class fighting
man. At various points in the poem he says:

> ''E squatted in the scrub an 'ocked our 'orses.'
> 'With 'is coffin. 'eaded shield an' shovel-spear'
> 'An' 'e's generally shammin' when he's dead'.

All of these characteristics are well illustrated in Brian Robson's account.
Having known the poem (nearly by heart) for many years, I had never
appreciated before how faithful an account it provided of what were two
very hard and, at times, bloody campaigns.

But the present account is timely on other grounds. It records two
expeditions, both of limited duration and neither very large in scale as these
things go. Both were very restricted in geographical scope. Although the
tactics and fighting differs markedly from today, there are some strange
echoes today regarding the mobilization, despatch and support for these
expeditions. In the last ten years the British Army has been engaged in two
limited duration, overseas expeditions; both, fortunately, rather more
decisive in their way. There were enormous differences but remarkable
similarities – and we cannot say that we were able to execute the plans today
with noticeably greater swiftness or efficiency. Indeed, this account brings
out very clearly how well the arrangements for transport, water, medical
support and all other logistical functions were addressed – and how

expensive these matters can be in terms of manpower. In the recent Gulf deployment under Operation Granby, 35,000 soldiers were despatched to the region. The one armoured division of two armoured brigades and one artillery brigade accounted for some 12,000 men. What were the rest doing? As Kipling would have said, 'that is another story, my best beloved.' Some of the answers are to be found in the campaign described here.

There is also a fine account of the post-campaign analysis regarding weapons, particularly machine-guns, swords and bayonets. The latter two certainly came in for some use, as the soldiers could testify. I shall leave the last word to Tommy:–

> 'An 'appy day with Fuzzy on the rush
> will last an 'ealthy Tommy for a year.'

Preface

I AM indebted first and foremost to John Andrews, lately Chief Librarian of the Ministry of Defence Central Library, and his staff for their unfailing kindness and patience in digging out the documents and books I have asked for. I am indebted secondly to the former Director of the National Army Museum, Bill Reid, and his staff for similarly providing documents but above all for producing most of the excellent contemporary photographs. The Library of the University of Durham, a major centre of Sudan studies, provided the striking photograph of Osman in captivity; it repays close study.

Air Vice Marshal Jim Fleming, lately Director of the Australian War Memorial, Canberra, allowed me to consult documents relating to the New South Wales Contingent and presented me most generously with copies of relevant books.

I am grateful to Michael Barthorp, Bill Carman and Herbert Woodend, Curator of the Pattern Room at the Royal Ordnance Factory, Nottingham, for expert help on aspects of uniform and equipment. Brigadier P.N.R. Stewart-Richardson very kindly lent me the diary of his uncle, James Drummond-Hay, extracts from which have appeared in the *Guards Magazine*. Dr Hew Strachan, of Corpus Christi College, Cambridge, allowed me to see the photographs of his visit to Suakin and the surrounding country in 1973, and Mr Pat Shipp read the manuscript with his usual scrupulous attention to detail.

While I have received help and encouragement from many people, the errors and faults are entirely my own. Experience leads me to believe that, despite the most rigorous checking, some mistakes will inevitably have crept into this final version. I can only hope that, like the housemaid's baby, they are only little ones.

I have dedicated this book to my family. Not surprisingly, they have never shared my interest in military history. I suspect that in their hearts they regard it as a form of advanced eccentricity. They may even, I suspect, have derived a certain pleasure from having such a genuine eccentric on their hands. But, by tolerating untold hours of neglect, they have put me permanently in their debt. It is right therefore to make them this small present.

Hove, 1993   Brian Robson

Introduction

E VERY BOOK requires a justification. The justification for this book is that it fills a gap which should have been filled long ago.

Wolseley's expedition up the Nile in 1884-5 to relieve Khartoum and rescue Gordon has attracted the interest of many historians and writers, and it is not difficult to see why. The spectacle of one lone Englishman, cut off and besieged a thousand miles from civilisation, fighting against the hordes of darkness, and of a small British army fighting its way forward against terrifying odds and arriving forty-eight hours too late – that is the stuff of which heroic romance is made. And it would be so even if the colouring was not heightened by the dramatic contrast between the two main characters; Gordon, the archetypal Victorian hero, deeply religious, without fear, celibate in the best public school tradition, driven by humanitarian zeal, and the Mahdi, the self-proclaimed messenger of God, the son of an obscure boatbuilder, who in three years had united the desert tribes, massacred a European-style army of ten thousand men led by a British general, and conquered an empire. That the obvious dissimilarities between the two men hid some deeper similarities adds to the piquancy.

Moreover, the availability of the electric telegraph, the photographic camera and the fast steamer enabled the details of the campaign to be brought promptly to the breakfast table of every British citizen. The spectacle of the broken square at Abu Klea, of the famous traveller Fred Burnaby dying of a spear thrust in the throat as he fenced with three savage opponents, of the tiny handful of the Desert Column – the cream of the British Army – struggling forward against seemingly overwhelming odds towards the steamers that would carry them the last few desperate miles to Khartoum, of the first sight of that city with the Dervish flags flying over it, of Wolseley waiting alone in his tent at Korti for news of success or disaster, and, above all, the ever-present sense of a critical race against time – all of these things helped to give the campaign a glamour and a fascination rarely, if ever, equalled in British military history. Even twentieth-century film makers have succumbed to the glamour with such films as 'The Four Feathers', 'Storm Over the Nile' and 'Khartoum'.

No comparable attention has been paid to the two campaigns which Sir Gerald Graham fought in the same period round Suakin, in the Eastern Sudan, even though they were directly linked to Gordon's activities at

Khartoum and to Wolseley's expedition. Yet there was also much glamour and heroism in those campaigns. The fighting was of the bloodiest kind, the enemy was perhaps the most extraordinary and formidable that the British Army had ever encountered, and overwhelming disaster hovered on at least two occasions. The participation of a contingent from Australia and the numerous offers of help from many other colonies marked an important step in the evolution of the Empire. The retention of a garrison in Suakin when the rest of the Sudan had been given up marked the acceptance of a permanent British interest in, and responsibility for, the Sudan. For good or ill, Britain was, henceforth, by reason of its garrison in Suakin, a Red Sea Power and the rivals there of the French and Italians. In turn, the occupation of the Sudan, with its direct access to Uganda and the heart of Africa, was to engender in the minds of Cecil Rhodes and others the dream of an All-Red route from Cairo to the Cape. That, in its turn, clashed diametrically with French plans for an expansion eastwards across the great grasslands of Northern Africa, linking the French empire in the West with the Nile and Egypt. It was the destruction of the Mahdiist state in the Sudan which enabled the British to forestall the French at Fashoda. There is thus a direct link between the activities of Osman Digna round Suakin and the dramatic confrontation between Kitchener and Marchand in 1898.

But this book is not really about imperial dimensions of that kind. It attempts only to fill in a relatively small historical *lacuna*, and, in doing so, to produce a more complete perspective of Gordon's activities at Khartoum and of the Relief Expedition which set out to rescue him.

Even given this modest aim and canvas, Graham's two campaigns have an interest and a compelling fascination of their own which deserve the attention of military historians. There is, first, the extraordinary nature of the British Army's adversaries. Religious fanaticism was nothing new for the British to encounter. They had come across it many times on the North West Frontier of India – from the Ambeyla campaign to the onslaught of the Afghan swordsmen at Ahmed Khel only a few years before. It had been a factor in the Great Mutiny in 1857 and in the New Zealand Wars. Equally, in their time, the British had encountered formidable foes of many kinds – Gurkhas, Burmese, Zulus, Pathans, Maoris, Sikhs. But the Hadendowa and their allies were something else, as Kipling recognised. No one had ever seen men who could take several Martini-Henry bullets and keep coming forward, men who, if they could not walk, crawled forward in the hope of striking a blow, men who would not be succoured but would instead try to kill those who tried to give them water. If one adds to that their extraordinary mobility and hardiness and the deadly nature of their weapons at close quarters, then the 'Fuzzy-Wuzzy' made an individual enemy who was not really matched until the British encountered the Japanese infantry in 1941. Killing the enemy wounded, while it happens on occasion in any army, has never been a British tradition; indeed, the reverse is true. Yet, in

Graham's campaigns, it became the norm for probably the first and, hopefully, the last time in our history. Kipling, as usual, caught exactly the sentiment of the British soldier in those campaigns – enormous admiration for his enemy, combined with intense regret that it should be necessary to fight and kill such remarkable people. (It seems, incidentally, to have been Kipling who coined the name 'Fuzzy-Wuzzy' under which Osman's men have entered into the British folk memory – there are relatively rare allusions in the memoirs of the period to 'Fuzzy-Wigs' but 'Fuzzy-Wuzzy', with its subtle implication of affection, seems to have been Kipling's own coining.) At the end of it all, we are still not really very close to understanding what it was that drove those men on to such feats of bravery.

The campaigns are a testimonial also to the steadiness and imperturbability of the Victorian soldier. Plucked at a moment's notice out of his peacetime barracks or from a troopship, and thrust almost immediately into action in a furnace of a land, against an extraordinarily formidable enemy, the soldiers of Graham's armies fought hard and emerged the victors. Perhaps the qualities of the Victorian soldier were never better shown than in the case of the men of the York and Lancaster Regiment in the 1884 campaign. Homeward bound from Aden, after thirteen years abroad, their wives and families with them, and looking forward keenly to seeing England again, they found their troopship diverted in mid-ocean, themselves disembarked with only the kit they stood up in, and in action within the week, while their families sailed on to England. At El Teb and Tamai the regiment bore the brunt of the action although woefully under-strength, a clear testimony to its dependability. And if, towards the end of the campaign, they started to grumble about their hard luck, that was, in the circumstances, both understandable and forgivable – as well as being in the British soldier's tradition. Equal admiration is due to the men of the Guards Brigade in the 1885 campaign. There could hardly be a greater contrast than that between performing public duties in London one week and campaigning in the Sudan three weeks later. Yet they took both in their stride.

The campaigns were significant on the British side for another reason. The campaigns in the Sudan, and particularly the two expeditions to Suakin, demonstrate the very high degree of logistical skill which the War Office and the Army had acquired by the last quarter of the 19th century. No one studying the proceedings of the Confidential Mobilisation Committee can fail to be impressed by the speed and efficiency with which the expeditions were equipped and despatched. In part, this was due to the availability of the electrical telegraph and the associated world-wide cable system. In part, it was due to the steamship, and, in turn, to the position of Britain as the dominant industrial and shipping power of the world. But it was also due to the way in which a better-trained staff corps and a professional, meritocratic civil service was able to focus the enormous amount of campaigning experience which the Army had accumulated. No army in the world possessed the depth and range of experience in all parts of the globe which the late Victorian Army had. That experience was now being harnessed in a thoroughly professional way and the results were becoming obvious. A very clear example was the speed and efficiency with which the Indian Government was able to assemble and despatch a brigade to Suakin in February 1885. Impartial observers commented on the way in which the Indian troops disembarked ready immediately for action, and on the high efficiency of their camp arrangements. This was a reflection of the constant campaigning experience which the Indian armies had at their disposal. It emphasised the role of India as the true strategic reserve of the British Empire, a role already vividly demonstrated seven years before, in 1878, with the despatch of the Indian contingent to Malta at the height of the Near Eastern crisis with Russia; and with the use of Indian troops in the campaign in Egypt four years later.

The campaigns round Suakin produced no significant technological innovation, except perhaps that it was the first time that the British Army had gone to war totally dressed in khaki. Nevertheless, a surprising range of technology was deployed in the two campaigns – the machine gun, the breech-loading rifle, the field telegraph, the optical rangefinder, the balloon, the railway, chloroform, sun-glasses, tinned provisions, distilled water, ice-making plant – none of these was new but it was perhaps the first time that all of them had been brought together in the same campaign. Although, in terms of tactics, Graham's two campaigns were old-fashioned, in their technology they represented a distinct step forward.

What is nowadays called 'media coverage' was fairly full but with gaps. The London newspapers were all represented in both campaigns but (with the exception of Bennett Burleigh) not by the major war correspondents, who preferred to wait and accompany Wolseley up the Nile. (Readers of Kipling will remember that the hero of *The Light That Failed*, Dick Heldar, was a war artist at Suakin when he first met his friends, the professional war correspondent, Torpenhow.) Again, while there is a fair photographic coverage of the 1885 expedition, I have found no photographs that can indisputably be dated to 1884. Both campaigns produced some splendid large scale paintings, notably by Giles and Fripp, but the only major writer who has been attracted to the campaigns is, inevitably, Kipling, in his poem *Fuzzy Wuzzy* and in his now largely-disregarded novel *The Light That Failed*. Not only is the hero of the latter present at Suakin in the earlier campaign but he meets his death dramatically from a Dervish bullet in the second campaign, after a journey on the armoured train which ran on the ill-fated Suakin to Berber railway (although Kipling takes some liberties with the chronology of the two campaigns). Kiplingites will, I hope, forgive my borrowing one of his titles for one of my own chapter headings. (Although I have used a quotation from one of Sir Henry Newbolt's poems because I thought it apt, the poem itself appears to have been inspired by Abu Klea rather than Tamai or Tofrek.)

The media coverage has to be balanced against a relative dearth of private accounts and, most particularly, of those of private soldiers and sailors. It is difficult, therefore, to catch the true flavour of life round Suakin for the ordinary soldier. What I have found, I have tried to use to maximum effect. On the Sudanese side, the dearth is total. Apart from the surviving pages of Osman Digna's so-called letter book, the *Daftar Waqa'i Uthman Digna*, which in any case does not cover the 1885 campaign, we know virtually nothing of Osman's thinking or planning, nor of the attitudes of his individual soldiers except insofar as these can be deduced from their actions. In particular, one is still left wondering about the precise mechanism which transformed the Hadendowa and their allies into such fanatical warriors in this period. During the long years of his captivity, Osman refused to speak of his experiences and thinking; with oral history techniques so much a part of the modern military historian's stock-in-trade, one would give much now for some carefully conducted interviews with him.

A word is inevitably necessary about the spelling of Sudanese names. Every author faced with the prospect of translating Arabic words into English faces the same problem – is he to use the most up-to-date, academically correct translations, or is he to use those versions which, however philologically corrupt, are nevertheless more familiar to his likely readers and will best enable them to make sense of contemporary documents?

Is it to be Suakin or Suakim or Sawakhin? Mohammed or Muhammad or Mahomet or Mahmet – the variations are almost endless. Osman Digna or Uthman ibn Abu Bakr Dignai (or Diqna)? The problem is not made any easier by the contemporary misunderstanding of local place-names, and by the British soldier's incurable habit of corrupting every foreign name into something he can get his tongue round – 'Wipers' being the most famous example, I suppose, although I have a strong regard for the man who corrupted Wadi Halfa into 'Bloody Halfway'. The problem is not confined to Sudanese names. M'Neill appears in that form in the Army List but elsewhere, in contemporary letters and books, as McNeill. This book is intended primarily for British readers and for non-Sudanese specialists so I have used those spellings which are the most familiar – so it is Suakin and Osman Digna. The purists may sniff but I hope they will at least understand.

Hove, 1993   BER

Prologue

IN OR ABOUT the year 1840, the wife of Abu Bakr Dignai, a prominent trader in Suakin, on the Sudan coast of the Red Sea, presented him with another son.

Abu Bakr was a Hadendowa, one of the five great tribes making up the Beja group. Arabised and converted to Islam several centuries previously, their ancestry included an infusion of immigrants from Asia Minor; the tradition in Abu Bakr's family was that they were descended from a Kurdish tribe from Diabekr, in what is now Eastern Turkey.

The Hadendowa were basically nomads but some of them had settled round Suakin. Across the water lay Arabia, with its insatiable demand for domestic slaves, and Suakin was on the great slave-trading route from Darfur, far in the west, to Jedda on the Arabian coast. Abu Bakr dealt in slaves as well as in other merchandise.

The son showed some academic bent and received a thorough education in Islamic law, theology, and astronomy. He joined his father's business, travelling as far as Darfur and Arabia. Slave trading was a precarious, if profitable, business. It attracted the envy and cupidity of Egyptian officials and, from 1854 onwards, the Egyptian Government attempted to limit, and then abolish, the trade altogether. In the course of this trading, Abu Bakr's son fell foul of officialdom and suffered captivity, confiscation and financial ruin.

By 1882 the Sudan was aflame with the news of a new Messiah, Muhammed Ahmad ibn Abdallah, who had proclaimed himself the Mahdi, the 'Expected Leader' of Islamic tradition, come to deliver the tribes from the corruption and tyranny of an alien administration, and to restore the purity of the True Faith. The fall of El Obeid, the capital of Kordofan, to the Mahdi at the beginning of 1883, sent a shock wave through the Sudan. What had seemed simply another minor rebellion now appeared to many to be a true revolution. In common with many others, Abu Bakr's son made his way to El Obeid in the early part of 1883 where he contrived to meet the Mahdi and his principal lieutenant, the Khalifa Abdallah. They were impressed with him and he with them, and in May 1883 he was appointed Amir (or Commander) of the tribes round Suakin, and despatched to conquer the area for the Mahdi.

For the next seventeen years, he was to be a dedicated and deadly opponent of the Egyptians, and of the British who succeeded them. Many thousands of British soldiers were to curse, and come to respect, his name as they sweated and toiled to catch and defeat him. He and his followers would be immortalised by Kipling, and the memories of 'the square that broke' would become part of the British folk memory.

His name was Uthman ibn Abu Bakr Dignai, which the British in their usual rough and ready way soon corrupted to Osman Digna.

1
Britain, Egypt and the Sudan

BRITAIN'S direct involvement in Egypt and the Sudan began at the end of the eighteenth century. Up till then it was a land known only to sailors, merchants and the occasional traveller; a land whose mysteriousness was symbolised for most people in Britain by those sinister travelling folk to whom the appellation 'Gypsy' was applied.[1]

Napoleon's invasion of Egypt in 1798, however, threatened the growing British empire in India. Whether Napoleon ever seriously considered emulating Alexander and invading India, and, even if he did, whether it was a practicable proposition is perhaps doubtful, but simply by occupying Egypt he was cutting off the most direct route to India. The instructions of the British military mission to Constantinople to enlist the aid of the Turks in expelling the French made the strategic interest quite clear: 'you will be particularly solicitous to direct the efforts of the Porte in such a manner as may destroy even the possibility of General Bonaparte's using any part of his force to the annoyance of the British Dominion in India.'[2]

Despite the destruction of the French fleet at the battle of the Nile in 1798, the French army remained in Egypt and it was clear that only a British force could expel them. Accordingly, in March 1801, a British army under Abercromby landed at Aboukir Bay and proceeded to destroy the French forces. A supporting expedition from India, under David Baird, landed on the Red Sea coast and reached Cairo in August 1801, just too late to play a major part in the campaign. Despite its strategic importance, and much to Napoleon's contempt, the British evacuated Egypt in 1803 but they were back in 1807 to forestall a threatened French re-invasion. This time, the force was too small and its objectives inadequately thought out; and it was unfortunate enough to be faced with a man of genius, Mehemet Ali,[3] who had seized power in Egypt from the ruling Mamelukes two years earlier. The unfortunate General Fraser was forced to agree to evacuate Egypt.

The defeat did not diminish the strategic importance of Egypt to Britain. Indeed, as the Indian empire expanded and its trade with Europe increased, the value of Egypt on the direct route grew. In 1820, Francis Chesney demonstrated that, contrary to previous professional opinion, a sea-level canal through the isthmus of Suez, connecting the Mediterranean with the Red Sea, was perfectly possible hydrologically. Five years later, an enterprising former naval officer, Thomas Waghorn, started a direct service, using barges and horse-drawn carriages, between Alexandria and Suez, whence fast ships took the traveller to Bombay and Calcutta.[4] By 1858, a railway traversed the route and played a major part in transporting troops to India to suppress the Mutiny. Even so, there was no interest in England in taking a more direct interest in Egypt: as Palmerston put it, 'We do not want Egypt or wish it for ourselves, any more than any rational man with an estate in the north of England and a residence in the south would have wished to possess the inns on the North Road. All he could want would have been that the inns should be well-kept, always accessible and furnishing him, when he came, with mutton chops and post-horses'.[5]

Two events in the 1860s destroyed that comfortable perception – the opening of the French-built Suez Canal in 1869 and the bankruptcy of the ruler of Egypt, the Khedive Ismail. It was the latter which gave Disraeli (and the Rothschilds) the opportunity to purchase a majority shareholding in the Canal in 1876. But this famous *coup* had two unfortunate consequences – it landed Britain in a potential entanglement in Egypt and it provoked a bitter rivalry with France, hitherto the dominant outside influence in Egypt. The entanglement could not, in practice, be avoided. By 1879, the finances and administration of Egypt were effectively in the hands of Britain and France. Much has been made in this context of the corruption and incompetence of the native Egyptian system but the fact was that much of the debt incurred by Ismail had gone very effectively into developing the economic infra-structure of the country. By 1879, exports were three times the value of imports and a British Government mission reported that the country was well able to manage its liabilities; what it could not do was to go on paying greedy European creditors at interest rates of twenty-five per cent. Ismail was nevertheless forced to resign in 1879 in favour of his son, Tawfik,[6] and under tight Anglo-French financial administration, the country prospered. Increased prosperity was, however, accompanied almost inevitably by an increase in nationalist sentiment. This had a number of sources – simple xenophobic resentment at the Anglo-French domination, Islamic revi-valism, the growth of liberal aspirations among the new middle-classes and the resentment of native-born Egyptian army officers at the dominance of the Turkish officers who monopolised the senior positions. As *The Times* put it, 'The army, we must remember, is the only native institution which Egypt owns. All else has been invaded and controlled and transformed by the accredited representatives of France and England.'[7] The rise of the nationalist movement was symbolised by the formation of a Nationalist Party, led by an Egyptian officer, Ahmad Arabi. In a bloodless *coup* in September 1881, Tawfik was forced to call a Parliament with power over the Budget. Arabi made a favourable impression on outside observers but his position was undermined by Tawfik, who intrigued at Constantinople for Turkish inter-vention, and by the French, who feared the effect of an Egyptian Islamic, nationalist movement on their North African possessions, particularly Tunis which they had only just occupied. Through the negligence of the Foreign Secretary, Lord Granville, and the ignorance of the Prime Minister, Gladstone, the British Government was induced to put its name to an Anglo-French Note to Tawfik in January 1882. The message of the Note was clear; the two Powers were united in supporting Tawfik's authority, to the extent of intervening directly against any influence, external or internal, which endangered the Egyptian *status quo*.

It is difficult at this remove to understand how Gladstone, that opponent of all foreign entanglements, could have been brought to support such a Note, especially when his own envoy in Cairo, Malet, had just warned the Foreign Office that the nationalist movement was genuine and should not be discouraged unless vital British interests were directly affected. Even more curiously, at the very moment when the Note was being delivered, Gladstone was writing to Granville that 'Egypt for the Egyptians' is the sentiment to which I would wish to give scope; and could it prevail, it would, I think, be the best, the only good, solution of the Egyptian question'.[8]

The effect of the Note was predictable and wholly destabilising. Tawfik was encouraged to continue with his malevolent intrigues, the Parliament was stimulated to widen its demands, and Arabi and his supporters were forced to conclude that the British and French were hostile to all legitimate Egyptian aspirations. A riot in Alexandria led to the deaths of some fifty Europeans, including a Royal Navy petty officer, and was followed immediately by the summoning of a Conference of the Great Powers at Constantinople at the end of June 1882 which applied pressure to the Turkish Government to intervene militarily – at Egypt's expense. The Conference was overtaken by events. As a result almost certainly of misunderstanding and inadequate communication, the commander of the British naval squadron off Alexandria became convinced that the forts there were being prepared for a bombardment of his ships. Accordingly he opened fire on 11 July and landed a force of sailors and marines to occupy the city. The British were now faced with the need for a major military intervention, without the aid of the French who had disassociated themselves from the bombardment as unjustified and inimical to French interests elsewhere.

We need not concern ourselves with the details of Wolseley's successful Egyptian campaign. At the end of it, Britain found itself with a *de facto* protectorate over Egypt which was to last through seven decades and two World Wars. All historical events reverberate to the end of time and the events of 1882 resound in the Middle East today. The lineal political descendant of Colonel Ahmad Arabi was Colonel Abdul Nasser.

Among the problems which Britain inherited in Egypt was the Sudan and the religious uprising which was beginning to shake that country to pieces. Despite the vital importance to Egypt of the Nile, whose two basic constituents, the Blue and White Niles, unite at Khartoum, Egypt had paid little attention to the Sudan until 1820. There was little obvious incentive to do so

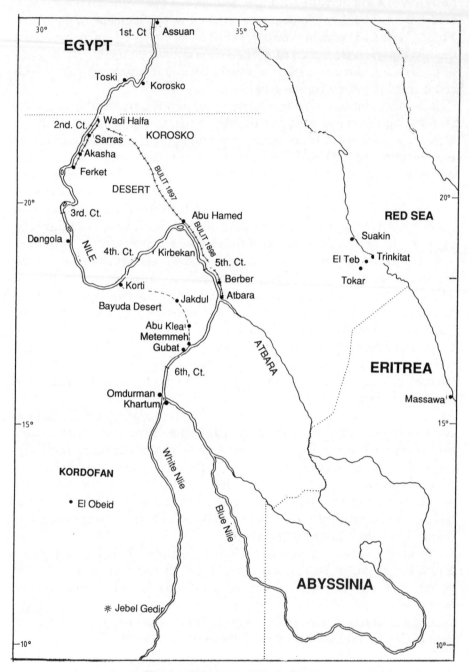

Map 1 Egypt & the Sudan

4

since the Sudan produced little of value except slaves, some ivory and a little gum, and was known to be a hell-hole of heat, dust and noxious pests. There was not even a proper boundary – Egypt simply petered out beyond the Second Cataract. Only a handful of trading posts along the Red Sea testified to any Egyptian interest at all.

Mehemet Ali saw a different vision.[9] For him, the Sudan was a potential producer of manpower and gold. Its possession would enable him to consolidate his control of the Red Sea and the huge pilgrim traffic to the Holy Places of Arabia. It would enable him to dispose finally of the remnants of the Mamelukes, who had taken refuge in the Sudan. Above all, there was the lure of opportunity; the Funj Sultanate of Sennar, the main power in the Sudan, was disintegrating and the fragments were unlikely to be able to stand up against a disciplined Egyptian army.

In 1820, Mehemet Ali's son, Ismail, invaded the Sudan and by 1824 Mehemet was master of the Sudan north of Khartoum, which was founded in the same year. The conquest was not easy or bloodless but when Mehemet Ali died in 1849 Egyptian rule had been largely consolidated in the Sudan, law and order and taxes introduced, and major strides made in the economic development of the country. There was alas! no gold and attempts to revive on a commercial scale the iron industry of Kordofan, with European help, had not been successful. But cotton growing and woollen manufacture had proved very successful, and the production of indigenous products such as ivory, ostrich feathers, cattle and palm products, and, above all, gum, for which the paper and confectionery industries of Europe had an insatiable demand, had greatly expanded.

The passing of Mehemet Ali was 'as though a gigantic dynamo had run down, leaving a silence broken only by the thin, metallic voices of the mechanics'.[10] With it came the end of the first great phase of Egyptian expansion in the Sudan. There was still much for the mechanics to do. To the west was the independent Sultanate of Darfur which menaced Kordofan. To the south lay the largely unexplored tropical regions of the Bahr al-Ghazal and Equatoria, inhabited by negro peoples and linking up with the Great Lakes of Central Africa. To the south-east was Abyssinia, the legendary Christian kingdom of Prester John, with whom the Egyptians had been carrying on a spasmodic border war since 1837. But, for the moment, the Egyptians in the Sudan largely marked time, the only major development being the decision to abolish the slave trade.

The succession of Ismail, a grandson of Mehemet Ali, as Viceroy in 1863 started the second great expansionary phase of the Egyptians in the Sudan. His objectives there were much the same as his grandfather's – to strengthen the government, to expand the economy (inter alia, by developing all forms of communications) and, significantly, to extend his territories. We have already touched upon Ismail's qualities. If, in the end, his personal extravagance and his failure to grapple adequately with the problems of public

5

finance were to bring him down, the fact remains that much of his debts was incurred in improving economic and social conditions in the Sudan and in extending its boundaries. Like his grandfather, he hoped ultimately that the Sudan would become a source of financial and economic strength to Egypt. Like him, he was to be disappointed despite the success of much of his policy.

Economic development under Ismail centred partly on the growth of cotton production, aided by the American Civil War which greatly reduced the world supply of cotton while it lasted and made cotton production in the Sudan increasingly profitable; the flourishing industry of today is largely a memorial to Ismail. No large-scale improvement in the economy of the Sudan was possible without major improvements to communications, internal and external. The creation in 1864 of a flotilla of steamers based on Khartoum was a major initiative. Equally important was the laying of a telegraph line which finally reached Khartoum in 1874 and linked it directly to Cairo. By 1875, both Suakin and Kordofan were linked to Cairo. In parallel the postal service throughout the Sudan was enormously improved. By 1874, the transit time of a letter from Cairo to Khartoum had been reduced to 28 days. Elsewhere, improvements in the mail service were aided by regular steamship services from Suez to Suakin and Massawa, the latter two ports being assigned once again in 1865 to Ismail in return for the revenues being paid to the Ottoman administration in Arabia. Most important symbolically, perhaps, was the inauguration in 1873 of a railway from Wadi Halfa across the desert to Metemmeh on the Nile, some ninety miles north of Khartoum. Alas! it had come too late, its start coinciding with the crisis in Ismail's finances. A short-sighted decision by the European Controllers of the Debt stopped the line at Sarras only thirty-three miles on from Wadi Halfa. The absence of a railway beyond Sarras was to have incalculable consequences in the fight against the Mahdi.

It could be argued that Ismail's greatest achievement in the Sudan was the huge extension of its boundaries. In 1873, Egypt took over the Bahr al-Ghazal although in practice its government was prudently left in the hands of Zobeir, the slave trader who had hacked out a private fief there. Sir Samuel Baker was hired in 1869 to extend Egyptian territory southwards from the Bahr al-Ghazal towards the Great Lakes. Baker was succeeded in 1874 by Charles Gordon as governor of the new province of Equatoria. By 1876, he had succeeded in pushing the limits of Egyptian influence, if not actual rule, to a point only some sixty miles from the northern shore of Lake Victoria and nearly a thousand miles from Khartoum.[11] On the Red Sea coast, Ismail pushed vigorously southwards from Suakin, at one point reaching Kismayu, within the area claimed by the Sultan of Zanzibar. Britain, the protector of the Sultan, forced Ismail to withdraw and an agreement in 1877 left Egypt in nominal possession of the Somali coast as far south as Ras Hafun, some four hundred miles east of Berbera. Such an extension, coupled with a vigorous extension of Egyptian influence in the area west of Massawa, was bound to create further causes of friction with the Emperor Theodore in Abyssinia. Fortunately for Ismail, Theodore was foolish enough to provoke a British expedition which occupied his capital and killed him. It was not until the Sudan was under Mahdiist rule that Abyssinia was in a position to wage serious war again. The crowning success of Ismail's expansionist policy was the conquest of Darfur at the end of 1874 although, in truth, the conquest was actually the work of Zobeir.[12]

Leaving aside for the moment the rise of the Mahdi's revolt, there were no significant changes in the Sudan between the abdication of Ismail in 1879 and the arrival of British rule in Egypt as a result of Wolseley's campaign in 1882. A snapshot of the Sudan in 1882 would have shown a country where trade, aided by steadily improving communications, was on the increase. The great central core of the country, from Wadi Halfa to Sennar and westwards into Kordofan, had been under Egyptian rule for sixty years and even if that rule was now exhibiting some signs of stagnation in the way of corruption and venality amongst its officials, it could not sensibly be described as cruel or tyrannical. A well-organised, if fragile, system of administration was backed by a comprehensive and not ineffectual code of law. An Egyptian army of some 33,000 maintained a reasonable semblance of law and order. Obviously, the picture was slightly different in the newly-conquered and distant provinces of Darfur, Bahr al-Ghazal and Equatoria. But, even there, energetic European governors were striving to bring peace and order and it is not unreasonable to think that, in time, the conditions of the northern Sudan would have spread to the outlying areas. From an Egyptian point of view, the great disappointment was that the Sudan was barely self-financing; the financial stream which Mehemet Ali and his successors had hoped would flow into Egypt had not materialised.

If there was a major cause of discontent among the Sudanese it lay in the attempts to suppress the slave trade. The impetus given by Said had never been wholly lost and under Gordon's rule at Khartoum between 1877 and 1880 the trade had indeed been virtually suppressed. But large numbers of the most influential Sudanese had derived profits from the trade. Its virtual abolition hit them hard and left them angry and ripe for trouble. And although much progress had been made in training and promoting Sudanese into government and military posts, supreme power still lay in the hands of Egyptians or Europeans, lumped together generically by the native Sudanese as 'Turks'.

It was into this situation in June 1881 that a religious man from Dongola stepped, proclaiming himself the Mahdi, the 'Expected Leader' long foretold by Islamic teaching.

7

1. Inaccurately, since they originated almost certainly in India or Central Asia.
2. Lord Granville to Brigadier General Koehler 11 November 1798 – see *Royal Engineers Journal*, Vol XIV (1911), p92.
3. Mehemet Ali was an Albanian who had started life in the tobacco trade and then entered Turkish service as an irregular (bashi-bazuk).
4. John Tillotson *The Overland Route to India* (London, 1928), p28-53.
5. A.E.M. Ashley *Life and Correspondence of Palmerston* (London, 1879), p338.
6. Ismail, prudently equipped with the Crown Jewels and £3M in cash, left in the Royal Yacht for Constantinople where he died in 1895. Until 1867, he had been legally only the Sultan of Turkey's Viceroy in Egypt but in that year he acquired the title of Khedive (or hereditary ruler) although the Sultan remained nominally his overlord until 1918.
7. *The Times of London* for 12 September 1881.
8. Gladstone to Granville 4 January 1882 – quoted in R. Robinson, J. Gallagher and A. Denny. *Africa and the Victorians* (London, 1961), p95.
9. I have drawn heavily in this section on Richard Hill *Egypt in the Sudan 1820-1881* (London, 1959).
10. I owe this felicitous phrase to Hill, op cit.
11. In turn, Khartoum is some 1200 miles, as the crow flies, from Cairo.
12. In fact, the Sultanate of Darfur ceased to exist only in 1916 when the last Sultan, Ali Dinkar, set out to seize Kordofan. It ended in his army being slaughtered by a British force in square in a battle not essentially different from Tamai or Abu Klea.

2

The Land and the People

'When God made the Sudan, he laughed' – Arab proverb

BEFORE 1882 only a handful of British travellers and adventurers like Gordon and Samuel Baker had penetrated the recesses of the Sudan. Unlike South, East and West Africa, it had little or no natural resources other than gum to attract European entrepreneurs. For the European Powers, it had no strategic value and nothing to offer the tourist. Hence they knew little of either the land or the peoples.

In classical times, the Sudan (which literally means in Arabic 'Land of the Blacks') had applied to the whole wide belt of territory stretching across Africa from the Red Sea to the Atlantic, roughly between the twenty-second and tenth parallels of North latitude. By the 19th century, the term had become more constricted, covering roughly the area of the modern Sudan, from approximately 5° North to 22° North, and westwards from the Red Sea to 22° East. To the east it was bounded by the Red Sea and the mountains of Ethiopia. To the west, it merged into the great grasslands of Central Africa. Northwards there was no obvious boundary except the Second Cataract at Wadi Halfa which marked a navigational limit for large sailing vessels. To the south, the swamps and tropical vegetation of the Equatorial Province merged into what is now Uganda and Zaire. Within the area of the modern Sudan lay the classical area of Nubia, stretching along the Nile from the first Cataract at Aswan to the sixth Cataract, just north of the confluence of the Blue and White Niles.

The Sudan embraces a wide variety of climates and topography and peoples. North of Khartoum, where the Blue and White Niles merge, the country is largely sandy desert, hot and dry. The only real areas of cultivation lie along the Nile itself. This is the land of the camel-owning Arab tribes. Their natural gaze is northwards down the Nile to Egypt or eastwards along the caravan trails to the Red Sea and Arabia from which many of their ancestors came originally. South of Khartoum is the land of the cattle-owning Arabs. Between the Blue and White Niles the area known as the Gezireh is enormously fertile, watered as it is by the overflowing of the two Niles. Southwards and westwards, into Kordofan and Darfur, the land is savannah, suitable for cattle raising but still hot and dry, with the location of villages and towns predetermined by the wells and waterholes. As one goes further

9

south, the Arabised tribes give place to negroid tribes – the Shilluk and the Dinka, the Nuer and the Azande, the Acholi. The country becomes steadily more humid and tropical. This is the land of the Sudd, the great floating islands of vegetation which block the flow of the Nile from its source in the mountains of Ethiopia and force it into a thousand channels, forming a huge waterborne maze through which the canoes of the tribesmen find their way easily but where steamers and large sailing boats could be totally halted. The Equatorial Province is part of Central Africa; it has little or nothing in common with the Northern Sudan.

The peoples were equally varied. In the Northern Sudan the tribes were Arabised, speaking dialects of Arabic, following Islam and sharing Arabic concepts of culture. While essentially Arab in culture, language and beliefs, they were an admixture to a lesser degree of the original Nubian inhabitants, tribal emigration from Arabia and the immigration of Turkish or Armenoid peoples via Egypt. Along the Red Sea littoral, the Beja tribes, while Arabised in religion and culture, continued to speak their own Hamitic languages although understanding Arabic. South of Khartoum, the Arabised tribes contained an increased element of negroid blood. In Kordofan, small pockets of the original negroid inhabitants, the Nuba, survived in the Nuba mountains where they maintained a degree of independence, not merely of the Egyptian Government but, in due course, of the Mahdiist state as well. In Darfur, the Fur people retained their dominance, negroid but Muslim. In the Bahr al-Ghazal and the Equatorial Province, the inhabitants were primarily negroid and non-Muslim although Arabs formed the ruling class, having gone there in search of slaves and ivory.

The Northern Sudan struck Europeans as harsh and bleak – a hell of heat and dust, with few, if any, redeeming features. G.W. Steevens, the famous Victorian war correspondent, who accompanied Kitchener's expedition up the Nile in 1898, wrote 'People talk of the Sudan as the East; it is not the East. The East has age and colour; the Sudan has no colour and no age – just a monotone of squalid barbarism. Nothing grows green. Only yellow halfa grass to make you stumble and sapless mimosa to tear your eyes; dom palms that mock with wooden fruit and sodom apples that lure with flatulent poison. For beasts it has tarantulas and scorpions and serpents, devouring white ants and every kind of loathsome bug that flies and crawls. Its people are naked and dirty, ignorant and besotted. It is a quarter of a continent of sheer squalor. Overhead the pitiless furnace of the sun, under foot the never-ceasing treadmill of the sand, dust in the throat, tuneless singing in the ears, searing flame in the eye – the Sudan is a God-accursed wilderness, the empty limbo of torment for ever and ever.'[1]

No doubt Steevens' description was deliberately heightened to exaggerate the hardship since he was, after all, in the business of selling newspapers and books. But probably few soldiers sweating up the Nile or trudging in dusty squares across the plains round Suakin would not have said 'Amen'. Even

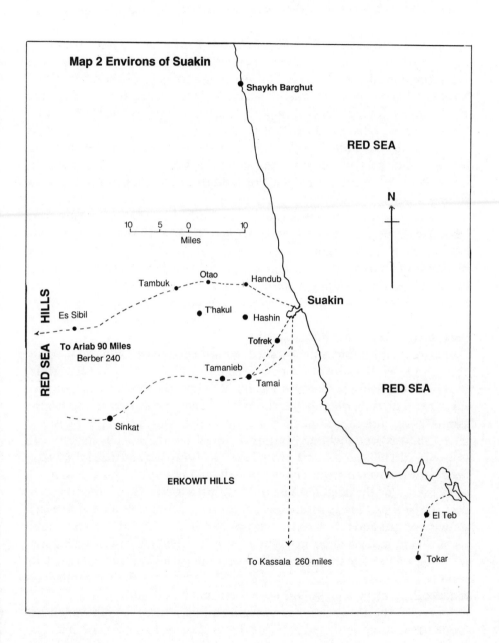

Map 2 Environs of Suakin

Shaykh Barghut

RED SEA

N

10   5   0   10
Miles

RED SEA HILLS

Tambuk   Otao   Handub

Es Sibil   T'hakul   Suakin

Hashin

To Ariab 90 Miles   Tofrek
Berber 240

Tamanieb
Tamai   RED SEA

Sinkat

ERKOWIT HILLS

El Teb

To Kassala 260 miles   Tokar

Steevens, however, could see that the Sudan had its attractions for some people: 'Perhaps to Englishmen – half-savage still on the pinnacle of their civilisation – the very charm of the land lies in its empty barbarism. There is space in the Sudan. There is the fine, purified desert air and the long, stretching gallops over the desert sand. There are the things at the very back of life, and no other to pasture in front of them – hunger and thirst to assuage, distance to win through, pain to bear, life to defend and death to face – You are unprejudiced, simple, free. You are a naked man facing naked nature.'[2] Steevens was certainly right about space. In 1882, the Sudan was roughly a million square miles in area – roughly a third of the size of the USA – with a population of perhaps eight millions.

This book, however, is concerned only with a tiny area of the Northern Sudan – that part which stretches along the Red Sea coast between the eighteenth and twentieth parallels of latitude, stretching inland for some twenty miles.

To the North the area was roughly de-limited by the main track from Suakin to Berber; to the south, it was marked off by the Erkowit Hills. Within that relatively tiny area, only some 40 miles by 20, was to occur some of the bloodiest and most critical fighting which the British Army was to encounter in the 19th century. When it was over, not less than 10,000 men had been killed or died of their wounds or sickness. When Sir Henry Newbolt wrote 'The sand of the desert was sodden red' he was scarcely exaggerating as regards the area round Suakin.

It started with a low, sun-scorched, coral-reefed coast, only a foot or two above sea level. Because of the coral, there were few harbours of any value, the chief ones being Suakin and Shaykh Barghut (the modern Port Sudan). Elsewhere, disembarkation was through surf and coral reefs on to swampy ground, as at Trinkitat. Inland, the country over which the fighting was to take place was overwhelmingly sandy or gravel desert, basically flat but with isolated small hills, and seamed with inumerable ravines and dried-up stream beds; it was covered with vicious, prickly mimosa scrub (Acacia arabica), often exceeding the height of a man. H.C. Jackson, who knew the area well, described it thus: 'The maritime plain extends inland for a distance of some ten or twenty miles and is covered in most places with scrub and the bushy adlib plant which, in years of normal rainfall, are sufficient to satisfy the undiscriminating wants of goats and camels. At certain periods of the year when the yellow, fluffy pompoms of the mimosa perfume the air with their gentle fragrance or the pink blossoms of the flowering tundub bush add a splash of colour to the scene, the desert assumes a peculiar attractiveness. Its inhospitality is hidden beneath a variegated covering that is pleasing to the eye, even if of no very great utility. The desert hare, ariel and Isabella gazelle are frequently to be seen. Bustards and the demoiselle crane wander about. Flocks of doves and sand-grouse flutter around a water-hole. The piping cry of a crested lark, as it rises just before the wayfarer, is borne plaintively upon the breeze'.[3]

This description underlines two aspects of the country – first, that all depended upon water supplies which were scattered and unreliable and, second, that the land had no natural resources of its own. The land is not waterless – in many places, water is available near the surface, by digging. But such supplies are restricted in quantity and it was extremely difficult to water any very large bodies of men or animals. Round Tokar, wheat was grown in some quantity but depended critically upon the main rainfall in the winter months. When that failed, as in 1888, the crops failed also. Suakin then acquired critical importance as the main importing centre for grain and rice. For the rest, goats and camels provided some milk and, occasionally, meat.

Inland, the Red Sea Hills, running north and south, roughly parallel to the coast, effectively shut off this part of the Sudan from the great central plain of the Sudan. Rising to heights of around 4,500 feet, the hills are not an impenetrable barrier to movement by men or animals, and water was available in the lower foothills. But their jagged ravines and boulder-strewn slopes presented a formidable barrier to the building of a railway or a road suitable for wheeled vehicles, of which, in 1884, there were virtually none in this area of the Sudan; all goods went by camel or donkey.

The combination of heat mirage, scrub and ravine meant that visibility at ground level was often poor, and the enemy's camps and villages difficult to locate at a distance.[4] Attackers could creep up unseen close to their enemy, fields of fire were usually severely constricted and cavalry movement was frequently difficult. It was a country which favoured the surprise guerrilla attack and placed a premium on effective defences being erected wherever troops halted for a night. It was a country where water was scarce. The native tribesmen were inured to it; but European or Indian troops could operate effectively only if adequate water supplies could be organised and carried. Fierce heat completed a picture which had led to the bitter Sudanese proverb 'When God made the Sudan, he laughed'.

The peoples inhabiting the Red Sea littoral belonged to the Beja group of tribes, the main sections being the Hadendowa, the Amarar, the Ababda, the Beni Amir and the Bisharin. Of these, the Hadendowa and the Amarar played the most important part in the events of 1884-85. The precise origins of the Hadendowa and the Amarar is still a matter of scholarly dispute. They still largely resemble the pre-dynastic Egyptians and this may well be the basic stock. But it has certainly been modified by some negroid influence, by the immigration of Arabs from Arabia and by immigration from Armenia. As we have seen, Osman Digna's family believed that its ancestors were Kurds from what is now Eastern Turkey.

The Beja tribes spoke a language which is part of the great Hamito – Semitic languages to which Arabic, Hebrew, Aramaic and Amharic also belong. As befitted nomads and traders, the Beja understood, and even spoke Arabic. Among the tribes, the Hadendowa had a reputation for being

13

proud, sullen and uncommunicative. (The name Hadendowa comes from two Beja words, 'had', meaning 'chief' and 'endowa', meaning 'people'. The Hadendowa were thus 'The (Head or Chief) People'). All Beja tribes wore their hair in the distinctive, frizzed style which was to give them the nickname among the British soldiers of 'Fuzzy-wigs'. Several Europeans, intrigued, described the way in which this hair style was created. 'I noticed some who wore the hair frizzed till it stood out fully six or eight inches on either side of their heads' wrote Gambier-Parry, 'This extraordinary thick growth, half hair, half wool, was then parted over each ear and round to the back of the head, the hair below the parting being brushed downwards and outwards, and that above the parting upwards. A long wooden pin or thin stick was run through the top part of this erection and the effect was complete'.[5] Wylde added some further details: 'The way in which the hair is generally worn is to concentrate it on the crown of the head; it is then brushed and frizzed, the hair that grows round the head being frizzed downwards to reach the shoulders, making a perfect protection to the back of the neck. The hair is thoroughly saturated with grease, on which sandalwood dust, or the dust of any other scented wood, is placed. It looks very smart at first, but after an hour or two in the sun, the grease begins to run, and the dripping falls all over the shoulders and clothes![6] As Wylde indicates, the hair style had evolved to give protection against the fierce sun.

If, ethnologically, the Beja were different from Arab tribes of the Central Sudan, such as the Baggara, they were at one with them in their devotion to Islam and its concept of a holy war against all unbelievers, in which those who died for the Faith had an immediate reward in Paradise. Unfortunately, as elsewhere in the Sudan, the Beja tribes were divided among themselves; some, such as the Beni Amir, never joined Osman; others, notably the Amarar, who rivalled, if not exceeded, the Hadendowa in strength, split among themselves, some joining Osman while others stayed loyal to the Egyptian administration. It was to prove a fatal weakness.

Since climate was to have such a dominant military influence, it is necessary to say something about it. It is always hot in the Sudan in day-time even if it can be cold at night. Along the Red Sea coast, breezes from the sea helped to alleviate the heat. But even in winter, day-time temperatures rarely fall below 80° in the shade. the main rains fall in the winter months (October-February) and as spring approaches, temperatures begin to rise. By the beginning of May the day-time temperature around Suakin averages 96°. Inland, away from the cooling sea breezes, it is even hotter. The most unhealthy period for Europeans was from August to October. Once the rains came and temperatures began to fall, sickness rates declined. The best campaigning time was in the late winter – January to April. May marked the end of practical campaigning for Europeans, and troops kept on through the summer and early autumn were likely to suffer heavily. The Royal Marines battalion which was in Suakin from May 1884 until April 1885 suffered some 1400 cases of invaliding or death – that is to say, the battalion had to be replaced in effect nearly three times; in September 1884 the sickness rate was fifty per cent. The main diseases were heatstroke, typhoid (enteric) fever and dysentery, diseases still largely not understood at that time. Nevertheless, providing the campaigning season was chosen carefully, the Red Sea littoral was not a particularly unhealthy place and in Graham's two expeditions the amount of sickness compared more than favourably with India, Afghanistan or South Africa.

NOTES

1. G.W. Steevens *With Kitchener to Khartum* (London, 1898), p324.
2. Ibid, p325.
3. H.C. Jackson *Osman Digna* (London, 1928), p20.
4. Bennet Burleigh, the war correspondent, setting out from El Teb, had great difficulty in finding Tokar, only six miles away. Bennet Burleigh *Desert Warfare* (London, 1884), pp78-79.
5. (Captain E. Gambier-Parry) *Suakin 1885* (London, 1885), p31.
6. A.B. Wylde *'83 to '87 in the Sudan* (London, 1888), Vol II, p76.

3

The Mahdi

A T THE END of June 1881, a religious teacher living on the island of Abba in the White Nile, some 150 miles south of Khartoum, announced to his disciples and the surrounding tribes that he was indeed the Mahdi, the long awaited leader foretold by Islamic teaching. His name was Muhammad Ahmad ibn Abdallah.

Although it does not appear in either of the two great collections of sayings of the Prophet – the Koran and the Hadith – nevertheless the concept of a leader, who would appear in order to eradicate wickedness, avenge the blood of the slaughtered Imams (the immediate successors of the Prophet Muhammad) and bring righteousness and justice to the world, had appeared early in Islamic theology. The word 'Mahdi' means 'the Guided One' or alternatively 'the Expected Leader', and the first pretender to the title had appeared as early as the seventh century. Other claimants had appeared at frequent intervals down the centuries – in the nineteenth century alone there had been a handful and it is frequently forgotten that Muhammad Ahmad himself had a contemporary rival in North Africa in the person of the leader of the Senussi tribe. Muhammed Ahmad actually invited the Senussi leader to be one of his four principal lieutenants (Khalifas) but the latter refused and never came to Khartoum.

Muhammad Ahmad was the third son of a carpenter and boat builder from the island of Labab, near Dongola. His father claimed descent from the Prophet and Muhammad Ahmad had been deeply religious from early childhood. His father had died soon after he was born and an uncle had taken over care of the family and the boatbuilding business. Muhammad Ahmad was thus free to concentrate on following the religious life. At an early age, he had become a member of a Sufi order[1] and had spent long years in the study of Islamic theology, law and military history. After various wanderings, he had settled on the island of Abba, where he assembled a band of disciples, including the future Khalifa, Abdallah ibn Muhammad, of the Taisha branch of the Baggara. Over the years, his reputation for sanctity had spread widely. In 1881, he was approaching forty and Ohrwalder, the Austrian missionary, who was his captive for ten years, described him as powerfully built, of dark brown complexion and carefully tended skin, with a pleasant smile which showed to advantage the prominent slit between his front teeth. According to Ohrdwalder, he had vigorously trained himself over the years to speak in a quiet, gentle manner, but he clearly had a magnetic, dominating personality and, as time was to prove, a strong strain of cruelty and ruthlessness in the service of the Faith. According to some Islamic commentators, the Mahdi, when he came, would be recognised by a V-shaped gap between his front teeth and a birth mark on his right cheek; Muhammad Ahmad was careful to emphasise that he had both.

During his years at Abba, Muhammad Ahmad (or the Mahdi, as it will now be convenient to call him) had made many journeys in secret throughout Kordofan and the Nuba Mountains. Thus, although the Ulema (the official college of Islamic theologians) in Khartoum denounced him as an imposter, the Mahdi could be sure of a substantial following when he made his announcement.

The Egyptian authorities were not slow to react to the news from Abba. Early in August 1881, Rauf Pasha, who had succeeded Gordon as Governor General of the Sudan in March 1880, sent one of his lieutenants, Abu Suud Bey, to talk to the Mahdi and to try to persuade him to go to Khartoum to submit his claim to the Ulema. The Mahdi refused and on Abu Suud's return to Khartoum, it was decided to send a company of troops with a gun to arrest him. The force was ambushed by the Mahdi and his followers and only a handful got back to the steamer and Khartoum; more than 120 were killed, including both officers. The alarm bells now began to ring in earnest in Khartoum and Rauf Pasha assembled all available troops from Khartoum, Sennar, Berber and Kordofan at Kawa, on the White Nile, a few miles north of Abba. But no attempt to advance on Abba was made and after hanging about at Kawa for a month, the force dispersed at the end of September having achieved nothing except to add to the Mahdi's prestige. In the meantime, the Mahdi had slipped away south-westwards towards the Nuba Hills, establishing his camp on the mountain of Gadir.[2] There was now no longer any attempt to hide or limit his objectives. To the tribesmen of Kordofan and anyone else who would listen, he set out his message clearly. He was the Mahdi, the Leader, the Divinely Guided One, come to restore the purity of the True Faith and to drive out the 'Turks'. His followers must trust in God, despise vanities of all kinds, look forward to the next world and rid the Sudan of the Egyptians who, by their corruption and pursuit of luxury, were betraying the Faith. What he was proclaiming was a Holy War in which those who died for the Faith were assured of a place in Paradise – 'God loves those best who fight for him'. It was a message of hugely powerful appeal to the unsophisticated, relatively poverty-stricken, desert tribesmen. Foreswearing all vanities was no great problem for people who had no resources or opportunities for luxury anyway; and although the Egyptian administration was scarcely oppressive, it was there, and essentially alien.

It may be as well to deal at this stage with the question of Egyptian rule as the major cause of the Mahdist rebellion. By 1881, the Egyptians had established an administration which covered the whole of the Sudan. But given the size of the country and the numbers of Egyptians (and other foreigners) deployed, it was a relatively fragile system. The power of the administration to enforce its rule and collect taxes rested essentially upon an Egyptian army which in 1881 numbered about 33,000, including many irregulars. That was a small enough force by any reckoning to control a country the size of Western Europe and measuring nearly one million square miles in extent. No doubt there was much petty oppression and corruption by local officials, and there is some evidence that taxation fell unfairly on those who were unable to evade it – that is to say, the city dwellers and riverain tribes. On the credit side, much had been done to stimulate trade, improve communications and establish a system of law; an increasing proportion of civil and military posts were being occupied by Sudanese. To view the Sudan in 1881 as a powder keg of discontent only waiting to explode is almost certainly an over-exaggerated view. Nevertheless, the spread of the Mahdi's rebellion makes it clear that there were serious factors of discontent present. Of these, the first was the fact that the Egyptian rule was an alien rule. The Sudanese did not distinguish over-much between Egyptians, Turks, Circassians and Europeans; they lumped them all together as 'Turks', foreigners and aliens. It was not so much the quality of the Egyptian rule as the fact that it was not an indigenous, Sudanese rule. Whatever their merits and efforts, the Egyptians were alien conquerors. Compounding this was a second factor. Although nominally Muslims like the great majority of their Sudanese subjects, the Egyptians and Turks were regarded as corrupt and impure Muslims, who debased the Faith and tarnished its purity. As with many primitive, unsophisticated peoples, the Sudanese tribesmen tended to be fanatical and austere in their religion. Twenty years before, the Wahabi movement had developed in much the same way among the primitive nomads of Arabia, as a movement to purify the Faith and bring it back to the simple, austere practice of its early years. Among the northern Sudan tribes, there was long-standing discontent at the Egyptian policy of suppressing the slave trade. Pursued with varying degrees of efficiency and success since 1854, suppression had been particularly effective under Gordon's reign as Governor General from 1877 to 1880. As a result, in 1881, many Sudanese, including the Danagla from whom the Mahdi came, were smarting at the losses they had sustained in the slave trade as as result of Gordon's crusade. Nothing in the Koran, and hence in the Mahdi's teaching, forbade the institution of slavery. Under the Mahdi, the slave-traders could look forward to a revival of prosperity. In turn, that would promote expansion elsewhere in the economy, including the great slave-trading port of Suakin on the Red Sea. Finally, there was a clear perception of an intangible slackening of Egyptian rule since 1879 when the Khedive Ismail had been deposed by Britain and France and the two Powers had assumed, through their control of the purse strings, the effective direction of the Egyptian administration. In the Sudan, the replacement of Gordon as Governor General by the gentler but weaker Rauf Pasha had contributed to the same perception that Egyptian rule was flagging. There was thus a reasonably favourable climate for the spread of a religious rebellion. Equally, the fact that nothing on the same scale had occurred before and that for the first three years it was essentially confined to Kordofan argues for the fact that Egyptian rule was both less oppressive and more effective than has sometimes been assumed.

The concentration, and then dispersal, of Rauf Pasha's forces in September 1881 had been watched with mounting impatience by Rashid Bey, the Mudir (Governor) of the province of Fashoda, 400 miles south of Khartoum, but only some 150 miles away from the Mahdi's camp in the Nuba Hills. He could see the danger far more clearly than the authorities in Khartoum and he pressed unsuccessfully for permission to attack the Mahdi. At the beginning of December, he took the law into his own hands and marched against the Mahdi's camp with some 1200 men. In the ensuing fight near the Jebel Gadir, Rashid was overwhelmed by the Mahdi's army, estimated now at some 8000. Rashid and most of his men were killed; a handful only escaped back to Fashoda. For the first time, the Mahdi was in possession of a considerable number of rifles and ammunition; overnight, the striking power of his forces had doubled.

It was becoming clear that a major campaign was necessary to crush the insurrection. To carry out such a campaign meant either the despatch of large numbers of fresh troops from Egypt or the concentration of the garrisons in the Sudan. Rauf Pasha was both unfortunate and weak. He was unfortunate because in the opening months of 1882, Egypt was distracted by the constitutional struggle in which the army, led by Arabi Pasha, was increasingly challenging the Khedive's government. No one was in a position to order large-scale reinforcements for the far-off Sudan. The only remaining recourse was to concentrate the existing forces in the Sudan and to seek to raise new troops locally. Denuding the existing garrisons in order to concentrate a striking force, while militarily the right course, meant exposing large areas to the risk of insurrection. Raising fresh regular troops was a long-term affair, while irregulars were increasingly unlikely to be able to cope with the fanatical fervour of the Mahdist forces. Faced with these dilemmas, Rauf Pasha followed no clear, consistent policy and he was recalled in March 1882 and replaced by the more energetic Abd al Qadir Pasha. There followed six months of widespread and confused fighting as the tentacles of the rebellion spread wider and wider. Early in April 1882, the rebels attacked Sennar, south of Khartoum, on the Blue Nile. They failed to overcome the Egyptian garrison but took and sacked the town, retreating when reinforcements arrived from Khartoum. At the end of the month, a small force of Egyptian troops was annihilated only some ninety miles south of Khartoum, but that was counter-balanced by two severe defeats inflicted on the rebels in the Sennar province by an Egyptian force led by Giegler Pasha, an Austrian soldier of fortune in the Egyptian service at Khartoum.

The main centre of the rebellion remained in Kordofan and at the end of May 1882 a large Egyptian force under Yussuf Pasha advanced to attack the Mahdi's main camp on the Jebel Gadir. In densely wooded country, the force, in hollow square and protected by a thorn fence (zariba), was attacked and destroyed by the fanatical impetus of the Mahdi's followers. El Obeid, the capital of Kordofan, 170 miles south west of Khartoum, was now under threat. Rebel attempts to seize Bara, the next largest town in Kordofan, a few miles north of El Obeid, were defeated in June and August, and El Obeid was re-victualled, only just in time, because at the end of August the Mahdi himself with his main army appeared before El Obeid and laid siege to it. The capital was defended by a large Egyptian garrison and after three assaults of mounting fury, the Mahdi was forced to withdraw with serious losses. Further success came for the government in September when a relief force managed to fight its way through to Bara, with very heavy losses, and drive off the rebels surrounding it.

But the occasional government success, counter-balanced by an equal number of defeats, could not disguise the ominous fact that the rebellion was spreading, the Mahdi was steadily growing stronger and the initiative was with him. Abd al Qadir Pasha was engaged in a despairing attempt to plug each leak as it appeared. Steps had already been taken to fortify the land approach to Khartoum from the south and in November 1882 work began on cutting a deep, water-filled ditch connecting the Blue and White Nile. Protected on two sides by the Nile and now on the third by the ditch, Khartoum had become an island. Given enough troops to defend its perimeter, it could become virtually impregnable. But troops were the problem. Throughout the spring, summer and early autumn of 1882, Egypt itself had been preoccupied with Arabi Pasha. Arabi himself, faced with a foreign threat of invasion, was in no position to weaken his army by sending a large part of it to the Sudan. Arabi's defeat at Tel El Kebir on 13 September 1882 and the establishment of British control over Egypt brought a new situation. The Egyptian army had effectively been disbanded and not yet re-formed. There were thus many thousands of Arabi's former soldiers roaming the streets of Cairo, penniless and a potential threat to the British occupation. When, therefore, Abd al Qadir-Pasha telegraphed urgently to Cairo in October 1882, asking for the immediate despatch of 10,000 men, his request fell for once on reasonably fertile ground. With the agreement of the British Government, the Khedive began to enlist a force of some 10,000 men from the unemployed soldiery of Arabi; a number of British officers were loaned to help. Service in the Sudan had long been unpopular and there was no great rush of volunteers. Not all indeed were volunteers. Major E.J. Montague-Stuart-Wortley, who was acting as Military Secretary to Valentine Baker, saw men tied together for despatch to Hicks. Some men had deliberately cut off their forefingers so that they could not fire a rifle; others had put lime in their eyes with the same object. Many had served for over thirty years in the

Egyptian Army already and were broken down. Nevertheless, by the middle of December, some 5000 men had been despatched to Khartoum via Suakin and Berber. Desertions were frequent and, as a precaution, the arms and equipment were sent separately. The first two battalions reached Khartoum early in December and went immediately into action. By the beginning of January 1883 nearly 5000 men with ten mountain guns had reached Khartoum and all 10,000 men had left Egypt for the Sudan by the middle of February. Abd al Qadir could thus look forward to building up the large striking force which he needed to tackle the Mahdi decisively.

It was not too soon. The rebellion had now taken a firm hold of the province of Sennar and fighting had been going on, with varied fortunes for the Egyptians, throughout January 1883. Abd al Qadir himself had taken command of the main operations and he ignored an order from Cairo at the end of January that he should suspend all operations and concentrate his forces at Khartoum, arguing very reasonably that, if he withdrew from Sennar now, that province and the others east of it would be lost to the Mahdi. What he did not know was that Kordofan was now wholly in the Mahdi's hands, Bara having fallen on 5 January and El Obeid itself on 17 January, after the food had run out. Some 6000 more Remington rifles and ammunition, together with ten guns, now fell into the Mahdi's hands. To use the rifles, he impressed into his army large numbers of the Egyptian prisoners, mainly Sudanese negroes from the south. From now on, Sudanese riflemen (the Jihadiya, as they came to be called) formed a major, permanent element of his army.

Clearly, if a major expedition was to be launched from Khartoum to crush the Mahdi there was no time to be lost. At the beginning of March, a new commander, Suleiman Nyasi Pasha, arrived at Khartoum, followed shortly by his British Chief of Staff, Colonel William Hicks, with a small British staff. At the end of March, Abd al Qadir, still campaigning in Sennar, learned that he had been replaced as Governor General by Ala-ed-Din Pasha.

Hicks had not had a particularly distinguished career in the Bombay Army. He had joined the Bombay Fusiliers in 1849 and after twenty-five years' service reached the rank of Lieutenant Colonel, having seen service during the Mutiny and on the Abyssinian expedition. His last post had been as Assistant Adjutant General of the Bombay Army from which he had retired in 1880. Events were to show that he was a competent, if not brilliant, officer, with a good deal of energy and courage. According to Montagu-Stuart-Wortley, a short list of three equally suitable British officers had been drawn up and the final choice was made by Valentine Baker drawing Hicks' name out of a hat.[3]

To spare Egyptian *amour-propre* and to avoid offending Muslim suscepti- bilities, Suleiman Nyasi was nominally appointed commander of the army in the Sudan but it had been made quite clear to him that in practice Hicks would command in the field and that Suleiman was to follow his instructions.

It was an arrangement almost guaranteed to cause difficulty, even given goodwill on both sides. Suleiman was, however, lazy, ignorant and jealous and took every opportunity to obstruct Hicks' activities. It was not an auspicious basis for a direct confrontation with the Mahdi and his army.

A major expedition into Kordofan to destroy the Mahdi remained the main objective and in May 1883 Cairo agreed to provide another 3000 men and resources for seven months' campaigning. But an expedition into the deserts of Kordofan could start only after the summer rains had re-filled the wells and pools. In the meantime, Hicks continued the campaign along the White Nile. At the end of April, he scored a major success only a few miles from Abba Island, utterly defeating a force of some 5000 Mahdists under one of the Mahdi's chief lieutenants, who was killed. The Egyptian troops had behaved reasonably well, although still very under-trained, and the guns and machine guns had played a major role. The morale impact on both sides was very considerable and needs to be borne in mind in considering the decision to march on El Obeid.

At the end of August 1883, with the rains over, Hicks was formally appointed to command the expedition into Kordofan, with the Egyptian rank of General of Division. He planned to move his force up the White Nile to Duaim, just over one hundred miles south of Khartoum as the crow flies, and about 150 miles north east of El Obeid. From Duaim he proposed to move westwards to Bara and then to come down from the north on to El Obeid, where he expected to meet the Mahdi's main army. His original plan was to set up a chain of fortified bases as he went to safeguard his communications. But this would have involved a significant weakening in his numbers and he was persuaded instead to keep the whole force together. In effect, when he left the White Nile, he was advancing into the unknown, with nothing to fall back on and with everything dependent upon finding adequate supplies of water. The initiative lay clearly with the Mahdi; his spies were able to keep him fully informed on Hicks' progress whereas Hicks' own intelligence was limited to the area immediately around his army. In a hostile countryside, swarming with fanatical tribesmen, long-range reconnaissance was impossible. Armed with superior intelligence, it would be the Mahdi who chose the time and place for battle. In these circumstances, all would turn upon the fighting power of Hicks' troops.

Hicks' army totalled some 8500 men, comprising 7000 infantry, 500 regular cavalry, 400 irregular cavalry (Bashi-Bazuks), four breech-loading Krupp field guns, ten mountain guns and six Nordenfeldt machine guns. The cavalry included 100 Circassian cuirassiers, clad in mail armour and wearing helmets with nasal bars such as the Normans had worn at Hastings.[4] He took with him supplies for 60 days, necessitating a baggage train of some 2000 followers and 5500 camels. Apart from the irregular cavalry, the bulk of the men had served under Arabi and since they had arrived in the Sudan Hicks had been hard at work, drilling them and teaching them minor tactics such as forming square. Many of the troops, however, had to be used almost immediately for operations against the rebels. That was not necessarily a handicap since soldiers tend to learn more and more quickly from actual fighting than on the parade square. Moreover, they had not performed badly and they had the victory at Marabieh in April to bolster their morale. Nevertheless, it could not be overlooked that Egyptian soldiers feared service in the Sudan and although the allegation that they had to be shipped there in chains is an exaggeration, few could have been entirely willing volunteers and they could scarcely fail to have been affected by the defeat at Tel-el-Kebir and the subsequent break-up of the old Egyptian army. The weakest element was undoubtedly the Egyptian officers who were badly educated and trained, and lacked dedication and discipline. Hicks' army was not the shambling rabble which history has tended to depict. As the British were to demonstrate later, with proper training and discipline and under good officers, the Egyptian and Sudanese negro soldiers were perfectly capable of standing up to the Mahdi's armies. But as events were to prove elsewhere in the Sudan, only the best-trained and led troops could be put up against the Mahdi's armies with reasonable confidence of success. Judged by that test, Hicks' army fell a long way short.[5]

By the autumn of 1883, the Mahdi had accumulated a formidable army. The men were hardy from years of battling against a harsh climate. They could go for days on a handful of dates or grain and a few mouthfuls of water, and cover immense distances on foot. Above all, they did not fear death – indeed, they welcomed it because they were fighting for the Faith. Had not the Prophet, speaking through the Mahdi, said that those warriors who went forth for the religion of God would be welcomed by God in the world to come, where they would be welcomed into Paradise with its palaces, wives, happiness and prosperity? There was no one good deed which could be compared to fighting for the True Religion; it was the highest gift which God could bestow on those whom he loved.[6] Such men feared nothing and would fight until they were killed. The vast majority of the Mahdiist army was armed with long, broad-bladed spears or straight cross-handled swords, clubs and shields. At close quarters they were formidable in the extreme. But the Mahdi also possessed large quantities of rifles and negro riflemen to use them. From captures at Bara, El Obeid and elsewhere, he had acquired at least 10,000 rifles, with huge stores of ammunition; he had also acquired a number of field guns. The rifles were mainly Remingtons – single-shot breech-loaders, using a hinged steel block to seal the breech at the moment of firing the heavy 0.43 inch lead bullet. In some ways they were better weapons than the Martini-Henrys used by the British Army, because they were lighter, less prone to jamming and used solid-drawn brass cartridges as against the weaker, coiled-brass cartridges used then by the British Army.

If Hicks' army was to defeat the Mahdi's troops, it could only be by maintaining its square formations and using its firepower to keep the Dervish hordes at a distance. If the Mahdi's troops could get to close quarters, then their superior numbers and their fanatical bravery were bound to be over-whelming.

The stakes for which Hicks was playing were very high – no less than the Sudan itself. As early as December 1882, when the idea of a major expedition into Kordofan to crush the Mahdi had first been mooted, Colonel Stewart had pointed out the risks; 'I would beg to point out how very important it is that the present expedition should prove a success. A failure would probably entail the total loss, if not of the Soudan, of at any rate many provinces'. Three weeks later, when he had seen more of the low fighting quality of the Egyptian troops then in the Sudan, he repeated his warning, writing to Malet: 'This move of Abdul-Kader is a critical one for, should he meet with any reverse, it will probably be a decisive one, as far as Egyptian authority in this country is concerned'. When he learned of the fall of El Obeid in February 1883, Stewart repeated his warnings: 'I am strongly of the opinion that to advance now on Kordofan would be exceedingly injudicious, and that the alternative policy of remaining on the defensive, rigorously putting down any attempted rising on the banks of the Nile, and waiting to see what will happen is the true one . . . A serious disaster, or, indeed, a check, would also very probably involve the loss of the whole of the Soudan'. Others, including Malet himself, were similarly pessimistic. What Hicks himself thought of his chances is not very clear. At no time does he ever appear to have advised against the expedition. Writing at the end of June 1883, he believed that as he advanced, the tribes 'though afraid of commencing hostilities against the Mahdi, would join [Hicks] as camp-followers'. He had had some minor successes against the Mahdi's followers in Sennar and on the White Nile, and, as a regular soldier, he may well have been predisposed to believe that organised, regular troops equipped with modern weapons should beat undisciplined savage hordes. Admittedly, he did not have quite as large a force as he would have liked but nevertheless, he was perfectly willing and confident; 'I am prepared to undertake the campaign with the force available; the risks are, as I have said, in case of a mishap, but I think this is not at all probable. Khartoum ought to be safe from outside under any circumstances'.[7]

One cannot, perhaps, acquit Hicks of the charge of misunderstanding the nature of his enemy and therefore of being over-optimistic. But did he, in fact, have any serious alternative? It is inconceivable that a policy of concentrating on the defence of Khartoum and leaving the Mahdi to take the initiative would ultimately have saved the Sudan. The balance of moral advantage would have continued to swing implacably in favour of the Mahdi and Khartoum would have fallen in the end, almost certainly without the assistance of Gordon. Moreover, military logic was on Hicks' side; given an adequate force, there was militarily everything to be said for tackling the Mahdi before he could grow even stronger. Time was not on the Egyptian side.

The main body of Hicks' army left Khartoum on 8 September and reached Duaim on the White Nile, 110 miles south, on the 23rd. Hicks, himself left Khartoum on 28 September and reached Duaim by steamer two days later. By 30 September, the army was some 30 miles south west of Duaim, with another hundred miles or so to go. The heat was intense and the camels were dying in large numbers. By 1 October, the force was 45 miles from Duaim and temporarily halted because of the uncertain water supplies ahead. Water indeed was, as expected, the critical parameter. There was ample food with the army, uncut forage was readily available and the health of the troops was good; all depended upon finding adequate supplies of water at frequent intervals.

Hicks was a reasonably experienced soldier who knew the basics of his business. His force marched in three columns, each column ready to form square instantly, with guns and Nordenfeldts disposed along the faces and angles of the square. Wherever the force halted, a zariba of thorn bushes was put up around the camp and each infantryman had four crow's feet (metal balls with protruding spikes, mainly used against horses) which he was trained to throw in front of him to delay the attackers.

Hicks, on the advice of Ala ed Din Pasha who was accompanying him, had abandoned his original idea of maintaining a chain of posts back to Duaim as he advanced since the posts were likely to be cut off by the enemy. The last despatch received from Hicks was dated 3 October. He was then at Sarakhna, some 60 miles from Duaim. He was worried about the uncertain water supplies and about having to abandon his lines of communication back to the Nile. He was now committed to advancing on El Obeid from the south, rather than from the north via Bara, because the Nubian King of Takalle in the Nuba Mountains south of El Obeid had promised assistance if the army entered Kordofan from the south. This may well have been a fatal mistake since it lengthened Hicks' march and, as it turned out, contributed nothing to his safety.

Nothing further was heard from Hicks. By the beginning of November, rumours were circulating that there had been a disaster. The rumours were confirmed on 19 November when a messenger despatched from Duaim to the army returned with news of the total destruction of Hicks' force. Even now, the full details are not known but it appears that the force struggled forward under increasing attacks which it managed to beat off at the cost of increasing exhaustion through heat and shortage of water. On 5 November 1883, as the army struggled in three squares through thick forest towards the lake at Fula, some 20 miles south-east of El Obeid and 225 miles from Duaim, it was attacked by the Mahdi's full army, estimated at some 40,000. Hicks' force disintegrated under the overwhelming attack and there was only a handful of survivors. Hicks himself died gallantly, sword in hand, and with him died all his European officers, the Governor General (Ala ed Din Pasha) and two European newspaper correspondents, O'Donovan and

Vizetelly. The whole of the ammunition, guns, rifles and stores fell into the Mahdi's hands; he now had nearly 20,000 modern rifles and 19 guns, with huge stocks of ammunition.

The news of the disaster to Hicks' army came as a staggering shock to the Egyptian authorities in Cairo. No disaster of such dimensions had occurred since the Sudan had been occupied sixty years earlier. At a distance of a thousand miles, it was difficult to understand the force of the tidal wave of fanaticism stirred up among the tribes by the Mahdi's preaching. But one thing was clear. Exhausted and bankrupt, Egypt had sent her last army. If the authorities in Khartoum were to be succoured and the Sudan held, it was the British who would have to do it. If not, there would have to be total evacuation and abandonment, as Stewart had warned.

If the news had shattered Cairo, its effect was scarcely less startling in London. For the first time, Gladstone and his Cabinet began to understand that if Khartoum fell, Egypt itself was defenceless; and if Khartoum was not to fall, then only the British could prevent it. As Northbrooke protested to Granville 'We have now been forced into the position of being the protectors of Egypt'. In these circumstances, there could hardly be any early withdrawal from Egypt as Gladstone had hoped.

Out of this unpalatable situation emerged the decision in January 1884, after two months of twisting and turning by the Cabinet, to send Gordon to Khartoum. It is not the intention of this book to go into the whole sad story of Gordon's tragic mission which ended in his death nearly a year later and the abandonment of the Sudan to the Mahdi and his followers for thirteen years. That story has exercised a permanent fascination on historians and, given Gordon's charisma, will no doubt continue to attract scholars, Sudanese as well as British, for decades to come. But Gordon's mission and subsequent death connects directly with the subject of this book to which we must now turn.

The fall of El Obeid at the beginning of 1883 had sent many men flocking to see at first hand the man whose successes seemed to prove that he was indeed the Expected One. Many came, were conquered by what they saw and stayed to serve. Among these was the man the British were to call Osman Digna. His family, the Dignai, were not pure Sudanese, as we have seen, but the family had inter-married with the surrounding tribes, including the Hadendowa, and Osman Digna regarded himself, and was regarded by others, as a Hadendowa.[8] The family's prosperous trading business, into which Osman had gone as soon as he had finished his education, had been largely destroyed by the Egyptian government's anti-slavery policy, stimulated and enforced by the British. In 1877, Osman Digna's brother, Ali, with a cargo of 96 slaves, had been intercepted and captured en route to Jeddah by HMS *Wild Swan*. The slaves and other goods had been confiscated and the loss exceeded £1000, a very large sum indeed. Shortly afterwards, the family's trading compound at Jeddah was searched, all merchandise and slaves seized and Ali, Osman and another brother, Omar, imprisoned. They and the rest of the family were then deported from Jeddah. The loss of the Jeddah outlet was a crippling blow and Osman was left an impoverished and bitter man.[9] At the time of Arabi Pasha's revolt in 1881, Osman Digna had tried to foment trouble in Suakin and bring the town over to Arabi's cause but he had been expelled by the leading townspeople. He went to Berber and set up in business as a broker. In 1882 he was back in Suakin, still trying unsuccessfully to stir up trouble in favour of Arabi and against the Khedive's administration. Foiled again, he made his way westwards to Kordofan to see the new Messiah amongst whose followers was already Osman's brother, Omar. Osman appears to have reached El Obeid shortly after it fell to the Mahdi in January 1883. Omar had died of disease during the siege; he had been well thought of by the Mahdi and his brother was sure of a welcome. In his turn, Osman Digna was captivated by the message and personality of the Mahdi; for the next forty years he was never to deviate from his allegiance, whatever the hardship involved.

When he first met the Mahdi, Osman was just over forty years old. Bennet Burleigh described him thus: 'Tall, gaunt, inclined to stoop – features ordinary Hadendowa type – chocolate-coloured skin, full high forehead, shaggy, crimpy hair, dark melancholy eyes, prominent nose, firm lips, dark brown beard.[10] Neither Burleigh nor, as far as can be discovered, any other Englishman had ever met Osman; even Wylde does not seem to have known him. Nor are there any contemporary photographs of him. Burleigh must therefore have got his description from other Sudanese, probably in Suakin. Nevertheless, his description accords fairly well with the photographs of Osman taken after his capture and we may accept it as a fair portrait of him at this time.

To the Mahdi, Osman was a valuable acquisition because he came from the eastern part of the Sudan, along the Red Sea, where the Mahdi's influence had not hitherto penetrated. No doubt also, he perceived Osman's valuable qualities – his natural leadership backed up by his persuasive, fiery oratory, his great physical endurance, his unquestioning loyalty. In the spring of 1883, he despatched him to raise the Beja tribes: 'Know that I am sending you an amir from this place to establish the Faith and revive the Sunna of the Lord of the Prophets and Apostles. He is Shaykh Uthman Digna, the son of Abu Bakr al-Sawakini. If he stays in your territories, gather round him, assist him and swear to hear and obey him. Assist him and go out with him to the war and the jihad and purify the earth of the Turks and the corrupters'.[11]

Armed with these powerful credentials, Osman Digna hastened to make contact with Shaykh al Tahir, the influential leader of the Majadhib sect, a sect to which Osman himself had belonged at one stage. The bitter rivals of the Majadhib were the Khatmiya sect, led by the powerful Mirghani family who favoured the Egyptians and were dominant in Suakin. Tahir and the

Majadhib were thus the natural allies of the Mahdi. They were particularly influential among the Beja tribes and the Jaaliyin. Thus Tahir's adherence to the Mahdi brought Osman a ready-made army which included the Hadendowa. There is no evidence that the Hadendowa had suffered particularly at the hands of the Egyptian adminstration but they had a grievance over non-payment for camels supplied to Hicks.

When Osman issued a proclamation on behalf of the Mahdi, summoning the tribes to join him in a holy war against the 'Turks', the leaders of the Khatmiya were quick to send a copy to the Egyptian governor of the Red Sea province at Suakin, Muhammad Tawfik Bey. He immediately summoned Tahir and Osman's brother, Ahmad, to Sinkat, in the Erkowit hills, some 50 miles west of Suakin, to explain themselves.[12] No doubt, he intended to seize them as hostages for the good behaviour of the tribes who were preparing to join the Mahdiist cause. Osman's response was immediate. He and Tahir collected a force and marched on Sinkat on 5 August 1883. They were repulsed with a loss of some 60-65 killed and wounded, the latter including Osman, and retired into the hills. In turn, Tawfik took out a force to follow up and disperse the rebels. He was attacked by Osman's men who failed however to penetrate the zariba which Tawfik had prudently erected round his camp. Despite the repulse, Tawfik was unable to advance any further and withdrew to Sinkat. From this position, the local initiative passed to Osman. At the end of October, a force of 150 Egyptian gendarmes on their way from Suakin to reinforce Sinkat were ambushed and annihilated. The rebels then proceeded to besiege Sinkat and Tokar, the centre of the grain growing district, 16 miles inland from the coast and roughly 50 miles south south east of Suakin. Tokar was particularly important to Osman because the availability of grain and water there made it the nearest place to Suakin where a large force could be maintained; and, since it could only be approached via Trinkitat, there was ample warning available of any attack. To relieve Tokar, a force of some 550 men was despatched from Suakin. The troops landed at Trinkitat,[13] on the coast 40 miles south of Suakin on 4 November and marched inland towards Tokar 20 miles away. The force was commanded by Mahmud Tahir Pasha, commander of all the troops in the Eastern Sudan, and it was accompanied, for reasons which are not entirely clear, by the British consul at Suakin, Commander Lynedoch Moncrieff, a retired naval officer who had been at Suakin for some eighteen months. At El Teb, about eight miles inland, the Egyptian force was attacked by an inferior force led by Osman.[14] Although in square, the Egyptians broke at the first attack and fled for the coast. Roughly three-quarters of the force reached Trinkitat, including its commander; the remainder, with Moncrieff, were killed and 300 rifles fell into Osman Digna's hands. Twenty four hours later and five hundred miles away, Hicks' army was slaughtered at Shaykan.

Sinkat and Tokar remained besieged and it was clear that something must be done to retrieve the situation if the whole of the Eastern Sudan, including

28

Suakin itself, was not to fall into the Mahdi's hands. The British gunboat *Ranger* was despatched from Aden to Suakin to stand by to evacuate British subjects if necessary and on 22 November, Rear Admiral Sir William Hewett, Commander-in-Chief of the East Indies Station was authorised to support the Egyptian authorities at Suakin, Massawa and elsewhere along the Red Sea coast; the gunboat *Coquette* was despatched from the Mediterranean Fleet to reinforce him. In Cairo the Egyptian government decided to despatch a large force of gendarmerie – the only disciplined force available – to Suakin, to safeguard Suakin itself, to relieve Tokar and to re-open the line of communication from Suakin to Berber which provided the quickest route to Khartoum.

The British were now willy-nilly being sucked in. The Mahdi's successes posed a threat to Egypt itself which the remaining Egyptian forces in Egypt were manifestly unable to contain. Baring in Cairo and Lieutenant General Stephenson, the commander of the British forces of occupation in Egypt, recommended that for the moment there should be no further evacuation of British troops. With reluctance, the Cabinet agreed but Granville emphasised to Baring that under no circumstances would the Government agree to be responsible for the Sudan.

At the end of November, the first detachment of gendarmerie left Cairo for the Sudan, reaching Suakin on 2 December. They arrived to witness the aftermath of yet another disaster. On the morning of the 2nd, a force of 500 negro infantry and 200 irregular cavalry, with a mountain gun, under the command of Kasim Effendi, had left Suakin to chase away the rebels who had nightly been firing into the town. At noon, the force had reached Tamanieb, near the base of the foothills west of Suakin. There it was attacked by Osman's troops. The negro infantry appear to have sold their lives dearly but their formation had been broken up by the panic of the irregular cavalry; split up into small groups, the infantry was overwhelmed by an enemy put at 3000. Fewer than 50 of the force returned to Suakin. Osman admitted losing 80 of his followers.

By 14 December there were available in Suakin some 2000 infantry (gendarmerie and the remains of the Egyptian garrison), plus some troops from Massawa and 300 irregular cavalry (Bashi-Bazuks). In the harbour, *Coquette* and *Ranger* were moored to provide gunfire support. Fortifications had been erected round the landward perimeter of the town and by the end of December 1883 Suakin could be regarded as reasonably secure.[15]

The operations against Osman Digna had been entrusted by the Egyptian Government to Valentine Baker Pasha, the commander of the Egyptian police. Baker had had an extraordinary career. The brother of Sir Samuel Baker the explorer, Valentine Baker had joined the 10th Hussars and commanded it from 1860 to 1872. Handsome, popular, well-connected, adventurous and dedicated to his profession, he seemed destined for a brilliant career but in 1875, when on the staff at Aldershot, he had been convicted of improperly assaulting a lady in a railway carriage and sent to prison. No one will ever know the truth but the whole affair seems improbable and at his trial Baker was the victim of emotional prejudice. Dismissed from the British army, however, he entered the Turkish Army and fought brilliantly in the Russo-Turkish war of 1877-78. By 1882, he was a Lieutenant General and he elected then to join the Egyptian service in command of the police.

Baker arrived at Suakin on 23 December, entrusted with full military and civil command of all parts of the Sudan which he might reach with his force. His instructions were to pacify the country between Suakin and Berber and re-establish a secure line of communication between the two places.[16] In a personal letter from the Khedive, Baker was instructed not to move before the black troops which Zobeir Pasha was raising had arrived, and in any event not to take the offensive except in favourable circumstances.

The situation facing him was unpromising. Sinkat and Tokar remained under siege by Osman Digna's forces and the garrisons were rapidly running out of food and ammunition while disease was beginning to take its toll. Osman's forces were put at some 4500 fighting men, mainly from the Hadendowa and Amarar tribes. Moreover, Abyssinia was threatening to seize Massawa as a result of a long-standing quarrel. At Suakin, Baker could field some 1700 infantry (regulars and gendarmerie), some 400 dismounted irregulars (Turks and Bashi Bazuks), some 400 mounted gendarmerie, 200 irregular cavalry and 200 Egyptian artillery – some 3000 men altogether. He could rely upon the Royal Navy for some assistance in protecting Suakin itself but, even so, the perimeter was two and a half miles long and he would have to leave a substantial proportion of his force to defend the town. The morale of his troops was low. The regulars were demoralised by Osman's successes and the ferocity of his troops; many of the gendarmerie had publicly protested against being sent to Suakin and had had to be shipped forcibly. Service in the Sudan was unpopular with Egyptians and the gendarmerie believed with some justice that they had not been enlisted to serve as soldiers there. Clearly, he was too weak in numbers to mount an expedition against Osman Digna with any prospect of success.

For the moment, all he could do was to wait for further reinforcements and, in the meantime, drill and train his motley collection of troops and endeavour to persuade the Abyssinians to refrain from attacking Massawa. The deteriorating situation elsewhere in the Sudan and the need to avoid further disaster led the Egyptian Government in January 1884 to amend significantly his instructions. Sinkat and Tokar were to be relieved *only* if he was confident of success and he was to refrain from attempting to re-open the Suakin-Berber road unless it could be done by negotiation with the tribes.

Throughout January, reinforcements trickled into Suakin, including a large contingent of negro troops raised by the famous slave-trader Zobeir Pasha.[17] On 22 January, in order to distract a portion of Osman's forces away from Sinkat and Tokar, Baker undertook a reconnaissance in force towards Handub. In the ensuing fight, the irregular cavalry panicked and bolted. Nevertheless, Baker was able to withdraw in reasonably good order, having inflicted casualties on his enemy. Two days later, he moved out from Suakin with a force of some 2000 and camped within four miles of Osman's camp at Handub. There was no serious fighting and when Baker learned that the enemy forces had retired to Tokar he returned to Suakin.

The situation at Sinkat and Tokar was now desperate. The commander at Sinkat, the gallant Tawfik Pasha, wrote on 30 January that he was in the last extremity. Even the dogs had been eaten and the daily ration was only half a pound of grain per day. Unless help arrived within a few days, he proposed to try to cut his way through to Suakin since he preferred death in battle to death by starvation. The commander at Tokar wrote in similar terms: 'It is impossible for us to be in worse condition than we are now. The enemy has filled up all the wells outside the town and the water in the inside wells is brackish and bad. The troops are suffering greatly from diarrhoea and I fear that in two or three days we shall be forced to surrender. We have dried grain enough for three months but no meat and only from ten to twenty rounds of ammunition per man. The rebels fire upon us night and day'.

Baker could afford to wait no longer if honour was to be satisfied. On 28 January he landed at Trinkitat with 1000 men, the first detachment of his force to relieve Tokar. By the 30th, he had assembled his full force of just under 4000 men with four Krupp field guns, two machine guns (Gatlings) and two rocket troughs.[18] The quality of the force was low. Many of the gendarmerie had had to be shipped forcibly to Suakin; none of them wished to be there. Zobeir's black infantry were raw recruits and scarcely knew how to load their rifles or to fix bayonets. The Sudanese negro infantry were in much the same position. The blacks were excellent fighting material, properly trained and led, as the British were to prove subsequently, but without drill and discipline, courage was not enough. The Turkish cavalry had not distinguished itself in the action on 22 January, bolting at a critical moment. The correspondent of the London *Daily News*, writing from Trinkitat on 31 January, was blunt: 'The fact is that diplomacy, rather than arms, must decide the fate of Tokar, as well as of Sinkat. The troops, especially the blacks, are good material, but even now, are wholly untrained in the use of their rifles. In today's practice almost every shot sighted for 100 yards fell 12 to 15 times that distance. Our 2000 blacks may certainly be depended on for the bravest resistance with the bayonet but it is equally certain that their fire cannot resist the rush of an enemy and that if the enemy be as numerous as supposed, the march, unsupported, against Tokar will entail a disaster . . . The native officers are most despicably cowardly and inefficient'.

So much must have been equally clear to Baker. He had therefore sought, and obtained, the promise of support from some of the friendly tribes around Suakin in attempting to relieve Sinkat and Tokar. In the upshot, it failed to materialise. He had also tried psychological warfare, using the presence of the important religious leader, Shaykh Muhammad-al-Mirghani, to exert pressure on the tribes to abandon Osman and the Mahdi. The Sheikh himself excommunicated Osman, who replied defiantly that he took his orders from the Mahdi.

Trinkitat was merely a landing place. There was no village there and the beach was separated from the mainland by a swamp some three miles wide, but there was 20 feet or more of water within a hundred yards of the shore. A fort was hastily constructed to cover the beach itself and the stores piling up there. A second fort, known as Fort Baker, was built three miles inland, on the crest of a ridge marking the edge of the swamp. It consisted of a strong earthwork, with a deep trench all round, with a thick parapet; held by 170 troops, it was virtually impregnable to attack by the Dervishes. On 4 February, at about 0730 hours, Baker began his advance with some 3500 men. The Egyptian cavalry formed a screen ahead of the main body. Behind them came Baker and his staff, followed by the Turkish cavalry, the artillery and then the infantry in massive columns, ready to form square. The baggage animals came last with instructions to move into the centre of the square when it became necessary to form it.

The morning was dull and misty, with occasional heavy showers of rain. The force had gone three miles when small bodies of Osman's troops appeared some two miles ahead, with a much larger concentration behind them. Two rounds from one of the Krupp field guns fell short and the gun was advanced another mile and a half. Its shells still failed to shift the enemy. The cavalry screen now commenced to fire aimlessly into the distance. Major Giles was despatched with the Turkish cavalry to pursue and disperse some mounted rebels on the right flank. At the same time, the cavalry screen began to waver and then retreat in disorder, closely followed up by the enemy. The lack of training of Baker's infantry now showed. The black troops from Massawa managed to form the left side of the square but Zobeir's troops could not be got to form up properly to constitute the rear face and the front and right faces were not formed at all. Confusion was made worse by the retreating Egyptian cavalry galloping through the infantry. Without a properly-formed square, Baker's force was lost. The artillery outside the square was overrun and every man killed. The guns inside the square could not be brought into action because the mules were out of control in the general panic. The Gatlings were brought into action but their fire was not enough to halt the enemy who followed the tactic which was to become almost Osman's trademark of attacking a corner and the rear of the force. A battalion of the gendarmerie appears to have broken first and the whole force then disintegrated, the panic-stricken troops throwing away their weapons and equipment as they fled towards the coast. Baker was unable to get the remnants of the cavalry to rally and charge, and it rapidly became a case of every man for himself. An attempt to rally the fugitives at Fort Baker failed and on the beach at Trinkitat there were ugly scenes as the panic-stricken men fought to get into the boats. Valentine Baker, with some of his staff, cut his way through the enemy and reached Trinkitat where he worked all night, evacuating the survivors. At 2200 hours on the 5th, the ships bringing back the remnants entered Suakin harbour. Baker had lost 96 officers and 2250 men killed, two thirds of his force; he had also lost 3000 rifles and all his guns. Given the circumstances, it is perhaps surprising that any got away at all since, man for man, the Egyptians and Sudanese were no match for their enemy. It seems probable that sheer weariness and the desire to pillage prevented Osman's force, which may have numbered only some 1200, from following up and killing every one. According to Osman's own letters, his troops were commanded by the amir Abdallah and they lost 300 men.[19] The famous Colonel Fred Burnaby, of the Royal Horse Guards, who had arrived without official leave to accompany Baker, was disgusted by the whole affair: 'The sight was one never to be forgotten, some four thousand men running pell mell for their lives with a few hundred Arabs behind them spearing everyone within reach'.[20] British involvement was now inevitable since it was obvious that Suakin could not safely be held by the troops at Baker's disposal. *HMS Ranger* had brought the news of Baker's disaster from Trinkitat to Suakin on the morning of 5 February and the news was telegraphed to London immediately.[21] As an immediate precaution, the Admiralty ordered the troopship *Orontes*, homeward bound from the Far East with sailors who had been relieved, to stand fast at Suez. Hewett, who seems to have been a thoroughly sensible, clear-headed officer, and who was already at Suakin in his flagship, had already landed a force of 100 marines and bluejackets with two machine guns to protect the town. At a Cabinet meeting on 6 February, the British Government decided to defend Suakin. Hewett was signalled and replied saying that he needed a total of 500 marines, including the 100 already at Suakin and 140 coming from *Orontes*. When the full force was available, Hewett recommended that all the remaining Egyptian forces, except for some Turkish cavalry to act as scouts and 500 Sudanese infantry, should be withdrawn because they were without arms and untrustworthy.

Baker still had some 3000 men in Suakin and wanted to retain them there but Baring agreed with Hewett, as did apparently the Egyptian Government. In consequence, Hewett was invested with supreme military and civil powers at Suakin with specific authority to send away the Egyptian troops if he thought it advisable. Hewett was also told that the troopship *Jumna* with time-expired British troops from India would reach Aden on 12 or 13 February and he was authorised to intercept her to obtain supplies or men if he needed them.

Further bad news now came in. On the 12th, news of the fall of Sinkat reached Suakin and was signalled immediately to London. The gallant Tawfik, having finished all his supplies, had spiked his guns, destroyed surplus ammunition and sallied out on 8 February to try to cut his way through to Suakin, only a tantalising 20 miles away. All but a handful of men and women were massacred within a mile and a half of Sinkat, Tawfik among them. By his conduct, he had done something to retrieve the reputation of the Egyptian army.[22] Only Tokar now held out. On receipt of the news of the fall of Sinkat, the Cabinet reluctantly decided to send an expedition to relieve Tokar. Stephenson was ordered the same day (12 February) to collect a force at Suakin to relieve Tokar if possible; failing that, the force was to be used to defend Suakin. He was instructed to send the three best British battalions in Egypt, together with the 19th Hussars. A Royal Artillery garrison battery in Egypt was to take over the guns, camels and equipment of the Egyptian Army camel battery. Hewett would provide a battalion of Royal Marines, and a naval detachment of three Gardner and three Gatling guns. In addition, the troopship *Jumna*, homeward bound from India with the 2nd Battalion Royal Irish Fusiliers, the 10th Hussars and M Battery, 1st Division, RA, was diverted to Suakin to land its troops there. The men had their Indian hot weather khaki uniforms and equipment but the 10th Hussars would have to pick up whatever horses could be found at Suakin; indeed, the original instructions envisaged the Hussars being used only to garrison the town. Baggage was to be on the lowest possible scale because the troops were expected to be back in Cairo in three weeks.

Of the two major generals available on the spot in Egypt, one (Major General William Earle, commanding the garrison at Alexandria) had seen virtually no active service and his career hitherto had been undistinguished; Wolseley wrote scornfully that his name was totally unknown in the Army.[23] The choice therefore fell on Major General Sir Gerald Graham, then commanding a brigade in the Army of Occupation at Cairo. He had distinguished himself in Wolseley's 1882 campaign in Egypt and Wolseley had known him since the Crimea where Graham had won the VC. Colonel Sir Redvers Buller was appointed to command the infantry and to be Graham's second-in-command. Since Buller was in England and could not reach Suakin for two or three weeks, Stephenson was authorised to send Major General Davis to Suakin temporarily; Davis could either return to Cairo when Buller arrived or, since there would be enough infantry to form two brigades, Davis could be used to command a brigade although Buller was to remain as second-in-command. Like Earle, Davis had seen very little active service and when he was misguided enough to complain later to Wolseley about Buller, a mere colonel, being appointed as second-in-command, he received a withering reply; Wolseley told him that in view of his lack of experience he could count himself fortunate to have been allowed to participate in the expedition and to be able to serve under two such distinguished soldiers as Graham and Buller.[24] In fact, Buller had had even more fighting experience than Graham; he was, moreover, a long-standing member of Wolseley's famous 'Ring'.

To command the cavalry, Colonel Herbert Stewart was appointed. He also was a close acquaintance of Wolseley, who regarded him as the best cavalry leader in the Army. He was to be killed while leading the Desert Column under Wolseley at Abu Klea in January 1885 before Wolseley's judgement could be proved.

Stephenson was told that the greatest publicity was to be given to the British Government's intention of relieving Tokar with British troops. Clearly the Government hoped that this would have a morale-boosting effect throughout the rest of the Sudan, especially since Gordon was now on his way up the Nile to Khartoum as Governor-General, with instructions to evacuate the remaining Egyptian garrisons and officials.

NOTES

1. Sufiism is a form of Islamic mysticism. The various orders are known as *tariqs* and the members are known as *darawish* (dervish), from a Persian word meaning beggar.
2. Abba Island continued to be the centre of the land holdings of the Mahdi's descendants until well into the 20th century.
3. E.J. Montague-Stuart-Wortley 'My reminiscences of Egypt and the Sudan' *Sudan Notes and Records*, Vol XXIV (1953) p18.
4. Colonel J. Colbourne *With Hicks Pasha in the Sudan* (London, 1884) p93.
5. Colbourne, who was perhaps understandably slightly biased wrote that 'with a steadier or more patient army I never marched . . . the Soudan Field Force was permeated throughout by a loyalty and a sense of duty beyond all praise' – Colbourne, op cit, pp137-38.
6. See the extracts from the Mahdi's letter book captured at Toski in 1889 and quoted in F.R. Wingate *Mahdiism and the Egyptian Sudan* (London, second edition 1968) pp48 and 63.
7. This, and the previous quotations, are taken from Lord Cromer *Modern Egypt* (London, 1908) Vol I, pp356-62.
8. What we know about the Dignai family is largely contained in Jackson, op cit, written by a former member of the Sudan Civil Service who knew Osman Digna.
9. Ismat Hasan Zulfo *Karari: the Sudanese account of the Battle of Omdurman* (translated by Peter Clark) (London, 1980) says that Osman had also been seized on a slave-raiding expedition to Darfur by Egyptian troops but had escaped during a rain storm. It is not clear, however, when this occurred.
10. Burleigh, op cit, p9.
11. Letter from the Mahdi 8 May 1883, quoted in P.M. Holt *The Mahdiist State in the Sudan 1881-1898* (Oxford, second edition 1970) p82.
12. Situated in the hills, Sinkat was cooler than Suakin and the Egyptian administration and wealthy Sudanese went there to pass the summer away from the heat and humidity of Suakin. It lies on the route from Berber to Suakin and was thus of some strategic importance.
13. More accurately, Kirinkakat – see Jackson, op cit, p63.
14. 'El Teb' appears to be a corruption of 'Andatteib' (the place of the hobbling of the camels). It is sometimes rendered as 'Et-Teb' in the early campaign despatches.
15. Mrs Sartorius, the wife of one of Baker's officers who accompanied him to Suakin described the fortifications thus:
'We went up to the fortified lines. These latter are only a shallow ditch, about four feet deep and three feet wide at the top, with the earth thrown up behind to a height of five or six feet. Into this parapet were driven six-feet long stakes, at about six inches apart; they were further bound together with a long line of transverse poles. The small forts, composed of detached buildings each surrounded by an extra large and deep ditch, were connected by these lines . . . a quantity of mimosa thorn, of the most prickly kind, piled

35

up to a thickness of six feet all along the outside, completely stops the possibility of rushing through them'. – Ernestine Sartorius *Three Months in the Soudan* (London, 1885) p126.

16. The instructions are printed in full in *The Insurrection of the False Prophet*, compiled by Captain J.J. Leverson, Intelligence Branch, Quarter Master General's Department, War Office, Part II, p13. Copy in MOD Central Library, reference W30.

17. Zobeir Pasha was the most powerful of the slave traders who had operated as independent rulers in the Bahr al-Gazal before Gordon came. He had assisted the Egyptian Government in seizing Darfur in 1874 and had been rewarded with the title of Pasha. He had quarrelled with the Government over the governorship of Darfur and had been detained in Cairo ever since. His son, Suleiman, had rebelled against Gordon, when the latter was Governor-General, and had been captured and shot on Gordon's orders. Zobeir's later history is part of Gordon's ill-fated mission to Khartoum in 1884.

18. Regular Egyptian and Turkish cavalry   450
    Gendarmerie infantry   1060
    Sudanese negro infantry   871
    Zobeir's negro infantry   678
    Egyptian artillery   128
    Europeans   <u>40</u>
        3656

19. See Osman's correspondence, *Daftar Waqa'i Uthman Digna*, captured in 1891, in the Central Records Office, Khartoum. I have used the translation in Wingate, op cit, for convenience although the translation may not be of the best.

20. Quoted in Michael Alexander *True Blue: the Life and Adventures of Colonel Fred Burnaby* (London, 1957) p157.

21. By good fortune, Suakin had been connected by submarine cable to Suez and thence to London on 31 January 1884. A message *en clair* took about two hours, which was the same as the time difference. Thus a message from Suakin at, say, 1400 hours reached London at 1400 hours London time. A message despatched from London at 1400 hours reached Suakin at 1800 hours local time. Letters took about ten days.

22. He was actually a Cretan. For an assessment of him, see Wylde, op cit, Vol I, pp20-21. Osman referred to him in a letter as 'one of the ablest of the God-forsaken Ala-ed-Din's men, and well known for his bravery and good administration – see Wingate, op cit, p511. Tawfik's reply to a demand for surrender, as recorded by Mrs Sartorius, deserves to be remembered: 'His life was the Khedive's, his honour his own, his daughter the Effendis had promised to look after, and therefore he intended to defend the place to the last'. – Sartorius, op cit, p64.

23. Despite this, Earle was appointed to command the River Column in Wolseley's Nile Expedition. He was killed in February 1885 at Kirbekan without having had much opportunity to distinguish himself. He was senior to Graham but made no fuss about being passed over in favour of the latter.

24. Wolseley to Davis 24 April 1885 – Wolseley Papers (Hove Library) P(rivate) L(etter) B(ook) 1, pp18-24.

4

A First Campaign
(February to April 1884)

'I suppose the policy at home was that, while the troops were there, they might as well kill someone, and the sentiment was that it will never do now we occupy Egypt to allow those that had beaten them in fair fight to rest on their laurels. Ours seemed rather a bullying kind of policy; the Soudan was abandoned and our fighting the tribes could not be defended altogether, although I suppose there was just as much argument in favour of fighting as there was against it.'

John Wylde.

IMMENSELY TALL and massively built, with a bushy grey moustache and penetrating blue eyes, holder of the Victoria Cross, Gerald Graham was the archetype of the successful Victorian general. Born in 1831 of a landed Cumberland family without any conspicuous military background, he had been educated, unusually, in Dresden, whence he joined the Royal Military Academy at Woolwich in 1847. 'The Shop', as it was always known until it was amalgamated with Sandhurst after the Second World War, was restricted to cadets intended for the Royal Artillery or Royal Engineers. When Graham graduated in June 1850, he was commissioned into the Royal Engineers. He was still serving in England when the Crimean War broke out and in February 1854 he embarked with his company for Malta. From there, with the advanced party of the 1st Division, he moved on to Gallipoli and then to Varna in what is now Bulgaria. Early in September 1854, he embarked for the Crimea itself. He remained there until July 1856, experiencing all the hardships and incompetence which characterised that curious and rather remarkable campaign. He emerged with a high professional reputation for coolness, courage and competence and he had made some friends, particularly Wolseley and Charles Gordon, who were to play a vital role in his later career. Above all, he had won the Victoria Cross, leading with great gallantry one of the storming parties in the unsuccessful attack on the Redan on 18 June 1855.

It is difficult for us now to understand the extent to which a VC was a key to professional success in Victorian times. We are accustomed to think of intelligence and brain-power and analytical reasoning as being more important for a general than physical courage displayed in the heat of the moment. But for the Victorians, war was a simpler business. Logistics were relatively

37

straightforward and the proper province of staff officers. The duty of a general was to plan his tactics and to lead his troops in carrying them out. Given that for most Victorian generals, the enemy was likely to be an unsophisticated one – Zulus or Maoris or Afghans or Chinese or Burmese – even the tactical problems were fairly straightforward. Thus leadership and courage became the pre-eminent virtues and what better proof of them was there than possession of the Victoria Cross? Not all successful generals were lucky enough to get it – Wolseley was the outstanding example. But against that, the long roll of VC holders who rose to the top – Roberts, Buller, Evelyn Wood, George White, Graham, Haines, Sam Browne and others – testified to the power of that supreme award.[1] The other side of the coin, of course, was that when the enemy proved to be as sophisticated as the British, leadership and courage were not enough, as the debâcles of the First and Second Boer Wars demonstrated.

Four years after his return from the Crimea, Graham was on his way to China to take part in the Second China War, having arrived in India just too late to take part in the suppression of the Mutiny. For Graham, the importance of that war lay in the fact that he added further to his professional reputation both as a soldier and as a professional engineer. Even more important, he was made a brevet lieutenant-colonel. At the age of 30, with only 11 years service, he was already well established on the professional ladder.

For the next twenty years, his career moved along quiet paths, steadily ascending all the time in professional terms, but without alarms or excursions into active service. Despite his acquaintanceship with Wolseley, the great rising star of the Victorian army, he did not become part of the famous Wolseley 'Ring'.

In 1881, at the age of 50, he reached the rank of major general and found himself temporarily on the unemployed list. Within nine months, he was rescued from that by the decision to send an expeditionary force to Egypt to tackle Arabi Pasha. Wolseley was to command the force and he chose Graham to command the 2nd Infantry Brigade of the 1st Division.[2] In the campaign that followed, Graham played a distinguished part. Wolseley chose him to lead the initial advance from Ismailia. He was present, leading his brigade, at the action of El Magar on 24 August 1882, and at Kassassin on 28 August he had his first personal victory when, with some 1900 men, he held and then defeated an Egyptian force nearly five times larger. Wolseley telegraphed home that 'General Graham's dispositions were all that they should have been, and his operations were carried out with that coolness for which he has always been well known'.

At the crowning victory of Tel-el-Kebir on 13 September, Graham's Brigade (2nd Battalion Royal Irish Regiment, 1st Battalion Royal Irish Fusiliers, 2nd Battalion York and Lancaster Regiment and a battalion of the Royal Marines Light Infantry) swept through a hail of fire to take the entrenchments in front of it and contribute powerfully to the general rout of Arabi's army. It is clear from the accounts of others that Graham had displayed that intangible gift of leadership – that mixture of gallantry, discipline and compassion – which endeared him to his soldiers and gave them confidence in him. Wolseley commented again in his despatch on Graham's coolness, gallantry and powers of leadership and command. Graham's reward was the KCB, the thanks of both Houses of Parliament and five mentions in despatches, plus the doubtful pleasure of being referred to publicly by Wolseley as having the heart of a lion and the modesty of a young girl.

On the breaking-up of the expeditionary force and Wolseley's departure for England, Graham was appointed to the command of a brigade in the Army of Occupation.

For Graham, life in the Army of Occupation consisted largely of inspections and parades, interspersed with a period of home leave during which he dined with Queen Victoria at Osborne House. But at the beginning of 1884, the tedium was broken by the arrival of Charles Gordon, en route to Khartoum and a hero's death. Graham and Gordon, fellow Engineers, had been close friends since the Crimean War. Graham accompanied Gordon on the first part of his last journey, as far as Korosko. On their final parting, Gordon gave Graham a silver-mounted kurbash (rhinoceros-hide whip) and took Graham's white umbrella, having lost his own. In an account written some time afterwards, Graham recorded his sense of foreboding that he would never see Gordon again.[3]

Graham was half-way back to Cairo when he received a signal on 14 February telling him that he had been appointed to command an expeditionary force going to Suakin. When he reached Cairo the following day, he found that Stephenson had already made most of the preparations for the despatch of the force, the first battalion (1st Battalion, Royal Highlanders (Black Watch)) leaving the same day. Stephenson had stengthened the force by adding the 26th (Field) Company, Royal Engineers. On Baker's advice, he had recommended sending some field guns in addition to the camel battery of mountain guns but the War Office refused. Baring had recommended on his own initiative that a battalion of the newly re-formed Egyptian Army should also be sent since this would create a good impression in Egypt; if it was not sent, it might prove difficult to attract British officers to serve with that Army. But the Home Government was not to be moved by pleading such as that; Baring was told by Granville that the new Egyptian Army had been raised to defend Egypt, not to undertake operations in the Sudan. The new Egyptian Army had been inaugurated by Khedivial decree on the 20 December 1882, with Sir Evelyn Wood as its first Sirdar (or Commander in Chief). It was based on conscription and initially comprised two brigades of four infantry battalions each; in 1883, the establishment was amended to include a cavalry regiment, three batteries of artillery (including a camel battery) and, later, a camel corps. The men were originally enlisted to serve for four years; subsequently, this was altered to four years in the army, four years in the police and four years in the reserve. In 1886, this was changed again to six years in the army, five in the police and four in the reserve. The first battalions were not in fact ready for service until 1885.

Once the decision had been taken to send a force to Suakin, preparations went forward with that extraordinary speed which characterised so many of the late-Victorian campaigns. Graham himself left Cairo on the 17 February with his staff and by the 22nd he and most of his force had reached Suakin, exactly ten days after the Cabinet's decision.

Back in England, the Confidential Mobilisation Committee,[4] under the chairmanship of the Adjutant General (Lord Wolseley) met on 13 February. The composition and command of the expedition had already been decided; the task of the Committee was therefore largely to arrange the supply of stores, equipment and ammunition, and additional medical personnel. Egypt already possessed sufficient stores and equipment to maintain the existing Army of Occupation of some 7000 men, but against the expected wastage inherent in any active operations, substantial quantities had to be sent out from England, including 250,000 rounds of carbine ammunition, 2000 sets of personal equipment, 700 saddles, 300 sets of mule harness, 400 carts, 500 double tents, a complete battery of 7-pounder mountain guns and six 40-pounder guns and carriages. From Malta, 200 rifles and 1500 sets of personal equipment were despatched to Egypt and the Indian Government was asked to provide 500 small tents (pals). Since clothing was always a casualty in operations, the reserves already in Egypt or on their way were supplemented with another 5000 pairs of boots, 5000 shirts, 10,000 pairs of socks and 1500 frocks (loose tunics). Finally, the Director General of Medical Services, having proposed an establishment of one General Hospital for 200 at Suez, a Field Hospital for 200 at Suakin, plus two mobile Field Hospitals, together with an addition of 200 beds in Egypt, despatched six Medical Officers, 50 NCOs and men of the Army Hospital Corps and equipment for three Field Hospitals and two Stations Hospitals. The India Office was asked to provide 200 camels, with drivers, from Aden. A thousand tons of miscellaneous supplies, including three months' groceries for 6000 men and 180,000 pounds of preserved meat, were also despatched. With that, the Mobilisation Committee rested on its oars and the action shifted to the Red Sea coast.

Graham reached Suakin on 22 February. The town of Suakin stands on an egg-shaped island, roughly five hundred yards by four hundred, and connected by a short causeway to the mainland where stood the much larger suburb of El Geif. The town is approached down a narrow winding channel fringed with coral reefs. Round the town, the channel broadens out to provide a fairly shallow harbour; large ships can moor only to the east or north-east of the town. North of Suakin Island there is a similar sized island, Quarantine Island (later Condenser Island), which was to form the main

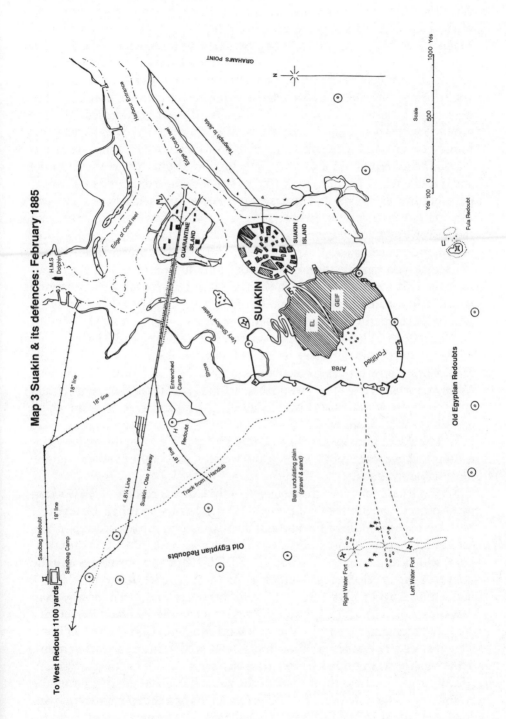

Map 3 Suakin & its defences: February 1885

41

logistics base. With its densely packed houses, Suakin's sanitation and cleanliness left much to be desired and the houses on closer inspection were often dilapidated. De Cosson recalled 'The small square houses built of rough blocks or coral without any pretence to architectural beauty but relieved by picturesque windows of carved and fretted lattice-work, the narrow, dusty lanes and various squares littered with piles of loose stones and rubbish; the squalid bazaar, darkened by heavy matting stretched from house to house, the rough kraals of the Arabs planted on every piece of waste ground, with their high fences or twisting mimosa stakes enclosing low round huts covered with skins and mats, in which dusky women are grinding flour between two stones while little brown, bright-eyed children run in and out like mice; the mingled odour of sea-weed and decaying offal which pervades the air.[5] It was not an easy port to enter, particularly at night, and Egyptian steamers preferred to lie off and wait until morning before braving the narrow, reef-edged channel. Prior to 1883, the town was largely unprotected by defences; a handful of earth redoubts, thrown up by the Egyptians in a semi-circle roughly three quarters of a mile out from the edge of El Geiff were the only fortifications which Colonel Harington found when he landed with the first batch of Baker's gendarmerie in December 1883. Harington proceeded to put the town into a defensible state and he built a chain of earth forts or redoubts, linked by a continuous mud wall, round El Geif.

To the north-west of these defences, covering the main Suakin-Berber road, Harington erected a large earth redoubt, called, after him, H Redoubt. More importantly, he built two earth forts, the Left Water Fort (Fort Shata) and the Right Water Fort (Fort Gemeiza), to protect the wells from which Suakin drew its main water supply. The two forts, 550 yards apart, were linked by a continuous earthwork. Some 1300 yards west of the main fortifications they were the most exposed and weakest part of the defences and the most liable to attack.

Suakin Island contained the residence of the Governor, some of the Government offices, the houses of the wealthier merchants and their businesses. Situated in the middle of the harbour and exposed to the sea breezes, it was cooler and therefore more desirable as a living place than El Geif on the mainland, which contained the bazaar, the smaller shops and businesses and the homes of the lower classes. Mythology had it that King Chosroes of Persia had sent to Abyssinia for seven virgins for his household. On their way from Abyssinia, the virgins had rested at Suakin; when they reached Persia they were all pregnant. Faced with this awkward situation, Chosroes' chief minister, the Vizier, blamed it all on the activities of a djinn (or evil demon). Thus Suakin was derived from either 'saba gin' (7 djinns) or 'sawwa-gin' (the djinn did it). Less romantically, the name is probably derived from the Arabic words for a market (suq). The Ottomans had occupied Suakin, with Massawa, about 1550 AD. The town had originally formed part of the Ottoman province of Abyssinia but with the decline of that province it had come

42

under the control of the Governor of the Hejaz, based on the port of Jeddah on the Arabian Red Sea coast. In 1843, Mehemet Ali had not unreasonably pressed for Suakin and its littoral to be transferred to him since he was now in control of the rest of the Sudan. The Porte had refused but he gained his wish in 1846. On his death in 1849, Suakin reverted to the control of Jedda where it remained for the next fifteen years until the Khedive Ismail acquired Suakin for Egypt for cash. Its importance lay largely in its position astride the trade route which ran from Darfur in the west, across Kordofan, the Nile and Eastern Sudan to Jeddah. In the late 19th century, Suakin's trade had expanded, due to the opening of the Suez Canal, the closure of the slave markets in Egypt and the opening of the White Nile route into Central Africa. In consequence, despite the navigational difficulties, a large trade in slaves, ivory, gum, ostrich feathers and incense flowed out through the port, with an equally large import trade in manufactured goods and food.

Osman Digna had laid siege to both Sinkat and Tokar but he had made no serious attempt on Suakin although there is little doubt that he could have occupied it in the twenty-four hours after his first victory at El Teb, on 2 December 1883. John Wylde, the leading European trader in the city, wrote later that 'Suakin that night was in a perfect panic and I never before saw such terror-stricken people. The position was, no doubt, critical and had the Arabs attacked us that night they could have carried all before them, as the town was a perfectly open one and no defence was organised'. The moment passed with the arrival of the first part of Baker's gendarmerie and the construction of serious fortifications around El Geif. Thereafter, despite the anxious period after Baker's defeat at the second battle of El Teb, the town was never in any serious danger. But almost nightly parties of Dervishes crept up close to the defences and fired into the town, occasionally cutting up sentries.

Why Osman failed to push home his advantage is not clear. A later Dervish prisoner claimed that Osman's programme had always been to take Tokar and Sinkat, then take and destroy Suakin and finally go on to Jeddah and Mecca.[6] Certainly Osman had no particular love for the inhabitants of Suakin who had expelled him and his family years before and who, by remaining loyal to the Egyptian Government, were implicitly denying the Mahdi and all he stood for. But Osman never deployed more than 6-7000 fighting men, most of whom were desert dwellers, and it may be that he was basically over-awed by the prospect of occupying a town the size of Suakin, a task for which he had no relevant experience and for which he could call on no expertise among his followers.

Graham arrived at Suakin with very precise instructions from Stephenson. He was to concentrate his expeditionary force at Suakin and then proceed with the utmost despatch to Trinkitat. From there he was to advance at once to Tokar and bring away the garrison and anyone else who wished to come. He was then to telegraph for further orders. If he received reliable news before he left Suakin that Tokar had fallen, he was to remain there pending further orders. If he received news of the fall of Tokar before advancing from Trinkitat, then he was to stand firm at Trinkitat until further orders, while at the same time detaching a sufficient force to hold Suakin.

Accordingly, the *Orontes*, carrying the Black Watch, and the *Teddington*, carrying 26 (Field) Company RE, proceeded direct to Trinkitat where they landed on 21 February, the Royal Engineers immediately beginning the construction of a landing pier. By the time that Graham reached Trinkitat two days later, the 3rd King's Royal Rifles, the 2nd Royal Irish Fusiliers, the 1st Gordon Highlanders, the 19th Hussars and some Mounted Infantry were already there and two condensing vessels, the *Tor* and *Teb el Bahr*, were producing 12,000 gallons of drinking water a day. A reconnaissance party from the 19th Hussars and the Mounted Infantry found Fort Baker unoccupied and small parties of the enemy in the vicinity retired as the cavalry advanced. It was clear that Osman had no intention of opposing the British landing. Three prisoners who were brought in said that they had been told that they would be fighting the Egyptians, not the 'fire devils' they had encountered.

Graham now received orders to prepare to advance even if Tokar had fallen and on 25 February, in pouring rain, the Gordon Highlanders and the Royal Irish Fusiliers, with supporting elements of artillery, mounted troops and engineers, advanced across the swamp separating them from Fort Baker and re-occupied the fort without opposition. The engineers then set to work to repair the damage which Osman's men had created.

Graham now added another battalion to his force. The 1st Battalion York and Lancaster Regiment, homeward bound in the *Serapis* after 13 years in India and Aden, was intercepted and diverted to Trinkitat which it reached on the 28th, the men having only the tropical kit they stood up in. Graham was now at full strength and ready to advance. He had received some days earlier a report from some fugitives who had escaped from Tokar that the town had already capitulated. He decided, correctly, that the report was not sufficiently reliable to justify delaying his advance. Baker had advised him that it would be impossible to find anyone foolhardy enough to take a message to Osman so Graham arranged for a letter to be fixed to a post in front of Fort Baker so that Osman's men could see and retrieve it. The letter called upon Osman to disperse his men and send delegates to Gordon at Khartoum to discuss the future settlement of the Sudan; while the British Government had no quarrel with the Arabs, it said, it was nevertheless determined to disperse the armed forces under Osman's command. The message was taken but no reply was received. On Friday 29 February, Graham moved out of Fort Baker with his whole force.

It was very much a scratch force. Three of the battalions (the Black Watch, the King's Royal Rifles and the Gordon Highlanders) had been plucked at a moment's notice from the sluggish peace-time routine of the Army of Occupation in Egypt; they all contained fairly high proportions of young soldiers who had never been in action. On the other hand, they were reasonably well-acclimatised. Two of the battalions (the Royal Irish Fusiliers and the York and Lancaster Regiment) were homeward-bound from long tours overseas. They had been hastily diverted to active service in the Sudan. Compared with the battalions from Egypt, they contained a higher proportion of older men, men who, by the simple process of survival in India, were likely to be tougher and more disease-resistant. As against that, they were likely to be less enthusiastic, having set their minds on England, and they were very noticeably weaker in numbers than the Cairo battalions.[7] A similar situation existed with the cavalry. The 19th Hussars had come from Egypt; because many of their English horses were not acclimatised they had been equipped on departure with Egyptian-bred horses taken from the Egyptian cavalry. The 10th Hussars, like the Royal Irish Fusiliers, had been diverted on their journey home from India and mounted at Suakin on horses taken over from the Gendarmerie. The 19th were 477 strong when they left Cairo; by contrast the 10th mustered only some 300 when they arrived at Suakin.

The remaining component of Graham's infantry comprised a battalion of Royal Marines, just under 400 strong, assembled from the ships of Hewett's East Indies Command and from the Mediterranean Fleet.

For artillery, Graham had 6 Battery, 1st Brigade, Scottish Division, Royal Artillery, a garrison battery which had been ordered to take over the guns, camels and equipment of the Egyptian Army's camel battery. When the battery reached Suakin, it was supplemented by 84 men homeward-bound from India in the *Jumna*, from 1 Battery, 2nd Brigade RA and G Battery, B Brigade, Royal Horse Artillery. At Trinkitat, 6/1's commander, Major Lloyd, managed to ditch his ancient bronze guns and obtain eight 7-pounder, rifled muzzle-loading guns from the Royal Navy. These were then fitted with some difficulty to the Egyptian carriages. Lloyd organised the guns and gunners into two batteries of four guns each. The 7-pounders threw a seven pound shell out to a maximum range of 3000 yards and fired common shell (i.e. high explosive) and shrapnel. In addition to these two batteries, Graham had three Gardners and three Gatling guns manned by naval crews provided by Hewett. These guns were hand-drawn.

To supplement his cavalry, Graham had brought with him a detachment of 124 Mounted Infantry, drawn from regiments in the Army of Occupation (KRRC, Royal Sussex, Black Watch and Gordons). With detachments from the various Departmental corps (Commissariat and Transport, Army Medical and Hospital, Ordnance etc.) and 26 (Field) Company, RE, Graham's force totalled just over 4700 men.

The infantry were equipped with the Martini-Henry rifle introduced in 1874. It was a single-shot breechloader, firing a heavy, 0.45″ lead bullet. Accurate out to a thousand yards, its effective range was considerably more. A trained soldier could fire 12 shots a minute with ease. It weighed nine pounds and, with its long, triangular, spike bayonet, the total length was nearly six feet. It was an excellent weapon, much beloved by the Victorian soldier, but it suffered from two defects; it had a very pronounced 'kick' and it was prone to jam in dusty or sandy conditions. The British cavalry were equipped with the Martini-Henry carbine, with the same action and cartridge but only three feet long and accurate to about 800 yards. The cavalry also carried the 1882 pattern sword, with a slightly curved, 35 inch blade and a sheet steel guard. It was, like its predecessor, a compromise design, intended for cutting and thrusting and not noticeably effective at either. Its other main defect was the scabbard which was metal and inclined to blunt the edge of the blade.

The Gardner gun was not a true machine gun but rather a volley-firing gun, using a number of separate barrels, varying between two and five.[8] Each barrel had its own breech and bolt which was cocked and fired by means of a cam-shaft operated by a manually operated lever. The barrels were loaded by gravity from a vertical hopper. The rate of fire was basically dependent upon the speed of operation of the lever which in turn was limited by the rate at which cartridges fell into the open breeches. The 0.45" calibre ammunition, unlike that of the Martini-Henrys, had a solid, drawn brass case. Apart from the bolts and barrels, the Gardner was made of brass and, given the very high temperatures encountered in the Sudan, it is not surprising that it was prone to stoppages. It was also extremely heavy. Mounted for use on wheels in the field, it weighed almost 800 pounds; with its ammunition limber, carrying 1200 rounds, the whole equipment weighed 1600 pounds or roughly three quarters of a ton.

The Gatling gun worked on a different principle. It had a number of barrels rotating round a horizontal axis by means of a manually operated crank handle, but with only a single bolt and breech. As each barrel came opposite the bolt, which was also cocked and released by means of the handle, a cartridge was fired. Thus, like the Gardner, the rate of fire was directly dependent upon the speed of rotation of the handle. Like the Gardner, it used solid-drawn 0.45" cartridges, gravity-fed from a vertical hopper or a drum. It was equally prone to jamming, as Roberts had discovered five years earlier in Afghanistan.[9]

Graham left behind at Trinkitat a garrison of some 150 men, including a company of the KRRC, with one Krupp field gun; at Fort Baker, he left three companies of the KRRC, with a Krupp field gun and two of the 7-pounders, about 250 men in all. Thus the total strength of the force he took forward was about 4300.[10] It was organised into three brigades; the 1st Infantry Brigade, under Buller, who had reached Trinkitat direct from England only on the 27th, the 2nd Infantry Brigade, under Davis,[11] and the Cavalry Brigade, under Stewart, who had arrived with Buller. Baker Pasha accompanied Graham because of his local knowledge and experience. The only transport animals accompanying the force were those carrying reserve ammunition and medical equipment; they numbered some 170. The infantry carried 70 rounds on each man, with reserves carried on mules. The artillery took 27 rounds per gun, all carried on camels, 18 rounds per camel.

Graham faced a formidable and well-armed foe. Accurate estimates of Osman's strength were impossible to come by but it could hardly have been less than 6000 fighting men and some estimates put it as high as 10,000 although that seems improbable. There is no evidence that the Mahdi supplied Osman at this stage with any of the weapons that he had accumulated in Kordofan but there was in truth no real need for him to do so. From the two disasters at El Teb, from the fall of Sinkat and now Tokar, and from the other minor clashes, Osman had accumulated a stock of at least 4000 rifles, with very large quantities of ammunition. He had also acquired four Krupp breech-loading field guns and two Gatling guns from Baker Pasha's defeat. The rifles were the excellent Remingtons. Osman was therefore well-equipped with modern weapons although collectively his troops were poor shots and lacked the disciplined fire-power of regular troops. Nevertheless, when added to the natural hardiness and fanatical courage of the tribesmen, the result was one of the most formidable opponents that the British had ever come across. The true qualities of Osman's men were, however, hidden for the moment; no British troops had yet been engaged and the experiences of the Egyptians were almost certainly discounted, given the low prevailing opinion of Egyptian troops, an opinion not without justification.

On the ship from Suez, Graham had worked out the tactical formation he would use. He proposed to stick with the well-proven square, with the front and flanks covered by the cavalry and Mounted Infantry, and the transport staffs and artillery moving inside the square. As compared, however, with the diagram recorded in his diary,[12] he made significant changes when the force advanced. Instead of the artillery being concentrated inside the square, he placed one battery in each of the rear corners, and he positioned two Gardners and one Gatling in the right front corner and two Gatlings and one Gardner in the left front corner. The KRRC and the Royal Marines were not deployed to form the square but were positioned as reserves inside. The final result, when it had been carefully marshalled, was a rectangle whose front and rear faces measured roughly 250 yards and the sides roughly 150. The front face consisted of the Gordons deployed in company columns of fours, in line abreast; when the square halted for action, the columns simply wheeled left or right to form a solid line. The rear face of the square consisted of the Black Watch deployed in the same way. These were the two strongest battalions. The right face consisted of the Royal Irish Fusiliers and some of the KRRC, in column of companies; on the command, they simply halted, and turned right into line. The left face was composed of the York and Lancasters and part of the Royal Marines in the same formation. Inside, were the Royal Irish and the remainder of the KRRC, forming, as it were, a second line; the rest of the Royal Marines were deployed in the same way behind the York and Lancasters. The front and sides of the square were protected by a wide screen of cavalry about 1000 yards ahead provided by one squadron of the 10th Hussars and a troop of the 19th Hussars, under Major Gough, 10th Hussars. The remainder of the cavalry, under the direct control of Stewart, followed the square, 600 yards behind the left rear. They were in three lines, the first line consisting of the remaining two squadrons of the 10th under their colonel, Edward Wood, the second and third lines of the 19th under the second in command, Percy Barrow, and the colonel, Edward Webster, respectively. Graham and his staff, 26 Company, RE and the medical and transport details were inside the square. The Mounted Infantry were initially in reserve behind the cavalry.

The square as a tactical formation had a long history in the British army. Originally, its purpose had been to defeat the attack of enemy cavalry by presenting a solid, impenetrable, continuous line of bayonets, backed by musketry. It had been used in this way at Waterloo. In the course of the late 19th century, it had been adapted for use against the charges of savage foes. Its great advantage was that it enabled maximum firepower to be developed by the infantry and it presented no flank for an enemy to turn. But it had a number of tactical drawbacks for any foe clever enough to utilise them. It was excessively difficult to control when moving; gaps and bulges were bound to develop in the faces of the square, presenting opportunities for penetration. The corners of the square were to a large extent unprotected because the fire of the adjacent faces diverged; the use of machine guns or artillery to protect these corners produced a gap which was liable to became an easy point of penetration. Finally, the square presented an enormous target for enemy marksman; given the range of modern weapons, the formation was untenable in face of concentrated musketry or artillery fire. Nevertheless, it had been used with success in Ashanti and in Zululand, and Graham was correct in his initial decision to use it against Osman Digna. Since the first troops had landed at Trinkitat, Graham's force had been under constant surveillance by Osman's mounted patrols. With the information readily available from his adherents in and around Suakin, Osman must have been fully informed both as to Graham's intentions and the composition of his force. The only matter on which he was unavoidably ignorant was the fighting power of the British troops, whom the Mahdiist armies had never encountered. Graham, too, had had his patrols out and had some intelligence from spies. All the evidence indicated that Osman had concentrated a large force in and around the village of El Teb; other forces were at Tokar and near Suakin. But whereas Osman knew the country intimately, Graham's intelligence was hazy even about the precise location of El Teb and he knew nothing of the composition of Osman's forces or about their position at El Teb. In their turn, the British troops knew little about the fighting power of the Dervishes other than that the Egyptian troops had been no match for them. To the British soldier that signified very little.

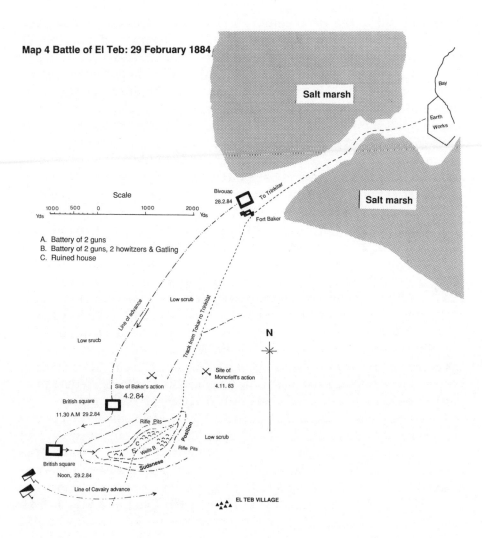

Map 4 Battle of El Teb: 29 February 1884

Salt marsh

Bay

Earth Works

Salt marsh

Scale

1000   500   0   1000   2000
Yds   Yds

Bivouac
28.2.84

To Trinkitat

Fort Baker

A. Battery of 2 guns
B. Battery of 2 guns, 2 howitzers & Gatling
C. Ruined house

Line of advance

Low scrub

Track from Tokar to Trinkitat

Low srucb

N

Site of Moncrieff's action
4.11. 83

Site of Baker's action
4.2.84

British square

11.30 A.M 29.2.84

Rifle Pits

Position

Low scrub

C
Wells B
A

Rifle Pits

British square

Sudanese

Noon, 29.2.84

Line of Cavalry advance

EL TEB VILLAGE

49

Graham moved off at 0815 hours on 29 February. It had rained heavily just before daybreak and that may have been the reason for his surprisingly late start. Since his troops were taking only one day's rations with them, it might have expected that he would have made an earlier start, both to give his troops the benefit of the cool early morning for their march and to give himself the maximum amount of daylight for the fighting which obviously lay ahead.

The ground for the first couple of miles was heavy from the overnight rain and the task of the Royal Artillery and the Naval Brigade in pulling its guns was correspondingly heavy. Frequent halts therefore had to be made. By 1000 hours, the force had advanced only three miles. Reports now came in from the left of the cavalry screen that the enemy were entrenched to the left front of the advancing square. 'My troop were the scouts of the front line of the Army, one mile in advance to feel and find the enemy. At about two miles from Teb, we sighted the enemy's scouts. They commenced a heavy fire on us but we did not return fire but marched steadily on them. I received an order from Major Gough to take three men and gallop to the front and find the strength of the enemy if possible, which to the best of my ability I did. I found their trenches all lined with men and the Krupp guns they took from the Egyptians at the slaughter three months before. They commenced a heavy fire on my poor section but were not clever enough to hit us. We moved about a bit too fast for them. My troop soon joined us in support. We again advanced under their fire, not attempting to return it. At last, we arrived on the right flank of their fort, right under the mouth of their guns, while the remainder of our Army advanced in square', wrote Sergeant Danby, of the 10th Hussars.[13] Graham now directed the square to incline to its right, away from the enemy, while the Mounted Infantry moved up to cover the left front of the square. By 1120 he was abreast of the position, of which he had not been aware, and, as it opened fire, he inclined the square further to the right. By 1130 he was abreast of the rear of the position.

Osman had clearly expected Graham to advance directly on El Teb and had constructed his positions accordingly. They were laid out with some skill. On the right of the main track from Trinkitat and facing towards it was a V-shaped earthwork, revetted with earth-filled sacks and barrels. In front of this was a ditch two or three feet deep. Behind this earthwork, Osman had mounted two of the Krupp guns and one of the Gatlings captured from Baker. To the right of this work the ground was thickly strewn with rifle pits, with the earth piled up in front to form a small parapet. To the left of the track, low hillocks were densely covered with rifle pits, row upon row, many carefully hidden behind the scrub bushes. Behind these positions lay the wells and huts of El Teb village covered by another Gatling and two old bronze guns. Further back, behind the village and some 950 yards from the first position, was another, semi-circular earthwork, covering a mound on which another two Krupps were mounted. This position faced at right angles to the other positions and covered their rear. The weakness of the position lay in the fact that the batteries were not laid out to provide cross-fire to each other and the whole position was laid out on the assumption that Graham would advance up the main track from Trinkitat. The Dervish force was led by three of Osman's best leaders, Idris, Osman's nephew, Hamed, and the amir Midani.

Whether by luck or good judgement, however, Graham had followed a route north of the main track.[14] Thus he found himself moving down the left flank of the enemy position, about 1200 yards away and relatively immune from the enemy fire although at least one Krupp shell landed near enough to wound a number of men. Baker himself received a piece of shrapnel in the face.

Graham halted roughly abreast of the last enemy position at about 1130 hours. The left side of his square, composed of the York and Lancaster battalion and the Royal Marines were thus closest to the enemy. The infantry were ordered to lie down to avoid the enemy artillery and rifle fire which was heavy if not very accurate. Four of the Royal Artillery camel guns and three Gatling and Gardner guns were now run out in front of the square and began to play upon the enemy position at a range of some 900 yards. The enemy guns were soon silenced and at mid-day Graham ordered the square to advance by its left flank on the enemy position. This automatically put the York and Lancasters and part of the Royal Marines into the front line, with the Black Watch and Gordon Highlanders on the left and right flanks respectively. The York and Lancasters advanced steadily, firing as they went. As they advanced, the line became irregular as some men hung back to maintain contact with the Gordons on the right while others charged forward, temporarily outdistancing the Marines to their left. As they got to within 200 yards of the earthwork, several hundreds of Osman's men leapt over the earthwork and charged the York and Lancasters. The enemy, armed mainly with spears and large, cross-hilted swords, were a daunting sight even for seasoned men such as the York and Lancasters. Those soldiers who had outrun their comrades began to fall back. Seeing this the Marines quickened their pace and the line was quickly re-formed. The enemy continued to come on, despite the relentless fire of the Martini-Henrys. Wounds seemed not to halt them and many of them got to within five yards of the square before being finally shot down. Some of the York and Lancasters were caught in front of the rest of their comrades and found themselves fighting hand-to-hand. Bennet Burleigh observed one such encounter: 'An Arab running out, spear in hand, rushed for one of the soldiers. The man fired, and at eight yards distance missed the savage; then the soldier appeared to be swayed by two instantaneous impulses – one to charge and give the foe his bayonet, the other to fall back on the line out of which he and other equally rash comrades had run to engage the Arabs. It ended by his furtively looking over his shoulder, a caving in of his chest, swaying to the rear for a step or two, and the Arab, who had not halted, bounded upon him, burying his lance deep in the wretched man's throat. Before the soldier had time to fall, he was lanced again and again; but the savage was the same moment himself shot and bayoneted by two of the 65th – too late to rescue, but in time to avenge'.[15] Assisted by two Gatlings and the Gardner gun which had been positioned in the corner of the junction of the York and Lancasters and the Gordons and which now advanced into line, the earthwork was quickly carried at about 1220 hours. The first VC of the campaign was won here by Captain Arthur Wilson accompanying the Naval Brigade. In protecting the machine guns, his sword snapped off at the hilt and Wilson, who was a huge man, proceeded to knock out his attackers with his fists. The two Krupps which had been captured were now turned on the other enemy batteries. The square now had to wheel to the left to roll up the remaining enemy positions from the rear. Inevitably the formation began to distort. The Black Watch, galled by fire from a house in front crowded forward abreast of the Royal Marines in order to fire at this house. On the right of the square which had now wheeled through nearly 180°, the Gordons brought one half-battalion up into line with the York and Lancaster while keeping the other half-battalion back as a flank guard. In this somewhat untidy formation, the troops swept through a series of huts and houses which were defended to the death of Osman's men. As Graham wrote 'The enemy's infantry, however, still clung with desperate tenacity to the numerous rifle pits and entrench-ments they had constructed, and large numbers occupied some buildings in the village, which were afterwards found filled with dead bodies; they seemed not to dream of asking for quarter, and when they found their retreat cut off would charge out singly or in scattered groups to hurl their spears in defiance at the advancing lines of Infantry, falling dead, fairly riddled with bullets'.[16] No quarter was given or expected on either side. 'It was almost impossible to save wounded Arabs, or take prisoners, as the dying savages, in their last throes, strove to thrust or cut with the keenest knives, lances or swords. The troops had to shoot or bayonet all as they advanced, for the wounded often started up, killing or maiming soldiers, and a grim pleasure lit their faces whenever they could bury their weapons in a man's body.'[17] Burleigh noted a small boy of perhaps twelve lying dead in a trench still clutching his small spear.

This was a new enemy for the British soldier. They had fought other foes – Zulus, Afghans, fanatics of all kinds – who had not flinched in face of the Martini-Henrys and the Gatlings but even these had had their breaking-points. No one had hitherto encountered a foe who never gave up and stopped only when he was dead or crippled. Several officers had narrow escapes. Captain Littledale of the York and Lancasters bent his sword over the head of one of the enemy, then pulled out his revolver and missed. He was promptly wrestled to the ground by the Arab who was about to kill him when he was rescued by some of his own troops who bayoneted and shot his attacker. Fred Burnaby, armed with a double-barrelled shot gun, was one of the first to reach the first battery. He was promptly attacked and forced to retire into the shelter of the other troops. At close quarters, the shotgun proved a devastating weapon, creating such massive and inhuman wounds that Burnaby (although not others) quietly abandoned it.

By 1400 hours, after two and a half hours' bloody fighting, Graham's infantry was in possession of the whole position. In the meantime, the cavalry under Stewart had got themselves into trouble. Stewart's instructions had been quite clear; he was to keep out of the way of the infantry square and to charge only when the enemy was completely broken and in retreat.[18] Stewart honoured the first part of his instructions until after the first battery had been taken. It would appear that then, seeing large numbers of men apparently retreating from this battery, he assumed that this was the main body in retreat and decided to charge. He swept round the rear of the infantry square, which was by now deep into the enemy entrenchments, and charged in three lines up the southern side of the village, the 10th Hussars leading, followed by the first line of the 19th under Lieutenant Colonel Barrow and then the second line under its regimental commander, Lieutenant Colonel Webster. What actually happened next is not entirely clear. Stewart was actually charging, not a defeated rabble, but large bodies of fresh troops who had hitherto not been seriously engaged. The first two lines charged through these masses, only to find them springing up again as they passed, hurling clubs and sticks at the horses' legs to bring them down and cutting at them with the heavy Sudanese swords to try to hamstring them. The first two lines, beset by the tenacious enemy, turned and charged back again, the first line of the 19th now leading followed by the 10th. Webster and his men appear to have become separated during the first charge, probably failing to get through the enemy masses. The affair now degenerated into a melée in which the British troopers were by no means at an advantage. Their swords were unable to reach the enemy lying down, and with their heavy stabbing spears which could also be thrown with great effect, the enemy were extremely effective at close quarters. Many of the troopers had not had time to school their Egyptian horses, hastily acquired just before leaving Suakin, and the unsteadiness of the horses was a factor in Stewart's difficulty. Quartermaster Sergeant Marshall of the 19th Hussars won the VC here for going to the assistance of Barrow who had got a spear in his side and had fallen to the ground. Marshall seized Barrow's hand and dragged him to safety. In the end all three lines of cavalry had to dismount some of their men and open fire with their carbines. By this time, the infantry had driven the enemy out of his main positions and the remaining Dervishes began to melt away into the scrub.

When the battle was finally over, Graham had lost 29 killed and 157 wounded; five men died of wounds subsequently. The cavalry lost roughly six per cent of the strength engaged; the infantry just under four per cent. Osman's force had numbered possibly 6000 and he admitted subsequently to losing 1500 killed and the same number wounded, including his nephew, Hamed, the amir Abdallah, the amir Midani, who had actually commanded the force at El Teb, and the amir Tahir, a cousin of Shaykh Tahir.[19] It was a staggering loss rate and Graham could be forgiven for assuming that he had dealt the Mahdiist forces a mortal blow.

Although he had gained a victory and blooded his troops against a new and very formidable foe at what may now seem to us a very small cost, Graham was not entirely satisfied with his troops. The Royal Irish Fusiliers and the KRRC had scarcely been engaged and he had nothing but praise for the York and Lancasters, the Gordons and the Royal Marines; but he commented severely in his despatch on the Black Watch being 'out of hand', although he believed that this was mainly through eagerness to fire on the enemy who was galling them with his fire.[20] He was also clearly irritated with Stewart although the wording in his despatch is oblique. He had reason to be angry; Stewart had mis-read the situation and had suffered relatively heavy losses as a result. Moreover, when the time came to consummate Graham's victory with a cavalry pursuit, Stewart had to report that the horses were too exhausted to pursue the beaten enemy.

Graham bivouacked on the battlefield that evening, heliographing back to Trinkitat for tents and supplies for the wounded. A tiny handful of prisoners had been captured and one of them was sent off in the evening with a further message to the enemy leaders, reported now to be concentrated at Tokar, calling upon them for the last time to submit and disperse.

Next day, (1 March) Graham left most of the Black Watch at El Teb, with orders to bury the enemy dead from the previous day and the European dead from the two previous battles there. (The Black Watch found 26 European bodies, including those of Moncrieff and Forestier-Walker. The bodies had all been mutilated.) With the rest of the force, he moved on Tokar just before 1000 hours. A much looser and larger square was used this time, to give more room for the transport animals. The Royal Irish Fusiliers, the Royal Marines and the York and Lancasters formed the front face, the Gordon Highlanders the rear; the sides were formed by the KRRC, which had not been seriously engaged the previous day, and the remainder of the Black Watch. As before, the square was covered by a screen of cavalry and mounted infantry with the main body of the cavalry concentrated in rear of the square. It was an excessively hot day and it was necessary to halt frequently to rest the men, particularly the artillerymen and sailors pulling the guns.

Sergeant Danby, of the 10th Hussars, claimed to have been the first man to sight Tokar, at about 1330 hours: 'I was the first to sight the place, being in the front with my three scouts. We advanced on nearly into the town, not seeing anyone. Suddenly they opened fire on us. We retired to a walk and informed the General what had happened. I was again ordered to advance with a little stronger party and if they again fired, not to return it but to

54

watch them. In the meantime, our army came in full view of the place. They [the enemy] left the town from the back, leaving the Egyptians and those that had been killed and died of starvation in the town . . . All men gone but found great piles of stores, guns, ammunition etc. but nothing to eat or drink.'[21]

Major Gough, again in charge of the screen, had told Graham at 1415 that he believed the town to be strongly held. Accordingly, Graham moved his force towards the north of Tokar since that side seemed the most favourable for an assault. In fact, as Sergeant Danby noted, the enemy had abandoned the town and it was occupied without incident at about 1630 hours. It proved to be a fairly unexciting place, consisting largely of reed matting huts with a few mud brick buildings which proved on closer acquaintance to be tumbledown and dirty. The fort was basically an enclosure roughly 300 yards by 200 yards, surrounded by a mud wall four to seven feet high with a six-foot ditch in front. In parts, the ditch was non-existent and the walls of some of the buildings of the fort provided the only cover. There was plenty of cover close up to the fort so it is unlikely that it could have been held indefinitely against the sort of fanatical attack which the Dervishes practised.[22] In fact, the garrison had capitulated ten days earlier. The Dervishes had looted and plundered but had otherwise not attacked the inhabitants. Nevertheless, the survivors of the garrison and the remaining townspeople were only too delighted to see Graham's men, their one objective being to get back to the coast, out of reach of Osman's men.

Graham's troops bivouacked outside the town, only those on specific duty being allowed inside, as a precaution against attacks by hidden fanatics. Water was available from wells and a convoy of food and forage arrived the same evening from El Teb.

On the following day (2 March), Graham, with a mounted party, searched villages around Tokar and found 1250 Remingtons, a brass field gun, a Gatling gun captured from Baker, and large stocks of ammunition. The rifles were destroyed, most of the ammunition buried and the two guns brought back to Tokar. Why Osman abandoned so many valuable rifles and ammunition is a mystery; one would have thought that, despite his losses at El Teb, he had enough men available to prevent this valuable booty falling into British hands. His defeat may simply have taken him by surprise.

Having already sent back the Black Watch, the KRRC, the cavalry and the naval contingent, Graham, pursuant to his orders, evacuated Tokar on 4 March and marched back to Trinkitat, taking with him 689 Egyptian soldiers and other refugees. Again, the troops started at 0800 hours and arrived back at Fort Baker at 1500, having covered some 17 miles without a man falling out. Sergeant Danby noted that they had been four days without a wash and had lived off biscuits and water; the preserved meat and potatoes which awaited them at Fort Baker was a positive feast. The wounded were embarked on the *Jumna* and sent off to the hospital at Suez.

55

Graham and Hewett had proposed that the force should return by sea to Suakin to undertake a further offensive against Osman to try to disperse his forces once and for all. The Secretary of State for War having given his approval, on condition that Graham did not operate at any considerable distance from Suakin, the force was shipped back to Suakin where it was concentrated on the evening of 9 March; Tokar, Fort Baker and Trinkitat being abandoned. Marling noted on return that an enterprising gentleman, half-Greek, half-Italian, called Sudrean, had set up a tent on the sea shore, imported a cargo of food and liquor, and started a restaurant.[23]

Graham had been warned by a friendly shaykh that Osman intended to fight again, and on 5 March Hewett and Graham issued a proclamation calling on the rebel chiefs to come in and submit to avoid the fate of those who had fought at El Teb. Graham had also been told by pilgrims bounds for Mecca from Darfur that the road from Berber to Suakin was completely free of Mahdiist forces. On 8 March, with preparations ready for an advance, Graham and Hewett issued yet another proclamation, calling upon Osman's adherents to disperse and warning them that the British intended to march on Tamanieb and deal with them as they had done at El Teb. It elicited only a scornful and defiant answer signed by a large number of hostile shaykhs. On the 9th, therefore, Graham reconnoitred along the road to Tamanieb, as far as the zariba which Baker had built in January, about eight miles from Suakin and roughly half way to Tamai and known as 'Baker's Zariba'. As a result, the zariba was occupied the following day by the Black Watch and some mounted infantry. Graham began his main advance on 11 March, moving his infantry and artillery to the zariba in the cool of the evening, the cavalry and Mounted Infantry following the next morning (12th). At about 1000 hours on the 12th, the Mounted Infantry reported that Osman was present in force six miles ahead. At 1300 hours, after the men had had their dinners, the whole British force began to advance in the usual square formation. Graham had left a hundred Royal Marines, plus the sick, at Suakin to defend the town and camp and he left two companies of the KRRC and Black Watch at Baker's Zariba. He was left with just over 4000 men, consisting of the 10th and 19th Hussars, the Mounted Infantry (124), 26 (Field) Company RE, and the original six infantry battalions, in two brigades. For artillery, he had Lloyd's two batteries of 7-pounders, the six Gardners and Gatlings manned by sailors, and M Battery 1st Brigade RA under Major Holley which had been returning home from India in the *Jumna*. Holley had, with great initiative, acquired four naval 9-pounder field guns, mounted them on Egyptian carriages and improvised the necessary transport. The battery had not been ready in time for El Teb but it was now to get its chance.

By 1700 hours on the 12th, the force had advanced some six miles, with constant halts to rest the men in the intense heat. The cavalry scouts now reported that the enemy were advancing in force to attack. Graham immediately halted the square on open ground and began to construct a mimosa-

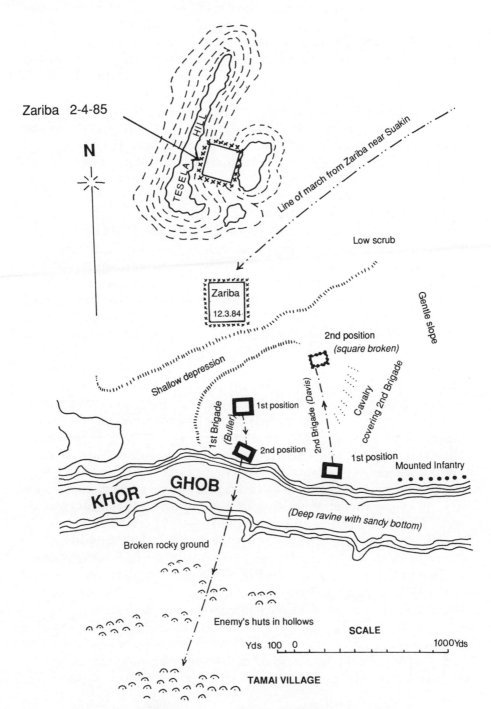

Zariba 2-4-85

N

TESELA HILL

Line of march from Zariba near Suakin

Low scrub

Zariba
12.3.84

Gentle slope

2nd position
(square broken)

Shallow depression

Cavalry covering 2nd Brigade

1st Brigade (Buller)

1st position

2nd Brigade (Davis)

2nd position

1st position

Mounted Infantry

KHOR GHOB

(Deep ravine with sandy bottom)

Broken rocky ground

Enemy's huts in hollows

SCALE

Yds 100   0   1000 Yds

TAMAI VILLAGE

Map 5 Battle of Tamai: 13 March 1884

bush zariba around his position. The cavalry and mounted infantry were sent back to Baker's Zariba and the rest of the force settled down to an uneasy night. The troops were then about half a mile from the Khor Ghob, on the far side of which was Tamai although it is not clear whether Graham knew exactly where he was. Osman's riflemen maintained a constant fusillade throughout the night but did not attack. Wylde, for one, was very glad: 'It is a good thing that the Arabs do not like attacking by night, as if they had done so when the troops covered such a lot of ground, what with the bush and the smoke from the guns it would have given the enemy a good advantage, and there would have been some hard fighting in which their numbers might have told. If they had been beaten off it would have only been after an enormous loss on our side and if once the troops had taken panic it would have ended in disaster.'[24] As the night wore on, the Dervishes grew bolder and came in closer, abusing the British troops and calling them infidels and Christian dogs. Just after midnight the whole force stood to arms, expecting an attack, but the firing began slowly to quieten down as dawn approached. Wylde was sent out with Abyssinian scouts that he had recruited at Massawa to see if he could drive off the Dervish sharpshooters but they were too numerous. He was able to see that the Khor Ghob, a large, wide ravine some 900 yards ahead, was filled with large parties of the enemy, the bright moon reflecting off their spear heads and rifle barrels.

Dawn eventually came on the 13th and, with it, the cavalry and mounted infantry from Baker's Zariba; the latter were immediately despatched to reconnoitre the enemy forces. Graham now knew from Wylde and from an escaped prisoner that the enemy was concentrated in the Khor Ghob which gave good cover. Graham's plan was to take up a position on the edge of the Khor from which he could rake the enemy with his artillery before committing his infantry. The morning was clear and bright as Graham's force moved forward, the infantry in two brigade squares in echelon. Leading was the 2nd Brigade under Major General Davis, with three companies of the Black Watch and three companies of the York and Lancasters forming the front face; the left side was composed of the remaining four companies of the Black Watch, the right face of the four remaining companies of the York and Lancasters and the rear face of the Royal Marines. M Battery was positioned inside the square near the front right-hand corner; three machine guns of the Naval Brigade were near the front left-hand corner. The 2nd Brigade moved off at around 0830 but the 1st Brigade was slow to form up and when it moved off it was in echelon some six hundred yards to the right rear of the 2nd Brigade. The cavalry remained in the rear. Graham was inside the 2nd Brigade square; M Battery had now been ordered outside the square, on its right flank.

As the 2nd Brigade approached the near edge of Khor Ghob, large numbers of the enemy appeared over the edge of the ravine immediately in front. Graham now ordered the seven companies of the Black Watch to charge, but either deliberately or through an oversight, left the York and Lancasters where they were. Galled by the unfair criticism of their behaviour at El Teb, the Black Watch needed no urging. In a twinkling, the lid had been largely lifted from the box. Into the gap now created in the front face of the square, Osman's men now poured. The Black Watch and the York and Lancasters found themselves attacked in rear and largely surrounded. The front face and sides of the square had in effect disintegrated into small groups of cursing, struggling fighting men. Some groups died where they stood. The remainder were forced back on the Royal Marines forming the rear face of the square. The Gardners and Gatlings, which Graham had hastily ordered over to the right-hand corner to stem the enemy inrush, were overrun although the sailors were just able to lock the guns before they were killed. With the front and sides of the square disintegrated and the enemy inside, hacking and stabbing, all depended upon the Royal Marines standing firm and providing a buttress on which the rest of the square could re-form. But even they were unable to withstand the pressure as the other troops were forced back upon them by the fanatical impetus of the Dervish enemy. In confusion, the whole brigade was forced to retreat, all cohesion lost. Succour came in the nick of time from Buller's 1st Brigade, from M Battery and from the cavalry. The 1st Brigade moved up on the right flank of the 2nd Brigade and, although attacked itself, was able to clear the ground between it and the 2nd Brigade with its steady volleys. At the same time, the cavalry moved up from the rear on the left flank of the 2nd Brigade and, dismounting some of its men, began to pour in volleys from its Martini-Henry carbines which at a range of only a few hundred yards were deadly. M Battery, which had been ordered outside Davis's square and caught unprotected, nevertheless proceeded to fight its guns pluckily and effectively, raking the enemy with case shot. Assisted thus by the fire power of the rest of the force, the 2nd Brigade was at last able to re-form into line several hundreds of yards behind its original position. Together, the two brigades were then able to advance, driving the remaining Dervishes before them. The enemy had not had time to remove the machine guns and, as the 2nd Brigade advanced again towards the Khor, the guns were recaptured, unlocked by the survivors of their crews, and turned on the enemy. The 2nd Brigade halted on the near rim of the Khor; the 1st Brigade, accompanied by Graham and some of the cavalry, moved down into the Khor, clearing it of the enemy as it went, and up the far side. Half a mile beyond were the scattered huts and tents which constituted the village of Tamai and Osman's headquarters. This was occupied just before noon, the Dervishes retreating sullenly. Graham then prudently withdrew all his troops, including the dead. The cavalry went back to Baker's Zariba for the night and the rest of the force re-occupied the previous night's zariba where it spent an untroubled night except for women's voices wailing from the battlefield. The next morning (14th), Graham re-occupied Tamai and destroyed the large stocks of ammunition found there, together with rifles and equipment captured by Osman in earlier encounters. Finally, the hundreds of huts were burned and in the afternoon the troops started the march back to Suakin. There was no possibility of using British troops to pursue the defeated enemy into the hills since, in the broken terrain, the Dervishes could move faster than regular troops, even cavalry, but Wylde, for one, felt that if steps had been taken earlier to organise a force of friendly tribesmen and Abyssinian scouts to pursue, there would have been a good chance of capturing Osman and his lieutenants and putting an end to the whole insurrection in the Eastern Sudan. A way would then have been open to Berber and thence to Khartoum. Hewett sent out 200 sailors to help with carrying the wounded and by mid-day on the 15th the whole force had been concentrated at Suakin.

Tamai had been an exceptionally bloody affair. Osman admitted to losing 2000 men killed and an equal number wounded. Including casualties on the night of the 12th/13th, Graham lost 109 killed and 112 wounded. As was to be expected, the heaviest loss was among the Black Watch, who lost 60 killed and 33 wounded; the Yorks and Lancasters lost 32 killed and 24 wounded. Out of their small numbers, the Naval Brigade lost 3 officers and 7 men killed and 8 wounded, mainly in the course of their guns being overrun. The wounded on both sides were killed virtually automatically; Wylde wrote of the Dervish wounded 'It was a cruel sight as soon as we got among the dead and wounded; the latter, although they could hardly move, would take no quarter, and it became absolutely necessary to put an end to them, as they were wounding our men and although in a crippled state, would fight to the last. It was useless taking their arms from them as they would try and crawl on to the nearest weapon to have a chance of killing a Christian in the hope of going straight to paradise'.[25] Burleigh recorded a typical incident; 'A fine-looking savage lay half-reclining . . . he was badly wounded in the leg, a bullet having shattered his knee. Grasping his heavy broad-bladed spear, he looked defiance and mischief at the soldiers as they approached. A Blue-jacket was the first to venture near him and although Jack had his rifle and cutlass attached, he liked not his far-reaching, quick striking spear. The troops were forbidden to fire and there was nothing for it but to tackle the man with steel . . . A soldier now stole up on the opposite side of the Hadendowa, but even then the savage, like a wounded stag at bay, was not to be trifled with. A mean subterfuge, cunning strategem or what you will you may call it, prevailed. A stone thrown at the Arab's head stunned him for a moment, and before he recovered the Blue-jacket had plunged his cutlass into him, bending the weapon into such a hoop shape that he could just barely withdraw it, and so closed the day of another life.'[26] One small boy, picked up and bandaged, tore off his bandages and tried to grab a soldier's bayonet; he had to have his arms tied to his sides. Given water by a priest, he spat it full in the priest's face. Half an hour later, he managed to get free, seized a spear and had to be knocked out with a camel stick. Even then, he refused to be re-bandaged and died the same evening, still cursing.[27] Apart from him, the only other prisoners recorded were a slave woman who had used the battle as an opportunity to escape, although speared in the process, and a Hadendowa warrior who had lost six brothers in the fight. The British dead were often unrecognisable because of the wounds caused by the heavy, razor-sharp Sudanese swords; many of them had been mutilated. Some of the British casualties were caused by cross-fire from the two squares. Graham himself had had a narrow escape. He had been inside the 2nd Brigade square and had posted himself immediately behind the York and Lancasters as soon as he saw the direction of the Dervish attack. He had been caught in the great melée when that corner of the square collapsed and at one stage was almost surrounded, one Dervish getting close enough to attack his horse.[28]

Two VCs had been won. Lieutenant Marling, KRRC, attached to the Mounted Infantry, won his at the beginning of the battle for giving up his horse to a wounded private and carrying him back to safety. Private Edwards, of the Black Watch, had been attached to the Naval Brigade as a mule driver. When the machine guns at the right front corner of the square were over-run, Edwards bayoneted two attackers, being wounded in the process by a spear, and succeeded in getting his mules, carrying ammunition, to safety. Graham referred in a General Order of 16 March to discipline having been forgotten at a critical moment, presumably a reference to the York and Lancasters. That regiment, whether by accident or design, had borne the brunt of the initial fighting both at El Teb and Tamai. It was little more than half the strength of the battalions from Egypt and the men, with their families, had been looking forward to reaching England when they were suddenly diverted to the Sudan; many were time-expired anyway. Bennett Burleigh noted that after Tamai 'the greatest dissatisfaction exists among all ranks, particularly among the time-expired men and others who think that, in common fairness, an arduous campaign like the present should have been reserved for fresh troops. There is more grumbling than I have ever heard among soldiers and officers about the whole business. They are constantly asking, "Why are we here? Why are we killing such brave fellows? Surely not for the sake of wretched Egyptians." It is impossible to magnify the intensity of the feeling thus indicated'.[29]

What tactical honours there were clearly went to the Dervishes who had been led by Osman's cousin, Muhammad Mussa; Osman, as was his custom, prudently stayed in the rear. They had had the patience to wait until the 2nd Brigade was almost at the lip of the Khor Ghob, thus greatly reducing the time during which the British troops could fire. When the charge of the Black Watch opened up the front face of the square, they were quick to direct an overwhelming attack on to the corner thus left exposed. But they had made the mistake of assuming at too early a stage that the square was doomed and many of them had gone off to attack the 1st Brigade. A con-

61

vergent attack on both front corners of the 2nd Brigade square must have annihilated it. Those who attacked the 1st Brigade were slaughtered because the distance involved (about 600 yards) allowed the British firepower to develop its maximum effect. Against the Martini-Henry volleys no flesh and blood could prevail. Nevertheless, Osman's men had smashed, and very nearly annihilated, a British square and captured its guns.

Graham accepted some of the blame for the near-disaster because he admitted in his despatch approving the charge of the Black Watch.[30] In truth, the whole blame was his. He had known since the previous night that the enemy intended to fight him on the Khor Ghob and that they were concentrated there in great force. Despite that, he had pushed the 1st Brigade too close to the edge of the Khor. If he had halted the square earlier, it would have had time to develop its maximum fire power before the enemy could close with it. He had then compounded his error and made disaster unavoidable by ordering the Black Watch to charge, thus opening up the box which depended wholly for its strength on remaining unbroken. Why he allowed the Black Watch to charge is to some extent unexplained but there are strong clues. Before the square had moved off that morning, he had addressed the Black Watch. There are slightly different versions of his actual words but the gist is clear. He had expected the regiment to charge the enemy at El Teb and fight them hand to hand, instead of merely firing at them. He was now giving the regiment another opportunity to prove itself. It seems clear therefore that in ordering the Black Watch to charge he had allowed reasons of sentiment to outweigh simple tactical commonsense. That he had not suffered a major disaster was due entirely to the courage and discipline of his troops and, in particular, to the timely intervention of Buller's 1st Brigade. Nevertheless, with Tamai, he could now claim that he fulfilled both objects of his expedition. He had rescued the garrison of Tokar even if he could not prevent the town falling to the enemy, and he had certainly dealt Osman and his forces a massive blow. Osman was still at large with a considerable army still at his disposal but he had lost more than 3500 men plus many who would either die of their wounds or be incapable of further fighting. Such a loss among the sparse population of the Eastern Sudan could hardly be made up. Moreover, the prestige of both Osman and the Mahdiist cause had been severely damaged. The bodies of the Faithful were not, after all, proof against the bullets of the Infidel and the long run of victories which had followed the Mahdi since 1881 had been decisively halted.

Now, if ever, was the time to push through to Berber and open up communication via the Nile with Gordon. As early as 5 March, Graham had suggested to Stephenson that Gordon should be asked if he would recommend that a force under Graham should operate along the Berber road, and if so, what co-operation he could offer.[31] Gordon confirmed on 7 March that he attached great importance to Graham following up his success at El Teb by sending a small force to Berber. On the 10th, he said that he was instructing the Mudir of Berber (Hussein Pasha Khalifa) to be ready to advance to Obak (roughly a quarter of the way from Berber to Suakin) to meet any force that Graham might send. Stephenson, however, was against Graham marching to Berber because of the shortage of water en route. The Secretary of State sided with Stephenson and instructed Graham not to undertake operations at any considerable distance from Suakin. Graham did not abandon hope of persuading the Home Government but he realised that it would now need to be done with greater finesse. Accordingly, he reported on 9 March that he proposed to advance on Tamai and thereafter, if practicable, to send a flying column on to Sinkat. The Secretary of State was not clear what the purpose of an advance on Sinkat was but he did not forbid it, contenting himself with suggesting that the road to Berber might be opened up by enlisting the aid of the friendly tribes. Graham exerted some more pressure on 14 March after the battle of Tamai by relaying to the Secretary of State the advice of a local shaykh that, once the news of Osman's defeat had spread, the Berber road would be clear very quickly.[32] The Secretary of State did not bite but acquiesced in Graham advancing to Sinkat; provided it could be done without risk and was not regarded as the first step in a series of advances.

After reconnoitring Handub on the Berber road on 15 March, Graham sent a long appreciation of the situation to London two days later. Two heavy blows had been struck and it was essential to follow up their impact by a demonstration towards Berber, giving the impression that the British could go anywhere that they wished. As far as Es Sibil (50 miles on), the road was in the hands of the friendly Fadlab section of the Amarar tribe. From Es Sibil to Arriab, the road was controlled by other sections of the Amarars, the greater part of whom were still loyal. From Arriab to Berber, the Bisharin tribes were in control and they would have to be dealt with from Berber itself. Graham recommended that Gordon should be asked to open the Berber road from his end and send a force through to Suakin.[33] The Government was not to be shifted. Four days later, Baring was told to instruct Graham to enlist the aid of local friendly tribes to open the Berber road; he was not to attack Osman but, if possible, negotiate to secure his submission in return for Osman becoming responsible for the government of the road.[34] Baring used his discretion and left it to Graham to decide whether to attack Osman or no. Baring was by this time cautiously in favour of attempting to march on Berber in co-operation with Gordon. The Government was, however, adamant; it was determined not to extend operations beyond the vicinity of Suakin, particularly since the hot weather was approaching. Behind its attitude lay a determination not to be sucked into a major expedition to aid Gordon who was wilfully disobeying his instructions to evacuate the Egyptian garrisons from Khartoum and elsewhere.

Graham always regretted afterwards that he had not taken the bold course and sent troops through to Berber without waiting for permission. Writing after Gordon's death, he said 'the battle of Tamai was fought, after which, at the price of much bloodshed, the road from Suakin to Berber was open for British or Indian troops and the opportunity for rescuing Gordon and for saving Berber and Khartoum was actually within England's grasp . . . it is yet some small consolation to me to know that Gordon, in the midst of his bitter reflections when alone at Khartoum, acquitted me and the gallant little force I had the honour to command of all unreadiness or disinclination to advance to his rescue'.[35]

Clearly Graham had a bad conscience about his failure to advance on Berber. We need therefore to look at the logistic and other risks involved. The principal road to Berber ran thorugh Otao, Es Sibil, Arriab and Obak and was 241 miles long. It had been traversed by a number of military observers in recent years, notably Captain De Cosson in 1873, Major Prout in 1877, and Colonel Colborne and Lieutenant Colonel Stewart in 1883. Information about the water supplies was therefore good although allowance had to be made for the unpredictable incidence of drought. The consensus of information was that from Suakin to Arriab (129 miles) there were supplies of water at reasonable intervals sufficient at least for a mounted force of several hundred men. It was the general view that these supplies could almost certainly be improved and increased. Close to Suakin, and again between Arriab and Berber, the water was inclined however to be brackish and salt. The real problem along the route lay between Arriab and Berber, a distance of some 112 miles. Beyond Arriab, water was not encountered for 53 miles until Obak where there were numerous wells of brackish, salty water. Beyond Obak, there was not water until Bir Mahobeh, 52 miles on; Berber lay seven miles on beyond Bir Mahobeh. The route itself presented no particular physical problems and Prout had declared it perfectly practical for wheeled traffic subject to some work at three places.[36] An alternative route lay to the south, through Sinkat, rejoining the first route ten miles from Obak. Yet another route, surveyed by Lieutenant C.M. Watson RE in 1874, left the main route at Otao and swung away southwards, rejoining the main route at Obak. Watson considered it the best route of all to Obak; it had water on nearly every day's march and it could quite easily be made suitable for wheels. The problem of the long, waterless stretch of fifty odd miles from Obak to Bir Mahobeh remained. De Cosson, however, believed that the existing water supply on all routes from Suakin to Berber had simply been developed to meet the actual traffic, and that more water could be found once the need was demonstrated. Taking all of the evidence together, it seems probable that the presence or absence of water would not of itself have prevented a substantial mounted force reaching Berber from Suakin; the use of infantry, however, would have required the transport of large stocks of water, particularly between Obak and Berber. The use of a large force was thus almost certainly ruled out in the absence of a railway. The question was whether a large force was required; that in turn depended to some extent upon the assistance which could be provided from Berber itself. None of the routes from Suakin was of very great difficulty but each of them traversed rugged, mountainous country with a number of narrow defiles. If these areas were held in strength by the Dervishes, then a small force could not be expected to get through. Moreover a small force could not be expected to take Berber if it had fallen into rebel hands. The passage of a modest force would not of itself open the Suakin-Berber road. That could only be achieved by garrisoning a chain of posts along the entire 241 miles and even then re-supply could prove a major military undertaking in face of determined opposition, as the 1885 campaign was to demonstrate. A secure route must depend upon the laying of a railway; once that had been done, the logistics problems could be solved and security ensured by the use of armoured trains.

But in the spring of 1884 there was a big prize to play for. If even a small force of British troops could get through to Berber, then it was only a few days steaming up the Nile to Khartoum. The effective presence of British troops in Khartoum in support of Gordon could have had incalculable effects on the general situation, as Gordon himself continually stressed. In March 1884, Berber was still firmly in Gordon's hands (it was not invested and taken by the Mahdi until May 1884) and Osman's power and prestige had been severely weakened around Suakin. It is difficult to avoid the conclusion that a great chance was missed in March 1884 to pass a force from Suakin to Berber and that ultimately the failure to do so sealed the fate of Gordon and Khartoum. Charles Royle, a contemporary historian of the campaign, thought so too; 'after the victory of Tamai Graham could have sent a few squadrons of cavalry through to Berber with ease . . . Two squadrons would, in the opinion of all the authorities in the Soudan, have sufficed to open the road and to save Berber, which was the key to the Soudan, and without the retention of which, evacuation [by Gordon] was hopeless'.[37] Wylde was of exactly the same view as, one suspects, were most of Graham's colleagues and subordinates.

All of this forms the background to Graham's operations after Tamai. Having despatched the wounded to the hospital at Suez in the *Jumna*, Hewett issued a proclamation, offering 5000 dollars for Osman Digna, dead or alive. This was too much for the Government's susceptibilities and Hewett was forced to withdraw it two days later. The Government preferred to proceed by negotiation and Graham and Hewett were informed on 18 March that Major Herbert Chermside, who had been on political duties in Egypt during Wolseley's campaign in 1882 and had since then been commanding a battalion of the new Egyptian Army, was being despatched to Suakin to negotiate with the shaykhs of the surrounding tribes for their submission and the abandonment of Osman and the Mahdi. In the meantime, Graham was authorised to make a demonstration of an advance along the Berber road. Accordingly, on 18 March, Stewart, with the 19th Hussars, the Mounted Infantry, the Gordon Highlanders and a detachment of Royal Engineers – just under 1100 men in all – occupied Handub, twelve miles out from Suakin, along the Berber road. The head of the Fadlab section of the Amarar, with some followers, accompanied him with a view to persuading other tribesmen to come in.

Handub[38] was only some 18 miles from Tamanieb where Osman was reported to be with 2500 men. It nestles at the foot of a hill and for part of the year has supplies of running water. In March, however, those supplies had dried up and the water provided by wells was brackish and regarded as suitable only for the horses. Drinking water for the men had to be condensed and sent up from Suakin. Stewart's camp was surrounded by a thick zariba against sudden attack and a fortified redoubt was constructed on top of the hill to provide a wide look-out.

On the 19th, Stewart, with most of the mounted troops, reconnoitred westwards along the Berber road as far as Otao, eight miles beyond Handub; another squadron explored southwards in the direction of Tamanieb. No enemy was seen. From Suakin, two days later, the 10th Hussars made a sweep of some 15 miles towards Tamanieb to intercept a convoy of 40 camels carrying grain alleged to be on its way from Tokar to Osman's camp. Again no enemy was met. The feeling was growing at Suakin that Osman was on his last legs and, since neither Graham nor Hewett had any great faith in the efficacy of the negotations, they succeeded, with Baring's support, in getting permision to attack Osman if they thought it desirable. Graham had already made plans to seize and destroy Tamanieb, and on the 23rd, six companies of the Gordons moved down from Handub and constructed a new zariba (No 4), only some six miles from Tamanieb.

On the 25th, at the somewhat curious hour of 1400 hours, Graham moved out from Suakin with his whole force and concentrated at No 4 zariba, leaving Suakin to to be guarded by seamen and marines from Hewett's ships. Graham believed that marching in the afternoon in the temperatures now being reached was preferable to marching in the morning when there was no breeze of any kind but, since more than 200 men fell out on this occasion because of the heat, the advantage is not immediately obvious. The majority of those who fell out were from the KRRC, which had a high proportion of young soldiers.

Next day, Stewart took out the mounted troops to try to find the where-abouts and numbers of the expected enemy. He was followed two hours later by Buller with the Gordon Highlanders, the Royal Irish Fusiliers and M Battery; Buller in turn was followed by a supply convoy guarded by the Royal Marines and 5/1, RA. Stewart encountered small parties of the enemy in the difficult hilly country close to Tamanieb and could get no further. On hearing this, Graham ordered Buller to construct a new zariba (No 5) close to the entrance to the hills around Tamanieb. The Black Watch and the KRRC were now ordered up from No 4 zariba, which was now garrisoned only by the York and Lancasters. Stewart bivouacked for the night in rear of No 5 zariba.

Stewart's reconnaissance had established little except that there were parties of the enemy around Tamanieb. That appeared to confirm the belief that Osman, with what remained of his troops was there, so next day (27th), at what was for him the unusually early hour of 0540, Graham moved out from No 5 zariba with virtually his whole force. As at Tamai, the force moved into two squares in echelon, the 1st Brigade leading, consisting of the Gordon Highlanders, Royal Irish Fusiliers and two companies of the KRRC. The 2nd Brigade followed, consisting of the Black Watch, the Royal Marines and a portion of the York and Lancasters. The two brigades were covered by a wide screen of cavalry and mounted infantry and accompanied by M. Battery. Graham and his staff, instead of being inside one of the squares as at Tamai, rode a quarter of a mile ahead of the first square. A couple of miles from Tamanieb, the route became winding and constricted by hills on both sides. The infantry therefore took to the hills and moved along a ridge while the mounted troops continued along the valley below. The mounted troops quickly became engaged with parties of Dervishes firing from behind rocks. The fighting which followed was conducted by the mounted troops dismounted. By the time the 1st Brigade was within shooting distance the action was over. A few shells from the artillery hastened the retreat of the enemy and the cavalry, pushing on, seized a stream of running water. As soon as the infantry had reached this stream, they were halted there and at about 1100 the mounted troops rushed on up the narrow valley and seized the village of Tamanieb. It consisted of some 300 huts, surrounded by precipitous rocks rising to a height of some 700 or 800 feet. Occasional Dervishes were seen occupying some of these rocks but were beyond reach. They had to watch in turn as the huts were burned. The British force then withdrew to No 5 zariba, Graham and the cavalry going straight through to Suakin. The British had lost two horses; Osman's casualties were not known but were unlikely to have been significant. By the 29th, all of the British troops were back in Suakin. A side-light on to the controversy about pushing a force through to Berber is afforded by Graham's signal of 27 March to London reporting that the road through Tamanieb to Sinkat lay through 'very difficult rocky country'. Graham had also had second thoughts about relying on local allies to keep open the road.

It was clear that in the absence of any agreement to push on to Berber, the expedition was virtually at an end. Gladstone and his Cabinet still saw no need to send troops to assist or relieve Gordon. The limited objectives which had prompted the despatch of Graham's expedition had largely been achieved and, on 29 March, Graham received instructions from London to disperse his force, keeping only sufficient men to garrison Suakin until a battalion of the new Egyptian Army could arrive.

The 10th Hussars, M Battery, the Royal Irish Fusiliers and the York and

Lancasters sailed from Suakin in the *Jumna* on 30 March, resuming the voyage to England interrupted some six weeks before. Most of the remainder sailed for Suez and Egypt on 1 April; Graham, with the Black Watch, left on 3 April. The KRRC and a detachment of Marines remained at Suakin pending the arrival of the Egyptian troops.

Graham reached Cairo on 7 April and left for England a fortnight later, on two months leave. He was much fêted, dining with the Queen at Windsor, with the officers of his own Corps at Chatham and receiving a sword of honour at Jarrow. He was offered the choice of a baronetcy or promotion and, on Wolseley's advice, chose the latter, being gazetted Lieutenant General on 21 May 1884. Like his troops, he received two clasps, 'El Teb' and 'Tamai', for the Egyptian Medal which he had received in 1882.

NOTES

1. I called attention in an earlier book (*The Road to Kabul*) to the extraordinarily high proportion of commanders with the VC in the Second Afghan War.
2. In the British Army it was relatively common at this time for brigades to be commanded by Majors General. In the Indian Armies, however, brigades were normally commanded by Brigadiers General, which was an appointment, not a rank.
3. There is a parallel with Roberts' farewell to Cavagnari in July 1879 – see Roberts *Forty One Years in India* (London, 1897), Vol.II, p179. Both accounts were written after the event so one must allow for a degree of sentimental hindsight.
4. The Mobilisation Committee was a major and highly effective addition to the Army's organisational system, filling the role which would now be done by a General Staff. Its work at this time may best be seen, however, in relation to Graham's 1885 expedition – see Chapter 7.
5. Captain E.A. De Cosson *Days and Nights of Service with Sir Gerald Graham's Field Force at Suakin* London, 1886; reprinted 1990) p30.
6. See *Warm Corners in Egypt* by 'One who was there' (London, 1886) pp223-24.
7. British battalions leaving India for home were likely to be very weak because many men chose to stay on in India and drafts were obviously held back in England. Two of the battalions from Egypt (Black Watch and Gordon Highlanders) left Cairo 750 strong; by contrast, the Royal Irish Rifles disembarked at Suakin only 350 strong and the York and Lancasters 479.
8. It is not clear whether the Gardner guns used in 1884 had two or five barrels but the evidence suggests two. In 1885 the five-barrelled version seems to have become standard although Gambier-Parry, op cit, refers to a two-barrelled gun with an experimental water jacket being tried at Suakin then.
9. The principle of revolving barrels has been revived in recent times and electrically-driven Gatling guns have had a vogue in aircraft and armoured vehicles because of the very high rates of fire which can be achieved.
10. The official strength was 4322, plus 30 native drivers – see *Insurrection of the False Prophet*, op cit, Vol.IV, p5.
11. Wolseley described Davis as 'a good, rolicking but very foolish Irishman' – see Adrian Preston *In Relief of Gordon: Lord Wolseley's Campaign Journal of the Khartoum Relief Expedition 1884-1885* (London, 1967) p221.
12. See R.H Vetch *Life, Letters and Diaries of Lieutenant-General Sir Gerald Graham* (London, 1901) p266.
13. Letter dated 1 March 1884 – NAM 7003-2.
14. Most accounts imply that this was deliberate, to provide easier ground for the guns and to avoid the earlier battlefields – see Burleigh, op cit, p45. Buller, who should have known,

believed the same – Buller to Duke of Cambridge 2 March 1884, RA Add. E/1/10663. I have some doubts about this. Graham's despatch of 2 March 1884 gives a clear impression that he did not know where the enemy was when he set off and Burleigh, in laying stress upon the difficulties of locating an enemy due to the nature of the country, may inadvertently have given the game away about El Teb.

15. Burleigh, op cit, p49.
16. Despatch 2 March 1884 to Secretary of State for War.
17. Burleigh, op cit, p65. Marling wrote later that 'We killed nearly all the wounded as it wasn't safe to leave them, as they would knife you like a shot'. Colonel Sir Percival Marling *Rifleman and Hussar* (London, 1931), p104.
18. Graham's orders, quoted in the Marquess of Anglesey *A History of the British Cavalry* (London, 1973-86), Vol.3, p312.
19. Wingate, op cit, pp516-17. Osman referred to it as 'The Third Battle of the Sea', the first being in the defeat of Kasim Effendi in December 1883 and the second Baker's defeat in February 1884.
20. Graham almost certainly misunderstood what had happened. Captain Stevenson, of the Black Watch, claimed that Davis had at one point ordered the regiment to charge but because the officers could not see an enemy to charge at, they had ordered the men to stand fast and to act only on the order of their colonel. Graham, hearing only from Davis that the regiment had hung back, put the worst interpretation on it. Given Wolseley's judgement on Davis and the fact that the latter had never been in action, Stevenson's explanations has the ring of plausibility about it – see 'Action at Tamai 13 March 1884', *Red Hackle* No.167 (April 1970), pp46-48.
21. Letters of 1 and 2 March 1884 – NAM 7003-2.
22. The followers of the Mahdi called themselves 'the Ansar (helpers)' and the term 'Dervish' really applied to the followers of the various Sufi sects (see Chapter 3, Note 1). But the term 'Dervish' came to be so generally applied by European observers to the Mahdi's troops as a whole that I have used it henceforth in this sense even if not strictly accurately.
23. Marling, op cit, p106.
24. Wylde, op cit, Vol.I, p137. Buller was very glad when the night was over. Buller to Duke of Cambridge 15 March 1884, RA Add. E/1/10692.
25. Ibid, p155.
26. Burleigh, op cit, p205.
27. Wylde, ibid, pp166-67.
28. It would have been surprising if, in the shock and confusion of the Dervish onslaught, some men had not panicked. Marling recalled one officer shouting 'D-mn it, men, don't run away from a lot of bare-backed (sic) savages' – Marling, op cit, p111. Buller, ibid, thought the Royal Marines had behaved badly. I owe this reference to Colonel Geoffrey Powell.
29. Burleigh, op cit, pp213-14. The adjutant was Herbert Plumer, who was to command the 2nd Army in France 1915-17.
30. Marling wrote that 'The Black Watch were very bitter about Graham and who can blame them' – Marling, op cit, p112.
31. Stephenson to Hartington 5 March 1884.
32. Graham to Hartington 14 March 1884. Despatched from Suakin to 1520 hours local time and received in London at 1500 hours GMT.
33. Graham to Hartington 17 March 1884.
34. Hartington to Baring 21 March 1884.
35. Vetch, op cit, pp277-78.
36. Colbourne noted that with swift riding-camels the journey took 8-10 days; a more normal journey was 15 days. Horsed cavalry might have been expected to match the swifter camel time. Colbourne, op cit, p16.
37. Charles Royle *The Egyptian Campaigns 1882-1885* (London 1900), p307. Burleigh concurred – Burleigh, op cit, p268.
38. Contemporary official documents refer to it as 'Handuk' but 'Handub' appears to be the more correct spelling and was used subsequently in official papers.

5
Reflections

'By the discipline of their armies the Government was triumphant. The tribes of the Red Sea shore cowered before them. But as they fought without reason, so they conquered without profit.'

Winston Churchill, *The River War*

A S THE LAST transport, the *Orontes*, pulled out of Suakin harbour on the morning of 3 April 1884, taking away Graham and the Black Watch, it was time for reflection.

In some ways, it had been a successful, if remarkably bloody, little expedition. From the moment of decision on 12 February to send a force to relieve Tokar until the moment when the last of the returning troops left Suakin, the whole affair had taken barely six weeks. In that time, a major force of some 5000 men had been assembled and despatched to Suakin, where it had fought two major and one minor engagement; the garrison of Tokar had been rescued and the Mahdiist forces under Osman Digna had suffered enormous losses in men. Suakin itself was now virtually impregnable. Clearly, the staff work had been impressive, even by modern standards. There had been no serious breakdowns in supplies or medical arrangements – indeed, the sick rate of under two per cent was extraordinarily low, given the climate and the conditions. The troops, hastily assembled from various sources, had shown admirable fortitude in coping with difficult and trying conditions and with an enemy of unprecedented ferocity. The fact that many of the fighting troops had been en route to England after lengthy service abroad and must therefore have been singularly unenthusiastic about being pitched at a day's notice into a severe campaign speaks well for discipline and morale, even if there were signs towards the end that some of the troops had had enough.

Graham had performed without much real distinction as a field commander. At El Teb, he had to some extent blundered into the enemy and while a square was an admirable formation defensively it was an unwieldy formation in which to attack; this had undoubtedly contributed to the early casualties. At Tamai, he had suffered a near-disaster for which he was wholly to blame. One must note also his very curious prediliction for moving late in the day in a climate where the only cool periods were very early in the morning and late in the evening. It was a point which did not escape comment

70

at the time. Nevertheless, he had handled the logistics side of the expedition adequately and he had maintained excellent relations with Hewett in an age when good army/naval relations were the exception rather than the rule.

The honours of the campaign were shared equally by the individual soldiers on both sides. Confronted with an enemy whose ferocity and animal courage exceeded anything that the British Army had ever seen before, the British troops had showed admirable pluck and steadiness, never more so than at Tamai where the 2nd Brigade, having been crumpled up and brought close to annihilation, managed to rally and advance again. The individual Dervish had proved himself a fighting phenomenon which had won the unqualified respect of his opposite number. Osman's commanders had shown some tactical skill but lack of discipline and effective firepower were handicaps which could only partially be made up by the extraordinary fighting power of the individual warrior. Nevertheless, not until they faced the Japanese sixty years later were the British to encounter individual opponents as savage and formidable.

The bloody quality of the fighting was not easily understood in London. Burnaby had attracted criticism in Parliament for using a shotgun at El Teb, since this was regarded as unsporting and inhumane. (Bowing to this criticism, he abandoned it when he accompanied Wolseley up the Nile, seven months later, although some others did not.) The practice of killing the Dervish wounded also aroused criticism in Parliament. Ministers themselves were unpleasantly surprised to learn from newspaper reports that it was virtually routine practice since wounded Dervishes were almost more deadly than the unwounded. Faced with a Parliamentary Question from Henry Labouchere about Tamai, the Secretary of State for War asked for information from Graham. Graham, in a signal of 19 March 1884, assured Hartington that no wounded man was killed unless he attacked a British soldier; generally speaking, the enemy neither gave nor accepted quarter and the British troops had been forced to kill them in sheer self-defence. He pointed out that the 2nd Brigade had actually taken 15 prisoners and that the British soldiers admired the Dervishes and were friendly towards them when they would allow it. Nevertheless, repugnant as it must now seem to us, it was true that wounded Dervishes were routinely killed; Private Storr of the 10th Hussars, for example, recorded that after El Teb 'my troop had a most unpleasant task to perform, that of despatching the wounded who would not accept quarter but threw their spears at us when we approached them and in their dying moments'.[1] Given the fanaticism which inspired them, there was probably little alternative and it seems unlikely that the Dervishes expected anything else. They certainly took no prisoners themselves.

There was some newspaper criticism also of Hewett's policy at Suakin of restoring escaped slaves to their Egyptian masters, the *Daily Telegraph* pointing out the absurd paradox of the British Navy patrolling the African coasts to prevent slave-trading while in Suakin soldiers and sailors were being employed as slave-drivers. Hewett was clearly anxious not to cause friction with the local Egyptian authorities but he would seem to have taken this too far.

There were aspects of the military operations which were less cheering. Given that the garrison of Tokar had ultimately been rescued although not until Tokar had fallen, and given that Osman's forces had suffered two major and bloody defeats, the fact remained that the Mahdiist cause in the Eastern Sudan had not been crushed. On the contrary, Osman was quick to claim, with a good deal of plausibility, that he was the victor since it was the English who had been forced to sail away. The route to Berber had not been opened and, within a month of Graham's departure, Berber was under siege, falling to the Mahdi on 26 May. From that moment, Khartoum and Gordon were doomed.

On the British side, there had been some ominous equipment failures. Both the Gatlings and the Gardners had proved singularly unreliable, as the Gatlings had done in Afghanistan five years before. At Tamai, in particular, the Gardners had jammed at a critical moment. They had also proved extremely heavy and cumbersome to drag through the sand and scrub. Captain Wilson VC, in a report to Hewett, pointed out that, with a combined weight of some two-thirds of a ton, gun and limber were exhausting to man-handle; on the other hand, mules were very unsuitable when the guns were placed in a square. His solution was to dispense with the limber and to carry the 1200 rounds it held either on pack animals or dispersed among the men; he also recommended larger and broader wheels and the substitution of twin shafts in place of the trail to aid pulling. His conclusion was that while the machine-guns were admirable when used statically (always assuming that they did not jam), their use in a moving square caused problems particularly when the square moved on and the guns had to be limbered up, with resulting confusion and the creation of gaps in the square. Wilson had, in fact, raised a fundamental tactical issue. Placed in the sides and, more particularly, the corners, of a square the guns created areas of weakness. Once the guns had been overrun or jammed, there were then gaps in the square through which the enemy could surge. It had happened at Tamai and was to happen again at Abu Klea, with near-disastrous results. Wilson's solution was to provide each gun with an infantry escort of at least 40 men but it is arguable that it would have been better to have treated the guns as artillery and fought them as batteries outside the square.

The cavalry sword had also proved ineffective against the tactics of the Dervishes who lay down and slashed at the horses' legs. The average trooper was unable in these circumstances to reach his opponent and Herbert Stewart after El Teb had equipped the cavalry with spears picked up from the Dervishes. At least one officer took to using a pig-sticking spear. In fact, there was a deeper lesson. Both at El Teb and Tamai, the cavalry had actually performed their most useful service when dismounted and using their carbines. In such circumstances it was mounted infantry, equipped with rifles instead of carbines and fully trained to their use, who were the more effective. Both points were taken on board. When the next expedition sailed for Suakin most of the regular cavalry were equipped with lances and they were to be supported by a strong contingent of mounted infantry equipped with rifles.

Writing in the *Birmingham Daily Post* a year later, Bennett Burleigh recalled that 'It was at El Teb that I was first struck with the inferior quality of the English bayonet and sword-bayonet . . . At Tamai, in the rush and scurry, it was put to a severer test than elsewhere in the Sudan. In that battle, the Hadendowas, as they rushed out of their grass cover with their short spears, fairly pitched themselves upon the weapons of our Black Watch and 65th, The York and Lancashire Regiment. The triangular bayonet oft-times bent and twisted. On the whole, however, it stood the test better than the sword-bayonet, I think. Like the sword-bayonet, it often bent like hoop-iron when a thrust was made, if bone interposed, and became cork-screwed in the struggle. It has two serious drawbacks, not so observable in the sword-bayonet. The wound it makes is slight, so that the fanatical savage or an infuriated man requires several thrusts before he is placed hors de combat, giving him a chance to run amuck among civilised troops. In the second place, the triangular bayonet, when thrust violently, goes too far and there is great difficulty in freeing it'. He contrasted this unfavourably with the opposition's weapons: 'Their swords and spears, sharp as razors, cut, as I saw scores of them do, through bone, sinew and every obstacle without turning the edges of the weapon'.[2]

Nevertheless, it was not until similar failures among Wolseley's troops in the Nile Expedition 1884-85 had caused a furore in the Press that the matter was fully investigated. The failures among the triangular bayonets of the ordinary infantry were partly due to Pattern 1853 bayonets having been adopted and altered in India and not subsequently inspected by the War Office. These bayonets, when used by the York and Lancasters and the Royal Irish Fusiliers at El Teb and Tamai, had failed in significant numbers. But it was also true that when the triangular bayonets in the hands of the troops in the United Kingdom were tested in 1884 and 1885, a large number failed also. This was ascribed to inferior quality steel and faulty manufacture – in particular, to grinding after the steel had been tempered only on the surface (case-hardened); grinding in these circumstances uncovered the soft inner steel.

The problem, however, was undoubtedly severest among the sword-bayonets used by the Royal Marines and the seamen of the Naval Brigade. These bayonets had been made in 1871, as an economy, by grinding down existing *curved*, 27" Snider sword-bayonets and some cutlasses to produce *straight* 25½" sword-bayonets. While there remains some dispute as to how precisely it was done, the great body of expert opinion was that the process of grinding-down and straightening had destroyed the temper of the steel. Indeed it is hard to see how it could have been otherwise. A subsequent naval committee of enquiry concluded that the bayonets were 'absolutely inefficient, untrustworthy and unfit for service'.[3] That this was Gladstonian economy gone mad was demonstrated by the fact that the cost of conversion per bayonet amounted to 9/9½d while the cost of a new bayonet was only 10/8½d.

Officers' swords, which were purchased privately and not subject to Government testing, seem to have been routinely useless except for the broadswords carried by officers in the Black Watch and Gordon Highlanders. The Pattern 1846 infantry officer's sword was indeed an unsatisfactory design with a compromise cut-and-thrust blade and a painfully weak brass guard. Even when made by the best manufacturers, such as Wilkinsons, it was hardly likely to stand up to blows from the massive Sudanese swords, and was liable to shatter when it hit solid bone. But that situation existed virtually throughout the 19th century. It was not until the introduction of a new, thrusting blade in 1892 that the British infantry officer had a sword worth fighting with, and, even then, it needed the introduction of a new steel basket hilt in 1895 to bring the sword to full perfection.[4]

On the credit side, Graham's troops do not appear to have experienced the major jamming problems with the Martini-Henry rifles and carbines which was to afflict Wolseley's troops in 1885. This was probably due to the short distances marched around Suakin.[5] The jamming which Wolseley's men suffered from at critical moments such as Abu Klea was almost certainly due to the soft, coiled brass cartridge cases becoming dented and deformed in the cartridge pouch and to sand clinging to these irregularities; when the cartridge expanded on firing, the sand formed a sticky seal against the walls of the chamber, making extraction difficult. Clearly, damage to the cartridges was likely to increase when the troops were marching long distances, day after day, and bivouacking in the open. The weakness of the extractor in the early models of the Martini-Henry compounded the problem. The problems with dust and the extractor had been known for years, but nothing had been done.

Much lay in the future. Within six months, another British army would be on its way up the Nile to try to relieve Khartoum and rescue Gordon. As a by-product, another force would try conclusions again with Osman Digna. But for the moment, he was master of the field round Suakin and he was not slow to rub home the point to the surrounding tribes. On balance, his prestige and that of the Mahdi had been increased rather than diminished by the 1884 campaign. The opening round had clearly gone to him on points.

NOTES

1. Letters in NAM 8107-16. Colbourne, serving with Hicks, noted the same treatment of prisoner:
    'We came across many wounded too. Sometimes the whole army would pass and leave a

poor fellow unscathed; but usually some ruthless hand would give him his quietus, perhaps after all in mercy, as in most cases the wounds were desperate.' – Colbourne, op cit, p173.

2. *Birmingham Daily Post* 7 May 1885.
3. *Report of the Committee on Cutlasses and Cutlass Sword Bayonets supplied to the Royal Navy.* C5014 (HMSO, 1886; also *Special Committee on Small Arms: Report on jamming of cartridges in Martini-Henry rifles and complaints with regard to bayonets in Egypt.* (War Office, 1886).
4. Brian Robson *Swords of the British Army: the regulation patterns 1788-1914* (London, 1975) pp119-20.
5. Gambier-Parry suggests that jamming did occur, and specifically at Tofrek – Gambier-Parry, op cit, p194. If it did occur, then it was presumably on a small scale since it is not mentioned in official reports or other memoirs.

6

Interlude
(April 1884 to February 1885)

A S THE LAST of Graham's troopships dipped over the northern horizon, bound for Suez (and, in the case of the *Jumna*, for England), Suakin began the struggle to get back to normality as a busy entrepôt for the trade from Middle Africa to Arabia.

Matters could never be quite the same again. There was now a British governor and a British official presence which would remain for the next seventy years. It was symbolised by the presence of British warships in the harbour[1] and by two British battalions garrisoning the fortifications. Outside Suakin, Osman Digna remained master of the field and the Mahdi was about to begin his march on Khartoum. For the tribes around Suakin, the situation was unstable. No one knew if the British would be back; the one certain thing was that Osman Digna and the Mahdiist cause were alive and kicking. Most of the tribes therefore prudently opted to keep a foot in both camps – trading with Suakin as before but maintaining relations with Osman who was reported in April to be near Tamanieb with a thousand men, planning to attack Suakin when he was stronger.

Colonel Sir Charles Ashburnham, who had commanded the KRRC in the late campaign, was left behind by Graham to act as Governor, assisted by Lieutenant Colonel Herbert Chermside RE, of the Egyptian Army, as his Political Officer. Immediately, Ashburnham had available his own battalion and a battalion of Royal Marines but on 11 April the transport *Utopia* arrived with the 1st Battalion of the 1st Brigade of the new Egyptian Army, replacing the Royal Marines who left for Suez four days later.

The intention had been to relieve the KRRC with a fresh battalion of Royal Marines from the Mediterranean Fleet but the lurking presence of Osman led the Admiralty in London to propose that the KRRC should remain as well as the Royal Marines. Ashburnham was given the choice but he was anxious to get his old battalion away from the unhealthy atmosphere of Suakin since it was largely composed of young soldiers who were suffering a high incidence of sickness. The new battalion of Marines arrived at Suakin on the 11th and the same troopship took away the KRRC the same day. Since there were now no troops from the British Army there, Ashburnham handed over the defence of Suakin to Commodore Molyneux, commanding HM ships in the Red Sea, and sailed for Suez with his battalion; Chermside became Civil Governor on behalf of the Khedive.

Life was not quiet. A meeting on 12 May between some of the friendly tribes and Osman at Handub broke down and in the ensuing fight Osman was victorious. His followers raided the outskirts of Suakin on the 17th and carried off a thousand sheep belonging to the inhabitants. Two days later, the Dervishes opened fire on the outskirts of Suakin and thereafter firing into the town became almost a nightly occurrence. By the end of the month, Osman's force was reported to have grown to some 3000. Morale on both sides was affected by the news on the 31st of the fall of Berber five days before. The effects were quickly shown in the increasing boldness of the Dervish attacks. The Water Forts were attacked on the night of 1/2 June; Osman's men were driven off and pursued at a discreet distance by some of the Egyptian infantry and some Egyptian cavalry who had been left behind in Suakin.

Chermside had already attempted to arrange a meeting with Osman but was peremptorily rebuffed; Osman made it clear that he was fighting a Holy War to the last man and would receive no letters or overtures. Chermside now asked for another battalion with which he was reasonably confident of holding the whole of Suakin. A second battalion of the Egyptian Army arrived on 14 June, bringing the infantry garrison up to three battalions, with a total strength of some 2000. Seven warships of the Royal Navy were moored in the harbour, able to contribute additional Marines and sailors if required. Suakin and the Red Sea to the north of it was now transferred from Hewett's East Indies Command to the Mediterranean Command, under Vice Admiral Lord John Hay who was directed to proceed to Suakin to examine what further measures were needed for its defence. All available Royal Marines at Port Said were to be sent immediately to Suakin to reinforce those already there.

Hay arrived to find Suakin still suffering almost nightly from rifle fire from the Dervishes. Molyneux reported that 'Almost invariably small bodies of the enemy fire at the town, forts etc. for a short time during the night, but their attacks have lately been much more feeble than formerly, and the enemy having suffered considerable losses do not often venture within 800 or 900 yards of the forts . . . The enemy invariably fire very high, the bullets flying about the forts, and striking the houses in the town without so far doing any harm, except on one night when two horses were killed'. The garrison was in reasonable health. Hay thought Suakin a healthy place because of its hot, dry climate tempered by sea breezes. While he was there, the day-time temperature varied between 85° and 111° Fahrenheit, the temperatures at night being only a few degrees cooler. The Egyptian troops were in excellent health but among the Royal Marines the sickness rate was roughly five to six per cent – by no means bad in the circumstances.

The arrival on 1 July 1884 of 17 (Field) Company, Royal Engineers was an event with very considerable implications. To understand why, we need to lift our eyes from Suakin and direct them to Khartoum four hundred miles to the south west.

Gordon had been despatched in January to evacuate the remaining Egyptian garrisons from the Sudan which the Cabinet was determined to abandon. Into the tangle of misunderstandings which surrounded Gordon's mission and objectives we need not penetrate too deeply. It is sufficient to say that, whatever the purpose of the mission as the Government and Gladstone saw it and as Gordon appears to have accepted it in England, by the time that he reached Khartoum he had rejected evacuation and decided instead to hold the Sudan and fight the Mahdi. How far he consciously or unconsciously counted upon effective aid from the British Government is a matter of specuation. Perhaps even Gordon himself was not entirely clear. Gladstone, however, was in no doubt that he had been humbugged and that Gordon, having been sent to evacuate, was now exerting moral blackmail to force the British Government and the British Army to come to his rescue.

As early as March 1884, Baring had warned the Government that Gordon and Khartoum were in grave danger and in April, Wolseley, still Adjutant General, told the Secretary of State for War that the British people would force the Government to act to relieve Gordon 'whether you like or not'.[2] When Berber fell on 26 May, the writing was on the wall, plain for everyone except Gladstone and some of his colleagues to see. With Berber in the Mahdi's hands, communications up the Nile to Khartoum were effectively blocked. The occasional steamer might run the gauntlet of the blockade at Berber, and native messengers, taking their life in their hands, could steal across the desert but, for all practical purposes, Gordon was now cut off.

To people like Wolseley, it was clear that intervention at Khartoum was inevitable. The question for them was simply 'Which route? – up the Nile or across the desert from Suakin to Berber?' Whichever route was chosen as the main one, it seemed clear that Suakin would have to play an important part, either as the base of the main expedition or as the base of a subsidiary expedition to link hands with the main expedition at Berber. It would be prudent therefore to begin the preparation of Suakin as a base. Graham's expedition had revealed the shortcomings of Suakin – the absence of landing facilities for large quantities of men and stores, the shortage of water supplies and storage, the absence of buildings and transport facilities. 17 Company was despatched on 26 June 1884 to start work on remedying these deficiencies.

Throughout July 1884, Suakin remained in effect under siege. Particularly heavy attacks took place on 7 and 24 July with the Dervishes getting to within 50 yards of some of the fortifications. On the 18th, a mounted patrol was attacked and an Egyptian trooper killed.

With the arrival of the Royal Engineers, it was decided to make the garrison into a brigade command and Major General Lyon Fremantle took over from Commodore Molyneux on 29 July. The Royal Marines battalion came under Lyon Fremantle's command and Molyneux was under orders to co-operate; some warships were now almost permanently moored in Suakin harbour in positions where their guns and, more importantly, their electric searchlights could bolster the defences.

Throughout the summer, Chermside and his political assistant, Brewster, remained optimistic about arranging a confederation of friendly tribes, notably the Amarar, to attack Osman. At the beginning of August, Brewster held a conference with friendly tribal leaders at Shaykh Barghut, north of Suakin. In return for 200 rifles and ammunition and food, the leaders undertook on the Koran to attack Osman's forces, reputed to be at Handub and Es Sibil, and to keep open their stretch of the Berber-Suakin road. Chermside, considerably cheered by this result, continued to believe that support for Osman was dwindling. The only thing, however, which was crystal clear was that there was no diminution in the nightly attacks on the town. At the end of August, Osman's men seized three native dhows, killing some of the crews but keeping the others to assist in navigating the vessels. The Egyptian gunboat *Jafferieh*, followed by *HMS Condor*, found the dhows beached fourteen miles south of Suakin but the warships were unable to retrieve them in face of large numbers of the enemy and the dhows had to be burnt. It was an interesting and potentially significant extension of Osman's activities.

In England, meanwhile, events had been moving which had profound consequences for Osman and Suakin. As early as 8 February, Wolseley had foreseen the consequences of Valentine Baker's defeat at El Teb; he told Hartington that unless something positive was done quickly, the tribes all over the Sudan would rise, Gordon would be cut off in Khartoum and the rest of the Egyptian garrisons would be forced to surrender or be slaughtered: 'This feeling that something should be done, like a rolling snowball, will go on increasing until the Government will be forced to adopt measures to save the Khartoum garrison . . . if nothing is done, that place will be besieged and we shall be, in my humble opinion, faced with a war on a large scale'. By the end of March, Khartoum was already coming under siege; from the middle of April, it was under regular siege by the Mahdi's forces although the Mahdi himself with the main body of his army remained for the moment in Kordofan dealing with local insurrections. At the end of May, Berber was taken by the Mahdi's forces and Khartoum was completely cut off.

While to Wolseley the course of future events might seem clear, Gladstone and most of his colleagues were unpersuaded. Gladstone had only agreed to Gordon going out to the Sudan to survey the situation and, if possible, to evacuate the garrisons. He had made it repeatedly clear that the Government was not in the business of defending the Sudan; and, as a corollary, if Gordon, in disobedience of his instructions, was to get himself shut up in Khartoum, then there could be no question of sending British troops to rescue him. To that view, he held unswervingly through the spring and early summer of 1884. Logic and consistency were undoubtedly on Gladstone's side; reality and perception were equally clearly on Wolseley's.[3] A factor

which Gladstone had perhaps overlooked was the presence of a *Times* correspondent, Frank Power, inside Khartoum with Gordon. The British public –
and the Opposition – were thus able to share vicariously in the tribulations of
Gordon and his troops. The Victorian public imagination was quickly
caught by the spectacle of a lone, gallant Englishman, cut off and surrounded
by the forces of darkness, waiting anxiously for the relief which his country
showed no intention of sending. Gladstone was a past-master at the art of
stonewalling, bolstered as he always was by an innate conviction of his own
rectitude. He was also a great Parliamentary performer. In consequence,
while the clamour for Gordon to be relieved grew in the Press and in the
House of Commons, Gladstone was able to defend his position of non-
intervention without undue difficulty. His colleagues, and, very particularly,
Hartington, his Secretary of State for War, were less easy in their minds.
Hartington had to live with Wolseley, and for Wolseley the question had
long since ceased to be 'Whether' and had become 'How and When'.

Throughout April, May, June and July, Wolseley had been locked in
battle with the Admiralty and the military authorities in Egypt over the
choice of routes for an expedition to reach Khartoum. In practice, the choice
boiled down to two; up the Nile from Cairo or across the desert from Suakin
to Berber and thence up the Nile to Khartoum. In theory, there were other
routes such as one starting from Massawa and another crossing the desert
from the Red Sea to Korosko. In practice, only the Nile route and the
Suakin-Berber route were serious contenders. From the start, Wolseley was
in favour of the Nile route, despite its length (nearly 1600 miles from Cairo
to Khartoum) and the immense obstacles to navigation presented by the
cataracts. Wadi Halfa, 760 miles from Cairo, could be reached fairly easily
by railway and steamer; beyond Wadi Halfa, a river expedition faced the
Third, Fourth, Fifth and Sixth Cataracts, growing in difficulty the further
one went up the Nile. Wolseley had never been up the Nile or seen the
cataracts but he had conducted the successful river-borne Red River
Expedition in 1870 and was confident that the methods and experience he
had acquired then could be successfully applied to the problems of the Nile.
In favour of the Nile route was the fact that it obviated the problem of water
for a large expedition and it also avoided, on the face of it, the need for huge
amounts of animal transport. Certainly, given reasonable conditions, boats
were an easier and a more efficient method of transporting large quantities of
stores and men; it was, after all, the reason for the spectacular growth of the
canal system in England.

The advantages of the Suakin-Berber route lay in its shortness – only 240
miles to Berber and only 400 to Khartoum. Its problems lay in the apparent
shortage of water (particularly over the last hundred miles to Berber), the
fact that the route was held by hostile tribes and that (after May 1884) an
expedition would have to fight its way into Berber or perish. Given these
difficulties, Wolseley believed that only relatively small bodies of troops

could be passed over the Suakin-Berber road, and even then only at the cost of maintaining substantial garrisons all along the route. Moreover, these garrisons would have to be British troops, given the formidable nature of the enemy, whereas on the Nile most of the troops on lines of communications duties could be Egyptian since they would be protected by the British troops pushing up the Nile ahead of them.

Others found it difficult to believe that the possible difficulties on the Suakin-Berber route could outweigh the fact that the Nile route to Berber was nearly five times as long and had its own, untested problems. Stephenson, asked for his opinion, rejected the Nile route completely and was in favour of Suakin-Berber; but the weight of his opinion was slightly weakened by the fact that as recently as March he had opposed Graham sending a force over the Suakin-Berber route because of the alleged shortage of water. The Inspector-General of Fortifications, Sir Andrew Clarke, was in favour of a railway from Suakin to Berber. Never having seen the route, he thought that the 240-mile line could be laid in just over four months; thereafter problems of supply would disappear. Finally, the Royal Navy and the Admiralty had a view. Lord John Hay had had the Nile route carefully examined; the conclusion was that it was quite impracticable and in any case the necessary boats could not be built in time. The Admiralty case owed something no doubt to its feeling that matters concerning navigation and boats were matters for professional sailors, not soldiers; but the case was to some extent based upon the misbelief that the Nile was at its lowest in the period after July whereas in practice it was at its lowest in May and June and rose thereafter. It was against this background of controversy that the decision was made to send 17 Company RE to Suakin to start preparing it on a contingent basis to receive an expedition.

It was not until the beginning of August 1884 that Gladstone, now under intense pressure both in Parliament and from his colleagues led by Hartington, bowed to the inevitable and took the symbolic step of asking Parliament for a grant not exceeding £300,000 to finance an expedition for the relief of Gordon should it become necessary. Even then, he continued to fight a rearguard action, arguing that he had only agreed to a brigade going as far as Dongola and suggesting that Gordon ought to be able to escape thence. But it was clearly a game – even Gladstone must have known that once an expedition was launched, neither public or military pressure would allow it to stop short of Khartoum if Gordon still hung on there. In these circumstances, the grant of £300,000 was a token sum, an earnest of intention only. The appointment of Wolseley, Britain's 'Only General', in late August to command the expedition made the point quite clear.

The detailed events surrounding the Nile Expedition are not the subject of this book except where they affect events at Suakin. Within ten days of Gladstone seeking his credit of £300,000 Stephenson was warned by the War Office that the probability of operations up the Nile meant that it was inadvisable to continue the Engineers' work at Suakin if it could be stopped without impairing credibility with the friendly tribes. Stephenson, after consulting Lyon Fremantle, replied on 13 August that cessation might have serious effects and lead to the friendly tribes making their peace with Osman Digna, thus blocking the Berber route completely and enabling Osman to operate against any force ascending the Nile. Grudging agreement was therefore given from London that most of the work being done by the Engineers at Suakin could proceed but the metre-gauge railway was to be stopped. The details of this engineering work will be dealt with later.

Matters around Suakin remained substantially unchanged. Hopes of the friendly tribes, led by the Amarar, combining against Osman rose and fell with a certain regularity. The tribes had been slow in producing any real action following the agreement reached at Shaykh Barghut but in the first half of September there were reports of several clashes between loyal Amarar and Osman's Hadendowa, in which the latter had been defeated with losses of over 150. In October there were reports of the Amarar along the Berber road having been dispersed by Osman and of many of the Amarar sub-tribes having made terms with him. Reports that Osman was concentrating a large force were succeeded by reports that he was not succeeding. The *Times* reported on 18 October that the recent rains had made the countryside very green, with abundant supplies of food and cattle, and that this favoured the rebels. At the end of October, the garrison at Suakin totalled roughly 2000 but it was still incapable of preventing nightly attacks and firing. A report prepared by Brewster on the tribes of the Eastern Sudan claimed that the Hadendowa were virtually all Mahdiists whereas the Beni Amir, who occupied the territory along the coast south of Suakin, and the Ashraf around Tokar and Sinkat, were opposed to the Mahdi and to Osman. The Amarar, who lived north of the Berber-Suakin road, were at present neutral but linked by friendship to the Hadendowa. The Bisharin, who occupied the country eastwards from the Nile as far as Arriab, were reported to be supporting the Mahdi, whereas the Rashida, south of Suakin, were allied to the Beni Amir and Ashraf. Numbers of fighting men were equally vague. The Amarar were put at something over 6500, the majority neutral or loyal. The Hadendowa were all Mahdiist and numbered some 10,000 or more; the Beni Amir and Ashraf some 16,000 the Bisharin the same.[4] It is clear therefore that there was still a great deal to play for in terms of hearts and minds.

By the end of October 1884, Wolseley's expedition up the Nile was well on its way. Wolseley himself, with an advanced guard of troops, was at Dongola, only some 300 miles from Khartoum as the crow flies but nearly twice that distance by water. The expedition was behind schedule and it would be an increasing race against time as the Nile began to fall and Gordon's food supplies began to run out. The scale of the expedition and the presence with it of Wolseley, its progenitor, made it clear that there would be little room for a supporting expedition from Suakin. Nevertheless work continued there on improving the defences and in laying light railways in and around the port. Basically, the situation remained unchanged. The confederation of friendly tribes had melted away, mainly because of the lack of a real leader; many had made their peace with Osman to protect their families and possessions. Osman was reported, not necessarily accurately, as being anxious to leave the area ostensibly to visit the Mahdi but was being prevented by his followers. He was reported to have a substantial force at Tamai and another at Sinkat. The news of Wolseley's expedition was already known among the tribesmen.

Optimism about Osman's position continued to rise and fall. After a lull, attacks on the outworks round Suakin began again on 4 November when 400 of the enemy attacked men working on the light railway; they were driven off by some of the Egyptian cavalry who behaved very well. A fortnight later, the Dervishes raided the cattle herds round Suakin and seized 40, killing a cowherd in the process. The grain crop around Tokar, Osman's base of supply, was unusually large and plentiful and the effect was immediately noticeable; Molyneux reported that 'The rebel forces are gradually regaining their strength at Tamai and Handub, and Suakin is now as closely invested as regards communication with the interior as ever. Osman Digna obliges the tribes who had lately been ready to cooperate with us, to rejoin him. Though any great success gained by the Nile Valley Expedition will undoubtedly have some effect here, the command of grain which the Tokar crops now give Osman Digna will enable him to hold his best men together easier than has lately been the case, when his supporters were reduced to a mere handful. People generally are heartily tired of the war'.

It is difficult now, as it was then, to be positive about Osman's real strength. It is unquestionable that the Hadendowa were solidly behind him. It is equally clear that the Beni Amir had never accepted the Mahdi's call and remained opposed to Osman and his activities. The Amarar were divided; Osman could not rely upon them as he could on the Hadendowa but equally the call of blood, of Islam, of xenophobia, meant that sections of the Amarar would support Osman when it came to serious fighting against the British. Much the same no doubt applied to the other tribes; the Bisharin, however, whose territory stretched from the Nile to the Red Sea and who were therefore more closely in touch with the Mahdi's activities than any of the others, were by now supporting Osman. No doubt, there had been a good deal of economic disruption around Suakin which affected the tribes' taste for war. Even so, as we have seen, crops continued to be grown and cattle and sheep raised. Suakin continued to function as a market and as a port, and this meant that trade continued to flow into it from the interior; in turn, this meant work for the Hadendowa, the Amarar, the Bisharin, who were mainly carriers by trade. The heavy losses in killed and wounded suffered at El Teb and Tamai must have had some effect on the will to fight and may well have accounted for the ambivalent attitude of the Amarar, but it had not prevented the Bisharin taking up arms late in the day and it did not prevent Graham encountering fierce opposition when he again appeared in 1885. That Osman was able to fight for so long and with such strength, with basically only the Hadendowa to rely on, makes one wonder now what might have happened if he had been able to unite all the tribes of the Eastern Sudan. For the moment, however, the relatively small garrison at Suakin was keeping some pressure off Wolseley. Proof of this was a report from Osman's camp that the Mahdi had asked Osman for help against Wolseley but Osman had been obliged to refuse in view of the possibility of a British attack from Suakin. The implications of the light railway work had not been lost on the Dervishes.

As Wolseley fretted at Dongola, waiting for his troops to arrive by the painfully slow boat route, activity seemed if anything to increase around Suakin. A sharp attack on the northern flank of the defences on 4 December was checked with the aid of the guns of *HMS Dolphin*. *Dolphin* was again engaged four days later when some 1500 of the enemy appeared on the plain in front of El Geif. They were driven off with some loss but in the interim a bold raid on the camel herd grazing some 1500 yards south of the Fula Redoubt resulted in 42 of them being driven off. At the end of December, a force of the Beni Amir was soundly beaten by Osman's men near Kassala and the leading Beni Amir chiefs killed.

The new year (1885) opened with Suakin even more closely invested than before. The *Times* correspondent thought that Osman's power was increasing; another correspondent calculated that since Graham had left in the previous April there had been 125 nightly attacks and more than 40 daylight skirmishes. Both Osman and the British authorities were predictably concerned about Wolseley's advance up the Nile which was now reaching its climax with the despatch of the Desert Column on 30 December on a last despairing dash to save Gordon. It was now even more necessary to keep Osman diverted.

The immediate origins of the second expedition to Suakin lay in fact in Gordon's message, received by Wolseley on 30 December 1884, warning him not to leave Berber behind him still untaken. It was important therefore not to allow Osman to transfer forces to assist in the holding of Berber by the Mahdi's forces. Baring immediately suggested a demonstration from Suakin towards Berber. Wolseley was still averse to diverting scarce resources to Suakin when he needed all he could get to assist him up the Nile. In his view, the most economical course was to concentrate all available warships from the East Indies Squadron at Suakin, where they could land their crews, and especially their Royal Marines, to give the impression of preparing for a serious attack on the Dervish forces; nothing more was required in Wolseley's opinion to prevent Osman reinforcing Berber. This low key approach did not commend itself to Hartington; he wanted to send two battalions, four squadrons of mounted troops, a mule battery and four field or horse artillery guns to make a real demonstration.

Wolseley replied from Korti on 8 January 1885. His advice was that to send troops to Suakin from England was an expensive and unnecessary luxury, but if the Government was prepared to afford it, then he believed that an expedition would be of value politically, provided that Osman was attacked and crushed *quickly*; to send a force which was not ready to attack the moment it landed would be a total waste. As far as a railway to Berber was concerned, it would take at least a year and could have no effect on his present operations to relieve Gordon.

Faced with this advice, the Secretary of State compromised; he would send one battalion only to Suakin, with two Horse Artillery guns and some cavalry. A battalion of Royal Marines was already there but it is difficult to see what could be effected by such a tiny force which could help operations on the Nile. Stephenson was instructed on 18 January to make the necessary arrangements and the 1st Battalion of the Berkshire Regiment disembarked at Suakin twelve days later, together with a squadron of the 19th Hussars and two guns of G Battery, B Brigade, Royal Horse Artillery.

Giving the new troops a day's rest, Lyon Fremantle moved out on 1 February towards the wells at Hashin, eight miles west of Suakin, which were known to be occupied by Osman's supporters. The Dervish camp was shelled but the enemy, who were in strength, could not be lured out of their strong position and Fremantle was back in Suakin by 0900 hours. Two days later, a troop of the 19th Hussars and a troop of Egyptian cavalry under Major Apthorpe was sent to reconnoitre in the direction of Handub. Apthorpe exceeded his instructions and occupied Handub where he burned the Dervish camp. He was ambushed in a ravine on the way back, losing 11 men killed. Stephenson was predictably very critical of this minor debâcle when reporting it to London.[5]

If this activity was intended to help Wolseley, it was irrelevant. A handful of the Desert Column had reached Khartoum by steamer on the morning of 28 January to discover that it had fallen to the Mahdi, and Gordon killed, two days earlier. The news was some time in reaching Osman but on 15 February Baring reported to London that the Mahdiists round Suakin were elated by the news from Khartoum and not in any way discouraged by the bloody fights at Abu Klea and Metemmeh; indeed, Osman was threatening to attack Suakin if the British would not come out to fight.[6]

The news of the fall of Khartoum, which reached Wolseley on 4 February and London on the 5th, transformed the whole situation. Whatever its earlier vacillations, the Cabinet when it met on the morning of 6 February was ready and willing to take the 'bold and decided course' which the Queen had already urged it by telegram to take. Wolseley was given carte-blanche to continue his operations against the Mahdi's forces and was assured of all necessary assistance, either by despatch of an expedition to Suakin or in any other way which Wolseley wanted. It was not yet ready to sanction the occupation of Khartoum but equally it was not keen for Wolseley to retreat because of the bad political effect both in the Sudan and at home.

Wolseley replied at once, suggesting an immediate expedition to Suakin to crush Osman. In amplification, he recommended the despatch there of an additional four battalions of infantry, a regiment of cavalry and the remaining four guns of G/B, RHA. He regarded this as sufficient to achieve the object of destroying Osman's power. Looking to a further campaign against Khartoum in the autumn, he recommended that Suakin should be held during the summer months by a brigade of Indian infantry and a regiment of Punjab cavalry. Asked by the Secretary of State as to what he saw as the precise objectives of the force for Suakin, Wolseley replied on 11 February that the objectives must be to destroy Osman Digna and then to link hands with Wolseley's own force at Berber, preparatory to an autumn advance on Khartoum. As regards the construction of a railway from Suakin to Berber, Wolseley was in favour of it but since he could not now capture Berber before the autumn, the railway should immediately go no further than Arriab (roughly half way). It should be continued after the summer when Wolseley hoped to take Berber.

On 11 February, Graham was sent for by the Commander-in-Chief, the Duke of Cambridge, and told that he was to command a second expedition to Suakin. The Indian Government had already been asked on the 8th to send a brigade of infantry and a regiment of cavalry as proposed by Wolseley.

While in some ways the obvious choice, Graham was not in fact Wolseley's own first choice. He had clearly had reservations about Graham's performance the previous year and he would have preferred Major General George Greaves to command the expedition. There was, however, a snag. It would mean promoting Greaves over the head of Lyon Fremantle. No matter that the latter had had no real active service experience and was therefore an unknown quantity; he was a Guards officer and that was enough to lead the Duke to oppose Greaves' promotion. Even Wolseley, as Adjutant General, was powerless. The options appear to have been Graham, Stephenson or Alison (the acting Adjutant General), each with Greaves as Chief of Staff. It seems to have been very much a question of 'better the Devil you know . . .' and Wolseley plumped for Graham in command, with Greaves as Chief of Staff.[7] It was a choice which Wolseley was later to regret since Greaves was arrogant and resented being under Graham whom he described contemptuously (although not necessarily inaccurately) as 'a fiddle-headed General'. Greaves, in turn, was described by Gambier-Parry as 'a short, sharp-featured individual, with a pompous and rather disagreeable manner, a loud voice, a quick temper, and a sense of his own importance which defied everything. He was not popular and he seemed generally to be absorbed in that wonderful thought 'I am'. A short answer was all you ever received from him, and one which often fell far short of ordinary courtesy'.[8]

NOTES

1. The scale of naval effort remained considerable throughout 1884. Visiting Suakin in June, Vice Admiral Lord John Hay found seven warships there. At the end of October there were still five, plus a hired transport, the *Belinda*.
2. Wolseley to Hartington 13 April 1884 – Wolseley Papers, Hove.
3. For a clear and perceptive treatment, see Julian Symons *England's Pride* (London, 1965).
4. Lieutenant Colonel H. Chermside and A. Brewster *Notes on Arab tribes of the Eastern Sudan* (Suakin, 1884).
5. Stephenson to Hartington 4/5 February 1885 *Egypt No.2 Correspondence respecting British military operations in the Sudan (C4280)* (HMSO, 1885) pp4-5.
6. Ibid, p11.
7. 'It never seems to have occurred to Greaves that he would not have been employed at all had I not insisted on it. I wanted to give him superior rank and put him over Fremantle. The Duke was angry, of course, and I was given the choice of three combinations and I chose the present one'. Wolseley to his wife 11 March 1885, quoted in Sir George Arthur *The Letters of Lord and Lady Wolseley 1870-1911* (London, 1922) p204.
8. Gambier-Parry, op cit, p120.

7

A Second Expedition, 1885

THE SECOND expedition was to be on an altogether bigger scale than the first.

The Confidential Mobilisation Committee under the QMG, Lieutenant General Sir Arthur Herbert, met for the first time at the War Office on 9 February 1885, only three days after the Cabinet decision; it was to meet on five further occasions. The QMG told the Committee that it had been decided to send a force to Suakin as soon as possible to crush Osman Digna, composed of the following fighting troops:

From England
    5th Lancers (2 squadrons = 13 officers, 270 men)
    20th Hussars (2 squadrons = 13 officers, 270 men)
    24th (Field) Company, Royal Engineers (6 officers + 194 men)
    10th (Railway) Company, Royal Engineers (6 officers + 149 men)
    3rd Battalion, Grenadier Guards (31 officers + 816 men)
    1st Battalion, Coldstream Guards (31 officers + 816 men)
    2nd Battalion, Scots Guards (31 officers + 822 men)

From Malta
    1st Battalion, Shropshire Light Infantry (27 officers + 813 men)

From Egypt
    1 battery Royal Horse Artillery
    1 mounted battery
    2nd Battalion, East Surrey Regiment (24 officers + 808 men)
    1st Battalion, Yorkshire Regiment (28 officers + 713 men)

Together with five companies of the Commissariat and Transport, elements of the Medical Staff Corps, Ordnance Store Department, Veterinary Department and various odds and ends, including a Telegraph Section of the Royal Engineers and a Balloon Detachment, this represented a force of nearly 7500 men.[1] This was already getting on for twice as large as the force Graham had operated with in 1884, but there was more to come. The Government of India was approached to send a force and accordingly the 9th Bengal Cavalry, the 15th (Ludhiana Sikh) Bengal Native Infantry, the 17th (Loyal Poorbeah)

Bengal Native Infantry and the 28th Bombay Native Infantry were nominated for service at Suakin.

In a more surprising development, as soon as news of the expedition became known, the Home Government was flooded with offers of men from the Colonies. As early as November 1884, Major General Lawrie, commanding the Canadian Militia, had offered to raise a force for service in the Sudan but his offer had been politely refused. Now, on 12 February 1885, the New South Wales Government offered by telegram to send a battalion of infantry and a battery of artillery, all expenses being met by New South Wales. Next day, the Government of Victoria offered help (unspecified), to be quickly followed by an offer of 250 men from South Australia and a colonial corps from Queensland. Not to be outdone, Fiji came up with the offer of 50 armed constabulary, and last, but not least, the Straits Settlements and Perak offered 250 Sikhs and a half-battery of mountain guns (or alternatively a Gardner and a Nordenfeldt gun).[2]

The offer from New South Wales was quickly accepted and the others diplomatically declined. The Home Government did not really need men – it had the resources of the Indian Army to call on, if necessary – and the offers from the Colonies, while gratifying, were something of an embarrassment. But it was clearly difficult to reject all the offers without creating resentment and setting back the policy of encouraging the Colonies to take over their own defence. Of the offers received, the New South Wales offer was the most attractive since it comprised formed, trained units.[3]

For artillery, Graham would have G Battery, B Brigade, Royal Horse Artillery, part of which was already at Suakin, equipped with 13-pounders; it was brought up to strength by a draft of 50 men and 80 horses from the United Kingdom. He would also have 5 Battery, 1st Brigade, Scottish Division, Royal Artillery, a garrison battery in Cairo which was hastily re-equipped with 7-pounder mountain guns (Kipling's famous 'screw gun') carried on mules. In addition, six Gardner guns and six rocket troughs (to fire nine-pound rockets) were sent from Cairo, to be manned partly by men from 6 Battery, 1st Brigade, Scottish Division, which had played an active role in 1884 but was now largely converted to act as an Ammunition Supply Column. Together with the New South Wales Battery and a detachment of six Gardners operated by the Royal Marine Artillery already at Suakin, Graham was well provided with guns.

Wolseley was asked by Hartington for his opinion on the size of the force proposed for Suakin, as opposed to a smaller one. Wolseley had never been enthusiastic about the Suakin-Berber route and while a force at Suakin had some value to him in diverting Osman Digna and his forces, it was not in Wolseley's interest for Suakin to lock up resources unnecessarily. Nevertheless, he raised no objection to what was proposed.

But it was not merely the size of Graham's force which affected the scale of effort involved; the objects of the expedition were also a significant factor.

In his instructions to Graham, dated 20 February 1885, Hartington laid it down that the 'first and most pressing object' of the campaign was the destruction of the power of Osman Digna; the second point 'of greatest attention' was the construction of a railway to Berber, although Hartington accepted that until the country round Suakin had been thoroughly pacified, it was unlikely that the railway could be pushed on beyond Tambuk.[4] Wolseley opined that unless he could take Berber before the hot weather, which was doubtful, then the railway could probably not go beyond Arriab, just over halfway from Suakin to Berber. On 27 February,the day after Graham had arrived in Cairo, Hartington again emphasised the importance of pushing on with the railway to enable Wolseley to re-equip and reinforce his troops on the Nile for further operations. Graham was told that Colonel C.B. Ewart had been appointed to command his lines of communication in the rank of Brigadier General with responsibility for choosing the exact line for the railway to follow.

It is perhaps time to deal with this railway. The idea of a railway from Suakin to some point on the Nile was not new in 1885. Ismail had carefully considered the matter in the 1870s before deciding on a railway due south from Wadi Halfa to link Egypt with the Sudan. In 1883 an Egyptian commission had condemned the Wadi Halfa route and recommended a Suakin-Berber railway.[5] Lieutenant Colonel Stewart, sent by HMG to survey the Sudan in 1882, also came out in favour of a Red Sea-Nile railway route.[6] By the beginning of 1884, the matter had assumed both urgency and importance in view of the success of the Mahdi's uprising which was threatening to cut off Gordon and the Sudan garrisons. Sir Andrew Clarke, the influential Inspector General of Fortifications at the War Office, knew the Sudan well through his involvement in the Suez Canal Company; he was also a Royal Engineer. He was convinced that the key to control of the Sudan lay in a railway from Suakin to Berber and on 10 February 1884 submitted a paper to Hartington, entitled *The Question of the Soudan* which strongly advocated such a railway. He followed this up with another paper at the beginning of March which Hartington circulated to the Cabinet. In consequence, Clarke was asked in May 1884 to submit a detailed plan and costing. His report, dated 18 May 1884, envisaged a line some 245 miles in length, with defensible stations at ten-mile intervals. The line would be metre-gauge, and the total cost, including rolling stock, telegraph line and water supply, was put at £1,250,000.[7] Clarke was against the use of a private contractor and recommended that the line should be built by his own Corps, although he did not exclude the possibility of using a private company to operate it once it had been built. He asked for an immediate grant of £310,000 to build the first 50 miles.

Clarke envisaged no great constructional difficulties even though a detailed route had not been chosen or surveyed. From Suakin, the railway would run across a broadly flat plain until it reached a range of hills which rose gradually to a maximum height of 2700 feet about fifty miles from Suakin. From then onwards, the land (and the line) descended gently downwards until Berber and the Nile was reached. Much of the ground was hard sand or gravel and the track could be laid with minimum grading. The major constructional problem lay in finding a line of acceptable gradient up the hills. The problem of water supplies could be solved by using the line itself to bring forward water as it advanced and by laying a pipeline and pumping equipment. But the threat from Osman meant that construction would require strong military forces to protect the construction gangs.

By now, of course, Graham's first expedition was over but the prospect of an expedition to relieve Gordon was looming larger, despite Gladstone's stubborn opposition. Wolseley and others were asked for their views on the value of a Suakin-Berber railway in the event of an expedition to relieve the Egyptian garrisons in the Sudan. Views as to the desirability of such a railway varied somewhat in enthusiasm, Wolseley predictably being lukewarm although not hostile. All agreed that such a railway should be narrow-gauge. The Secretary of State accordingly agreed on 13 June that some preliminary work should be put in hand at Suakin to facilitate its development as a base and as the starting point of a railway to Berber. As already noted, 17 Company, Royal Engineers was despatched from Cairo to Suakin for this work, arriving there on 1 July 1884.

Clarke's scheme envisaged a metre gauge railway to Berber, together with a narrow (18 inch), gauge railway network in and around Suakin for logistic purposes. Fortuitously, 18 inches was the gauge already being used for the railway then being laid in Cyprus and it was agreed that some five miles of track, two locomotives and some rolling stock should be diverted to Suakin. Similarly, two metre gauge locomotives being built by Neilsons in Glasgow for the Bengal and North Western Railway in India were taken over, by agreement, and despatched somewhat hastily to Suakin. Clarke, who was a forward-looking officer, was keen to install electric lighting at Suakin to speed up the work but experiments at the RE Depot at Chatham were not promising.

The decision in August 1884 to send a relief expedition to Khartoum did not immediately affect the work at Suakin. The Suakin-Berber route for the relief expedition was strongly advocated by many, including, unsurprisingly, Clarke. But, as we have seen, Wolseley ultimately came down in favour of the Nile route. With resources being concentrated on this route, Suakin would have perforce to take a back seat and so orders went out at the end of August to stop all work on the metre-gauge railway which at this stage had reached a point roughly a mile and a half from the coast. Out of the blue, however, the Ipswich engineering firm of Ransome and Rapier came forward with an offer to undertake construction of the railway and to equip it, the work to be completed to Berber by January 1885. This seems in the light of subsequent experience to have been a hugely optimistic offer but in any case the railway was not now seen as a necessity in view of Wolseley taking the Nile route. The offer was declined.

Clarke continued to fight hard for his project. As late as November, he was still advocating the advance of a small column from Suakin to the Nile to assist Wolseley's advance. In December, having changed tack, he was advocating extending the 18-inch railway to Berber to assist in bringing Wolseley's troops back from Khartoum. But the game was up for the time being and at the end of November 1884, orders were given to pack up and despatch the two metre-gauge locomotives to India, to their original owners, the Bengal and North Western Railway. They left Suez on 1 January 1885, leading subsequently to a merry little row about the condition of the locomotives when they reached India.

Clarke was not defeated. In the first week in January, he was busy pointing out the need to take decisive military action round Suakin with the threefold object of removing the threat from Osman Digna, giving general support to Wolseley's advance and clearing the way to link up with him at Berber. He therefore proposed to extend the 18-inch railway in the first instance to Tambuk, 26 miles from Suakin, and then, if the conditions were favourable, to Arriab, a further 11 miles on and just over halfway to Berber. None of this attracted much enthusiasm in the War Office so, undeterred, he proposed on 14 January to push the line on only to Handub, 12 miles from Suakin, with the object of over-awing the local tribes, protecting the western approaches to Suakin and providing a healthier camp for the troops. He asked for authority to send out another 15 miles of track, two more locomotives and another 30 wagons.

Clarke's initiative was not ill-timed. Although Khartoum had fallen on 26 January, the news was not known in London until 5 February. If the Desert Column was by then in process of retiring, the River Column under Earle was still advancing and there was every prospect of the campaign continuing with the object now of recapturing Khartoum and destroying the Mahdi. Wolseley was still unenthusiastic early in January about a Suakin-Berber railway, taking the view that it could have no effect on the immediate conduct of the war, although accepting that its ultimate value for the Sudan would be great. But the news from Khartoum changed a great deal. Assuming, as Wolseley and others now did, that there would have now to be a major, deliberate campaign to recapture Khartoum and defeat the Mahdi, a dual advance from Dongola and Suakin on Berber seemed the obvious first step. On 10 February, Hartington asked Wolseley to reconsider the railway project, particularly as a means of bringing up heavy artillery, which would be required at Berber and Khartoum, and river steamers to replace those now lost to the Mahdi. Wolseley, sensing perhaps that the Government was determined on the project, agreed that such a railway would be useful for bringing up men and supplies.

Although there was agreement on the desirability of a railway, there was still confusion and disagreement about the gauge and who should build it. Clarke's proposal for an 18-inch railway to Berber suffered from the disadvantage of low carrying capacity; assuming nine trains a day each way, and allowing for the need to transport water and coal for the engines, the net carrying capacity was put at only 243 tons a day, at an average speed of five miles an hour. This was clearly quite inadequate in relation to the effort involved in laying the line. Attention was therefore focussed again on a metre-gauge line and enquiries were made of the Government of India to see whether suitable rails could be made available by the Indian railways.

There was even fiercer argument about who should construct the line. The Royal Engineers were keen to do the work and the Deputy Adjutant General of that corps argued very strongly in a memorandum of 14 February 1884 that not only was his Corps experienced and available but, since they were trained soldiers, they could defend themselves whereas civilian contractors would need military covering parties. In anticipation of a favourable decision, 10 (Railway) Company RE was ordered to Suakin. But at the same time, a well-known firm of railway contractors, Messrs Lucas and Aird, were offering their services to lay the line. They were planning to use the standard, 4 feet 8½ inch gauge although it is not clear whether Hartington and Wolseley appreciated this.

As events turned out, it might well have been better to put the whole task of constructing the railway in the hands of the Royal Engineers. Better still, construction should have been handed over to the Indian authorities, using Indian coolies. Six years before, during the Second Afghan War, the Indian Government had laid a railway 133½ miles long from the Indus to the Bolan Pass in 101 days;[8] that was the sort of speed which was required in the Sudan if the railway from Suakin to Berber was to play any really useful part in a forthcoming campaign.

But it was the age of private enterprise. Wolseley had even depended upon Thomas Cook to provide part of his logistics chain up the Nile so it was not perhaps surprising that the Government decided to accept Lucas and Aird's offer, and the firm was duly informed on 16 February. Under the agreement finally signed on 6 March, Lucas and Aird were to build a single-track, standard-gauge railway to Berber. The firm was to be responsible for buying all materials (subject to Government inspection), recruiting and shipping out the necessary constructional staff and undertaking the construction and operation of the line. The work was to be on a cost-plus basis, the firm receiving a commission or fee equal to two per cent of the value of the work done, subject to a maximum of £20,000; it would receive a bonus equal to the commission earned, as and when sections of the line were completed to the Secretary of State's satisfaction. It was the sort of cost-plus contract which modern Ministries of Defence tend to eschew. There was no incentive to rapid completion or to economy. But in the circumstances, there was probably no alternative; no firm was going to offer a fixed price for a railway whose route had not been surveyed and where the logistics and military problems were undetermined.[9] To avoid confusion, Lucas and Airds were asked to take over responsibility for extending the 18 inch network in and around Suakin. But overall control, both of the construction work and of the operation of the railways, was to rest with Graham. It was an arrangement full of potential difficulties.

The first of Graham's troops, the Berkshire Regiment, had arrived to garrison Suakin in January. Since it was already there, it was decided to keep it there and substitute it for the Yorkshire Regiment, which joined Wolseley instead. The next battalion to arrive was the 2nd Battalion, East Surrey Regiment which began disembarking at Suakin on 24 February. Eight days later, it was followed by the first regiment of the Indian Contingent, the 15th Bengal Native Infantry. It was followed the next day by the 17th Bengal Native Infantry, who were accompanied by the commander of the Contingent, Brigadier General John Hudson, of the Bombay Army, with his staff. The speed with which the Indian troops had been despatched was really very remarkable. The Home Government's request for troops had reached the Indian Government on 10 February. Of the regiments selected, the 17th Bengal Infantry were at Benares, some 800 miles from Bombay, while the 15th Bengal Infantry was at Lucknow, 700 miles from Bombay. The 9th Bengal Cavalry was en route from Peshawar to its new station at Ambala, some 800 miles from Bombay. Despite the unexpected notice, the first unit, the 15th Sikhs, left Bombay only 12 days later, on 22 February, reaching Suakin on 4 March. The next day, Hudson and his staff and the 17th Bengal Native Infantry arrived, followed quickly by the 9th Bengal Cavalry and the 28th Bombay Native Infantry. The last to arrive, on 12 March, was F Company of the Madras Sappers and Miners which had come from Bangalore, 500 miles from Bombay.

The 9th Bengal Cavalry had had the additional problem of being required to convert, en route to Bombay, to being a lancer regiment, using lances drawn from the reserves maintained for the British cavalry in India. The need for lancers had been demonstrated during Graham's first campaign when it was found that troopers armed with the sword were unable to reach the enemy when the latter adopted the tactic of lying on their backs and slashing at the horses' legs. But there were already trained lancer regiments in the Indian Army and since the effective use of the lance was generally regarded as requiring at least two years training it is odd that the 9th were required to convert in this hasty way.

Both the 15th and the 28th had seen fighting in the Second Afghan War. The 15th had marched to Kabul with Sir Donald Steward in March 1880 and had then formed part of Roberts' relief force for Kandahar in August 1880, being present at the battle of Kandahar. The 28th had been beseiged with Primrose at Kandahar and had fought well during the disastrous sortie against Deh Khoja, Lieutenant Chase of that regiment winning the VC for helping to save a wounded man under fire. The 17th Bengal Infantry had also served in Southern Afghanistan in the closing stages of the war but had not seen any actual fighting. By contrast, the 9th Bengal Cavalry was the only Bengal cavalry regiment which had not served in the Second Afghan War, which may have been the reason for selecting it for the Sudan. It was commanded, however, by A.P. Palmer, who had served in that war and led the native levies at the taking of the Peiwar Kotal in December 1878. Hudson, the commander of the Contingent, was described to the Secretary of State of India as 'a cool, experienced officer of good judgement'. He had served in the Persian War, the Mutiny, the Abyssinian campaign and had commanded his regiment in the Second Afghan War.

The Guards Brigade had also been despatched very expeditiously. The first battalion (1st Battalion, Coldstream Guards) left Wellington Barracks on the morning of 19 February and disembarked at Suakin on 8 March, the 2nd Battalion, Scots Guards arriving the next day and the 3rd Battalion, Grenadier Guards the day after that.

When Graham himself arrived at Suakin on 12 March, the bulk of his force, amounting to some 10,000 men, was already there. Graham, with his Chief of Staff, Greaves, had attended the meetings of the Mobilisation Committee on 12 and 17 February but, returning home from the latter meeting, had severely damaged his ankle. By the time he reached Cairo on 26 February, he was in such pain, and the injury had become so serious, that he had to have an operation and was confined to bed for ten days. He sent Greaves on ahead and finally left Cairo himself on 9 March, reaching Suakin three days later.

Since he had left nearly twelve months before, an immense amount of work had been done at Suakin to convert it into a base for a major expedition. In July 1884, Major Peck, on behalf of the Inspector General of Fortifications, had selected Quarantine Island as the site of the main logistics base. The island was basically a coral reef, covered with sand and gravel, roughly eight to ten feet above high water level. On the eastern (harbour) side, shallow water extended to a distance of roughly 330-360 feet when it suddenly deepened to 19 feet. Apart from a few tombs and derelict graves, the only building was a large, stone coal store from which a coaling pier, about 13 feet wide, made of coral blocks, ran out 300 feet to the deep water.

Peck proposed to turn the coal store into workshops, stores and offices, to widen the coal pier to 24 feet to take a double-track, metre-gauge railway and to provide a T-shaped pierhead of timber. This would become the main pier, accessible to big ships. A new coaling pier and depot would be constructed to the south of the main railway pier and another pier, to take a double-track, 18 inch-gauge railway, was to be built to the north. Ultimately 12 piers or jetties in all were built at different points round the harbour (see Map 3). Finally, the island was to be connected to the mainland to the west by a long causeway, 18 feet wide, to take both metre- and 18 inch-gauge railway lines, and made of coral, sand and stones. The main supply depots would be on the mainland to the west where there was ample space for a large expeditionary force. The depots and camps would be connected among themselves and with the piers on Quarantine Island by an 18 inch-gauge railway network.[10] Work began on this plan immediately by 17 (Field) Company RE under Lieutenant Colonel Elliott Wood. By the first week in March 1885, Wood could report that the causeway was completed, five large piers, suitable for big ships of 4000 tons, were available, together with seven smaller piers and five miles of 18 inch-gauge railway had been laid. In addition, wells had been dug, acres of land had been reclaimed from the sea, and work on a new hospital was progressing. Although much remained to be done, what had been achieved was sufficient to enable Graham's expedition to start assembling at Suakin.

Suakin itself was protected by a chain of strong redoubts and forts, connected by a continuous mud wall three and a half feet high, with a ditch in front, which surrounded the mainland suburb of El Geif. The town's water supply, drawn from wells some three-quarters of a mile outside these fortifications, was covered by two large masonry forts (the Right Water Fort (or Fort Shata) and the Left Water Fort (or Fort Gemeiza) joined together by a continuous earthwork.

Among its other labours, 17 Company had constructed a large new redoubt (Sandbag Redoubt), a mile and a half north west of the causeway, on the line of the projected railway to Berber; a large earth and sandbag redoubt (H Redoubt), which had been built by Harington in 1884 and named after him, was converted into a two-tier stone structure. Suakin, virtually undefended before Harington arrived in 1883, was now, for practical purposes, impregnable, especially since its massive fortifications were backed up by the guns and searchlights of warships moored in the harbour.

Neither Quarantine Island nor El Geif could accommodate the massive force now pouring into Suakin. Supply depots and camps for the fighting units had to be located on the flat desert areas west and north west of the town, outside the main fortifications. It was here that the staff work began to go wrong. No clear plan of encampment seems to have been drawn up, whether through carelessness or contempt for the enemy. Unit camps seemed to spring up higgledy-piggledy, with no system of mutual support against attacks and no zaribas. The East Surrey Regiment and the Shropshire Light Infantry were camped near the Right Water Fort. A mile to the north were the three battalions of the Guards Brigade, their camps at right angles to the rest of the line. The Berkshire Regiment were near Sandbag Redoubt, nearly two miles from the other two battalions of the 2nd Brigade. The Marines and Horse Artillery were to the rear (east) of the Berkshires, as were the 19th Hussars, behind which was the HQ camp. The 5th Lancers and 20th Hussars were in the rear of the centre of the front line, while the Indian Brigade were south east of El Geif, near Fort Fula. No one arriving could make any sense of these dispositions. To Captain Gambier-Parry, it appeared that there was 'no particular system about it and we were told that military requirements had been allowed to sink before sanitary considerations in choosing the camping-grounds. It appeared to us as if everyone had been allowed to take his choice and regimental camps were scattered about pretty much like plums in a cake, and with just about as much foresight on the part of the chief cook'.[11]

Captain De Cosson was equally puzzled: 'Indeed I was much puzzled when riding home to understand the principles on which the camp had been planned – for the various camps were scattered so far apart that an enemy could pass between them, and yet were sufficiently near together to render it impossible for them to protect their flanks without firing into each other'.[12] Lieutenant Drummond-Hay, with the Coldstream Guards, noted that 'On the first night [8 March] we were encamping in the open, entirely separated from the rest of the force but although the Arabs made depredations on other parts of the camp they did not come near us, which was fortunate as in our unprotected position they might easily have crept into our camp and committed havoc'.[13]

It is surprising that Graham, a Royal Engineer, and his Chief of Staff should have allowed the force to be scattered about in this extraordinary way. No doubt Gambier-Parry was correct in assuming that health and sanitation had taken precedence over purely military considerations. The opportunity was not missed by Osman's men. Despite a line of pickets being thrown out each night to cover the west front of the base, the spaces were too great to prevent parties of the enemy slipping through, to snipe into the camps and to cut up sentries. On the night of 7 March, the camp of the East Surreys was attacked and two men stabbed; thereafter, the attacks came in every night. On the 11th, a particularly heavy attack was made on the Ordnance Store camp near the sea shore, close to the causeway. There was continuous sniping from 1900 hours onwards and by midnight virtually every unit was blazing away, from the Indian camp right round to the Guards Brigade camped near the Sandbag Redoubt. The Ordnance Store camp was protected on two sides by a barricade of Maltese carts but was wide open to the south and east; it was guarded by one NCO and 24 men of the Berkshires. The sentries were taken by surprise and cut down, and the rest of the guard were attacked and most of them wounded as they emerged from their tent. For a time all was confusion among the mountains of stores. Then *HMS Dolphin* switched on its electric searchlight and the attackers began to melt away to the north west, the ships being unable to fire for fear of hitting the British troops. The Berkshires lost three men killed and eight wounded. Osman's losses were not known although the leader of the attack, Abdul Adab, Osman's standard bearer, was killed. The affair had had the makings of a major disaster since the depot contained the main stores of the expeditionary force – many hundreds of thousands of pounds worth of everything from rifles and ammunition to stationery and boots. Its destruction would have set back Graham's expedition many weeks. The following night the Shropshires were attacked and lost four men wounded. On the 13th, during another alert, a Scots Guards sentry bayoneted and killed another Guardsman by mistake. So it went on, night after night. On 17 March, Graham at last recognised the folly of having the Guards' camps at right angles to the rest of the line and they were brought into line with those of the other infantry regiments. At the same time, the Indian Contingent's camps were brought round to link up with the left hand of the line held by the East Surreys, thus protecting the southern approaches. While it made the disposition marginally more effective from a defensive point of view, it made no difference to the nightly attacks. The nightly alarms were having a serious effect on the force, shaking the troops' morale and depriving them of sleep; as Gambier-Parry put it 'without sleep, especially in such an enervating climate as that of the Sudan, a soldier cannot be depended upon in daytime either to march or fight in the way he should. Added to this, a perpetual series of night attacks, carried on by a few determined and reckless individuals under cover of the darkness, tended so to shake the nerves of our men that the efficiency of the force was to a certain extent undermined'. No sentry could feel safe; every shadow, every bush, every trick of moonlight was liable to become a Dervish to tired, edgy men; the natural response was to open fire just in case. Fear and panic are contagious however; one shot was enough to bring a regiment to its feet, blazing away at everything in sight. Some regiments were clearly more jumpy than others, especially those filled with young, inexperienced soldiers. Others, were much less prone to open fire; the Indian regiments in particular, many of whose men had seen recent service on the North West Frontier or in Afghanistan, were notable for their steadiness. Writing on 21 March, on the eve of the advance, Lieutenant Alexander Edwards, of the Royal Irish Regiment but attached to the 28th Bombay Native Infantry, observed that 'the British soldiers are getting accustomed to being up all night and are not so jumpy as when we first arrived when they used to fire volleys half the night through. I must say that our gallant natives behaved much better as they haven't had a panic of any kind yet; at least, we have not though I believe the Sikhs got excited one night and fired a lot'.[14]

The attack on the Ordance Depot emphasised the scale of the logistic build-up for the expedition. The Mobilisation Committee had met in London on 9, 12, 17 and 25 February. It met again on 12 March.

The Confidential Mobilisation Committee played such an important role in the military operations of the British Army overseas in the last quarter of the 19th century that some account needs to be given of its activities. The second Suakin expedition provides an excellent illustration of its work. The Committee was normally chaired either by the Quarter-Master-General (Lieutenant General Sir A.J. Herbert) or by the acting Adjutant-General

(Lieutenant General Sir Archibald Alison). Its members comprised the heads of the principal departments of the War Office – the Inspector General of Fortifications, the Director General of the Army Medical Department, the Commissary General, the Directors of Clothing, Artillery and Stores, Supplies and Transport, the Principal Veterinary Surgeon, the Deputy Adjutants General (Auxiliary Forces) (Royal Artillery) and Royal Engineers, the Accountant General and the Assistant Under Secretary of State, (representing the Permanent Under Secretary) – together with the Director of Transports, from the Admiralty. The function of the Committee was both to settle the scale of stores, equipment and men required to carry out the objectives of the expedition and then to arrange their despatch. The Committee met at intervals of a few days to receive reports of progress from the various Departmental heads and to take further decisions. At the end of each meeting, its recommendations and decisions were reported to the Secretary of State for War himself for his formal endorsement; occasionally he would comment, or even amend the decision, usually in the interests of economy. On two occasions, Graham and his Chief of Staff (Greaves) attended the meetings of the Committee, prior to their departure for Egypt and Suakin. The Committee occasionally set up sub-committees to tackle particular problems – in 1885, for example, it set up a Sub-Committee on Water Supply at Suakin. In effect, and given the absence of a proper General Staff, it played the part of a modern Defence Logistics Executive, co-ordinating the logistics work of the Service Departments; the important difference is that the Mobilisation Committee was not in permanent session. In between expeditions, it did not meet and once an expedition had been despatched, the Committee stood down, reconvening only to tidy up the logistic loose ends after military operations were over. Thus in relation to Suakin the Committee did not meet between 12 March and 30 June when it re-convened to receive the final report of the Sub-Committee on Water Supply and to settle arrangements for the move of the Guards Brigade from Egypt to Cyprus. In addition to the expedition to Suakin, however, the Committee had been organising the logistics of Wolseley's Nile Relief Expedition.

The scale of its activities for Suakin in 1885 was immense; 20,000 sets of khaki clothing, 15,000 pairs of boots, 13,000 tropical helmets, 7000 pairs of goggles, 15,000 flannel shirts, 10,000 pairs of blue serge trousers, 3000 clasp knives and lanyards, 53,000 pieces of soap, 10,000 flannel belts to protect against cholera and sunstroke, socks, spoons, tallow, buttons, thread, needles, spine protectors, rifle oil, combs, bootlaces by the thousand – the list was seemingly endless. (When the cargo ship El Dorado was wrecked on the coast of Portugal on 2 February 1885, the losses from that ship alone included 1600 kilts, 3000 helmets, 4000 pagris, 5000 pairs of boots, nearly 4000 tunics of various kinds and 4000 pairs of braces.) Guns, ammunition, veterinary stores, medical equipment, tents for a force of some 13,000, tinned food, carts, pack saddles, telephone and telegraph cable and equipment, well-drilling equipment – all had to be sent out, either direct to Suakin or to replenish stocks in Egypt which had been depleted by calls from Suakin.

But in addition to stores, men also had to be despatched. From England and Ireland direct to Suakin went the Guards Brigade, the 5th Lancers, the 20th Hussars, Nos 10 and 24 Companies, Telegraph Section and Balloon Detachment, Royal Engineers, five Companies of the Commissariat and Transport Corps, 550 men of the Medical Staff Corps and tiny elements of the Ordnance Store Department, the Veterinary Department and the Military Mounted Police. But in addition, there were replacements to be found for the units in the Mediterranean earmarked for Suakin. The Shropshires were replaced at Malta by the 1st Battalion, the Dorsetshires from Chatham. The East Surreys were replaced in Cairo by the 2nd Battalion, Royal Dublin Fusiliers from Gibraltar, who in turned were replaced at Gibraltar by the 3rd Battalion of the Rifle Brigade from England. 5 Battery, 1st Brigade, Scottish Division from Cairo was replaced by 9 Battery, North Irish Division also from Gibraltar, which was in turn replaced by 1 Battery, Cinque Ports Division from England. From first to last, nearly 100 vessels of all kinds were employed between England, Egypt and Suakin, many of them making more than one voyage. The Indian Contingent, plus its store and transport, absorbed another 38 ships taken up from the Indian trade. It was an impressive demonstration of the size and ubiquity of the British shipping industry, then at the peak of its domination of world trade.

To a 20th century observer, what is most impressive is the speed with which all this was done. The Cabinet decision to send an expedition to Suakin was taken on the morning of 6 February. The Mobilisation Committee met for the first time on 9 February and the first transport, taking troops from Gibraltar to Egypt, sailed on the 15th; the first troops from England left in the *Arab* on the 17th. The first stores ship, the *Cameo*, sailed from England on 15 February. Matters were equally expeditious on the Indian side. The first transport, carrying the 15th Sikhs, left Bombay on the 22nd; since the request for troops reached Army HQ in India only on 10 February and the Sikhs had had to journey 700 miles to Bombay from their present station at Lucknow, this was good going indeed.

It was clear from Graham's previous expedition that the campaign would be dominated by two problems – water and transport. Among the first acts of the Mobilisation Committee was to arrange for the immediate despatch of vessels with condensing apparatus to distill water at Suakin. The problem was of sufficient importance to justify setting up a special Sub-Committee of the Mobilisation Committee under the acting Adjutant-General, which met for the first time at the War Office on 20 February. It had before it a report prepared in August 1884 by Major Clarke, of the Royal Engineers. Clarke noted that for many years Suakin had derived its water supplies from wells in the Khaur river bed near the Right Water Fort. These wells had never been known to run dry and it had been estimated that 20,000 men and 2000 camels had watered there on occasion. Valentine Baker had watered his force of 5000 men, with camels and horses, there without difficulty. Clarke reported, however, that in the previous cold season, the Suakin medical authorities had condemned the supply although it was not at all clear why since there had been no cases of disease among the Suakinese, or the Royal Marines when stationed there.

On the basis of Clarke's report, the Sub-Committee concluded that the wells should go far towards meeting the requirements of the animals in Graham's force, on the basis of 9000 camels, 2000 horses and 3000 mules requiring 515 tons a day. But water for the troops and followers should be provided by condensed water, initially from distilling ships. The Director General of the Army Medical Department advised that each man would need at least a gallon a day for cooking and drinking and another gallon for washing; in standing camps, such as those round Suakin, five gallons a day for all purposes should be allowed. Graham's 1884 expedition had produced a consumption of three gallons a day and the Sub-Committee decided to use this as a basis for their initial calculations. Assuming a force of 22,300 men, this produced a daily requirement of 344½ tons.

Against this requirement, the Egyptian condensing vessels already at Suakin could produce 90 tons a day; the *Calabria* now fitting out on the Thames would be able to produce 300 tons and the *Edinburgh*, fitting out at Malta, another 100 tons. Finally, the *Zurich* or *Osprey* would take out condensers capable of producing a further 590 tons.

That appeared to provide a comfortable margin of supply and the Sub-Committee turned to the problem of storing and transporting the water. The *Calabria and Edinburgh* could store 1000 tons or three days supply each. The Commanding Royal Engineer at Suakin was instructed to arrange for a further 1000 tons of storage on shore; in fact, work on building brick tanks had been going on under the supervision of 17 Company RE since July 1884. Two tank vessels, capable of discharging 60 tons an hour, would take the water ashore from the condensing vessels.

But having got the water ashore it was still necessary to distribute it to the troops. For this purpose, huge quantities of iron tanks, wooden barrels, canvas, leather and rubber water bags and troughs were ordered in England and Egypt, holding in all some 4500 tons. Finally, a contract was placed for 50 miles of four-inch iron pipe to convey water along the railway line towards Berber. The Sub-Committee nevertheless recommended as an aside that Graham should seize the wells at Tamai as soon as possible.

At its second meeting on 21 February, the Sub-Committee had had second thoughts about the force's requirements. Revised calculations suggested that a force of 8000 fighting men, plus 8000 followers and 1500 animals, would require 450 tons a day when on the move. This would leave an inadequate margin to cater for the troops left at Suakin and for the railway builders. The Committee therefore recommended that the distilling capacity at Suakin should be raised to 1200 tons a day as soon as possible. Since it now also appeared that the force might succeed in establishing its advanced base at Arriab, some 112 miles from Suakin, further four-inch pipes would need to be procured and sent out.

By the time the Sub-Committee met again on 3 March, three further condensing ships, the *Kangaroo*, *Cyphrenes*, and *International*, had been chartered. Together with the Egyptian vessels already at Suakin which could produce, it was now estimated, 150 tons rather than 90, this gave a total capacity of 1150 tons a day which the Committee regarded as sufficient.

The first of the large condensing ships, the *Calabria*, could not reach Suakin before 15 March, having sailed on 25 February; the *Cyphrenes*, *International* and *Kangaroo* could not arrive before the first week in April. It was clear that until then water would be a brake on Graham's offensive operations. Pumps, filters, funnels, canvas horse, repair materials, 560 tins of alum for filtering, 500 bottles of permanganate of potash for purifying, repair materials and tools for canvas, rubber and iron tanks all had to be delivered before the supply of water could be regarded as secure.

Transport for Graham's force posed an equal problem. At its first meeting on 9 February, the Mobilisation Committee was pressed by the QMG to take immediate steps to assemble at least 5000 camels at Suakin. Obviously every effort would have to be made to find camels and drivers in Egypt and round Suakin but no one expected that the full requirement could be obtained that way in the timescale allowed. The Indian Government was therefore approached to supply camels and drivers from India. The authorities in India responded handsomely. By the close of the campaign, they had supplied four camel corps, totalling over 4000 camels and 2000 drivers. In addition, they had supplied 150 bullock carts with 300 bullocks, 150 ponies for the Mounted Infantry, a corps of 300 muleteers, a corps of 300 bhisties (water carriers) and a corps of 500 dhooly bearers for carrying the wounded.* The Hadendowa and other tribes round Suakin were famed as camel drivers and a certain number of camels and drivers were procured in this way. Some camels came from Egypt and others were purchased in Aden but without the Indian contribution the expeditionary force would have been crippled for transport.

No aspect of logistics is more important than satisfactory medical facilities in sustaining the morale of the fighting troops. This was especially so in the Sudan where the enemy gave no quarter and disease was ever present. At the first meeting of the Mobilisation Committee, the Director General of the Army Medical Department proposed to send out some 45 medical officers and two bearer companies, together with four Field Hospitals of 100 beds

*A dhooly is a form of covered-in stretcher or litter carried suspended from the shoulders of four bearers. The Indian corps was actually equipped with Lushai dandies, an alternative form of dhooly, deriving, as its name implies, from the Lushai Hills in Northern Eastern India.

each, a fifth Field Hospital of 200 beds, a Base General Hospital of 300 beds, and a hospital ship and tender capable of taking another 250 patients; the existing base hospital at Suez was to be equipped to full war scale. Most interestingly, eight nursing sisters were to be despatched, four for the hospital ship and four for the hospital at Suez. Wolseley had had two nursing sisters with him at Wadi Halfa in 1884 and was much in favour of them: 'We have actually two lady nurses here in our hospital; they are a real boon. Before we got them recognised as part of our medical establishment the doctors pooh-poohed their value and tried to keep them at a distance. I wish we had plenty more of them; they serve moreover to keep the doctors and the hospital order-lies up to the work'. The Base and Static Field Hospitals should have light huts rather than tents. One bearer company would be equipped with light wheeled ambulances and wagons; the other would be equipped with stret-chers (litters) or cacolets carried on camels. All this would require at least 400 trained men who could not be found without calling out some of the Reserve, unless the home hospitals were so denuded of staff as to impair their efficiency.

At its next meeting on 12 February, the Committee was informed that the transport *Ganges* had been appropriated as a hospital ship and was expected to sail from England around 25 February, reaching Suakin on or about 15 March. The Director General reported that 53 medical officers of different grades and eight nursing sisters had been placed under orders for Suakin and that requisitions had been placed upon the Director of Artillery and Stores and the Director of Clothing for all the necessary equipment, stores and clothing for the various hospitals. He recommended that India should be asked to send a corps of 500 dhooly bearers.

The first party of 156 medical staff, with ten ambulance wagons, left Southampton on the *Arab* on 17 February 1885 and reached Suakin on 7 March. The *Ganges*, with its four nursing sisters, sailed from London on 26 February, reaching Suakin on 14 March. The bulk of the remaining medical staff reached Suakin in the *Calabria* a day later.

The Indian Government made its own medical provision for its troops. The provision was based upon the assumption that sick and wounded would not exceed twelve per cent of the fighting troops and three per cent of the followers. On this basis, provision was made for two Field Hospitals of 100 beds each and a General or Base Hospital of 288 beds. It was assumed however that those sick or wounded who were not likely to be fit for further service in the field would be shipped back to India at fortnightly intervals. In addition to the hospitals, 191 Lushai dandies and dhoolies were sent out, with some 500 bearers. Finally, the *Czarewitch*, which had taken the 9th Bengal Cavalry to Suakin, was detained there and fitted out as a hospital ship with 125 beds.

The scale of medical provision was therefore fairly lavish. For the British contingent of some 9800, the hospital provision worked out at one bed for roughly every nine men; for the Indian Contingent, one bed per six and a half men. In practice, casualties and sick never remotely approached these levels.

Of scarcely less interest to the troops was the question of food. The daily ration scale which was adopted for British troops comprised, in its essentials, 1¼ pounds of bread or 1 pound of biscuit, 1¼ pounds of fresh (or 1 pound of preserved) meat, ¾ pound each of potatoes and fresh vegetables or 1 ounce of compressed vegetables, together with tea, coffee, sugar, salt, pepper and jam or marmalade every day. When available, an orange was issued to each man and a lemon to every four men; surprisingly, perhaps, lime-juice was to be issued only when tinned meat was issued. Consumption amounted to some 20 tons a day. The Indian troops had, of course, a different scale, comprising basically rice, lentils, vegetables and a small amount of meat, together with tea, sugar and salt. Their requirements worked out at roughly 10 tons a day. It was one thing to prescribe a ration scale but quite another to ensure that it was available for issue. Fresh meat was always likely to be a problem but cattle were obtained for slaughter from Odessa, in Russia and Graham claimed in his final report that, except for certain operations such as those at Hashin and Tofrek, where it was considered dangerous to have cattle inside the square, fresh meat was issued most of the time. Similarly, bread was baked at Suakin and it was rarely necessary in camp to issue biscuit instead. Vegetables were available from Egypt, England and locally, but compressed vegetables were issued on occasions.

The preservation of meat in tins had become commonplace since the Crimean War but the Sudan, in an era without refrigeration, was not the most suitable climate for storing tinned meats. Graham complained that initially the supplies were mainly corned beef, which was too salty and caused excessive thirst; it was also in 6-pound tins which were inconvenient and wasteful. In the latter stages of the campaign, sufficient supplies of fresh, preserved meat were obtained, in 2-pound tins, and this proved much more satisfactory. For cooking, wood was obtained from Egypt, Cyprus, India and locally; on active operations, the troops cut down trees and bushes.

Impressive as the rations appeared to be on paper, in practice there were frequent grumbles about both quantity and quality. Gambier-Parry referred to 'indifferent food and no variety from the daily ration of bouilli Beef'.[15] During the time that M'Neill's zariba was occupied, the rations were mainly corned beef and biscuit so hard that it had to be soaked in water before it could be eaten. Gambier-Parry wondered why such uneatable and unsuitable meat should have been supplied: 'I knew many cases where men actually threw their rations away rather than run the chances of increasing their thirst by putting such stuff in their mouths'.[16] He was also critical about the failure to provide a plentiful supply of lime juice. A doctor told him that the force occupying the zariba, which was only six miles from Suakin, was on the edge of contracting scurvy. Private Thomas Mulready, of the New South Wales Contingent, told his family that on the expedition to Tamai the food was mainly biscuit. On balance, the food was probably no better and no worse than the British soldier was used to on most of his campaigns in the second half of the 19th century, and probably no worse than he got during the Second Boer War. The cooking and preparation of the rations was a more important factor than the quality of the rations. In the absence of properly trained cooks, there was little respite from the eternal stew.

As always, the officers were able to purchase luxuries not available to the men. Gambier-Parry recorded eating tinned Oxford sausages, tinned herrings and sardines, tinned vegetables, stewed beef steak, haricot mutton and even grouse with truffles – and, on one celebrated occasion, *paté de foie gras*. At one dinner party he attended in Suakin, the menu comprised soup, curried beef and rice, sardines, and preserved peaches, washed down with champagne, whisky and a cup of coffee. (The ability of the British officer to lay his hands on champagne and whisky in almost any situation is one of the minor revelations of military history.)

The Indian contingent quickly gained a reputation for being better organised and better-off than the British, their officers living in some luxury, with proper table cloths and glasses. This was ascribed to the experience and ability of their native servants but in truth it was really a reflection of the far greater campaigning experience of the average Indian regiment compared with the British regiments. The 5th Lancers had seen no active service since it was re-formed in 1858; the 20th Hussars had served on the North West Frontier of India in 1863 and 1867. The Scots Guards and Coldstream Guards battalions had not seen active service since Waterloo and the 3rd Battalion, Grenadier Guards not since the Crimea. Of the other British battalions, the East Surreys had seen active service in the opening phase of the Second Afghan War seven years before and the Berkshires had taken part in the Egyptian Campaign of 1882, but the Shropshires had last taken the field in the Crimea. Moreover, as a result of the short-service system introduced by Cardwell in the 1870s, the British units tended to be filled with young, unhardened soldiers. By contrast, the Indian regiments were recruited on long-service engagements only, the average length of service being closer to ten years than five.

The new railway to be built by Lucas and Aird had also got off to a prompt start. The *Zurich* sailed from London with railway material on 22 February, reaching Suakin on 11 March. Other ships, similarly laden – the *Seaham Harbour*, the *Norfolk*, the *Dromore*, the *Ashington*, the *Topaz* – followed in a steady stream. The first civilian navvies, 100 in all, appear to have sailed on the *Osprey* on 26 February. Others left on the *Albatross* five days later.

NOTES

1. Proceedings of the Confidential Mobilisation Committee 117th Day, 9 February 1885. The Proceedings of this Committee are of great interest and importance – see Brian Robson 'Mounting an expedition: Sir Gerald Graham's 1885 expedition to Suakin' *Small Wars and Insurgencies*, Vol 2 (1991), pp232-39.
2. *Correspondence respecting offers by the Colonies of troops for service in the Soudan* (C4325) (HMSO, 1885).
3. The political implications of the New South Wales initiative have been endlessly discussed by Australian historians in recent years. For a useful survey see K.S. Inglis *The Rehearsal* (Sydney, 1985).
4. *Egypt No.9 (1885) Further Correspondence respecting military operations in the Soudan (C4345)* (HMSO, 1885) p   .
5. *Report of a Commission on Sudan Railways* (Cairo, 1883).
6. *Report on the Soudan (C3670)* (HMSO, 1883).
7. It eventually cost £865,000 to lay 18½ miles of standard gauge line from Suakin to Otao.
8. See P.S.A. Berridge *Couplings to the Khyber* (Newton Abbott, 1969).
9. Asked in the House of Commons how long it would take to survey the line, the Under Secretary of State for War replied tersely 'The line cannot be surveyed as long as the enemy is in possession of it.' – see Hansard for 27 February 1885, col.1620.
10. Major Peck to Inspector General of Fortifications 13 July 1884.
11. Gambier-Parry, op cit, p61.
12. Captain E.A. De Cosson *Days and Nights of Service with Sir Gerald Graham's Field Force at Suakin* (London, 1886), p55.
13. Manuscript diary in the possession of Brigadier P.N.R. Stewart-Richardson.
14. Letters, NAM 8111-30, f75.
15. Gambier-Parry, op cit, p97.
16. Ibid, p220.

8

Hashin and Tofrek
(March 1885)

The sand of the desert is sodden red –
Red with the wreck of a square that broke;
The Gatling's jammed and the Colonel dead,
And the Regiment blind with dust and smoke.
The river of death has brimmed his banks,
And England's far and Honour a name.
Sir Henry Newbolt, Vitai Lampada

THE LAST OF Graham's fighting troops, apart from the Australians, reached Suakin on 20 March, although odds and ends continued to dribble in for weeks to come.

The size of the force was impressive. He had ultimately three brigades of infantry (the Indian, Guards and 2nd), a brigade of cavalry (comprising the 9th Bengal Cavalry, two squadrons of the 5th Lancers, two squadrons of the 20th Hussars and one squadron of the 19th Hussars), a horse artillery battery of 13-pounders (G/B), the New South Wales battery re-equipped with 9-pounders, a mountain artillery battery carried on mules (5 Battery, 1 Brigade, Scottish Division), a mixed battery of Gardners and 9-pound rocket launchers (manned by 6 Battery 1 Brigade, Scottish Division), six Gardners manned by the Royal Navy and Royal Marines, and a battalion of Mounted Infantry. In addition, there were three companies of Royal Engineers (including a Photographic Section), a company of the Madras Sappers and Miners, two Telegraph Sections manned partly by Post Office reservists, a Balloon Detachment, five companies of the Commissariat and Transport Corps and a medical establishment of nearly 60 doctors and 470 men of the Medical Staff Corps. In total, the force ultimately numbered nearly 13,600 fighting men, rather larger than Wolseley's own Relief Expedition, and nearly three times the size of the 1884 force.

The cavalry were to be commanded by Colonel H.P. ('Croppy') Ewart, a Household Cavalryman of impeccable social connections but, as events were to prove, of no great military talents. The Guards Brigade was to be commanded by Lyon Fremantle, himself a Guardsman; indeed, since under Queen's Regulations, a brigade of Guards battalions could only be commanded by a Guards officer, it may have been Fremantle's presence at Suakin which was the primary motive for sending out the Guards. The other

107

British infantry brigade was to be commanded by Major General Sir John M'Neill, a fighting soldier of immense experience and a long-standing member of Wolseley's 'Ring'. 'He was of middle stature, somewhat stout, and with a round, red, good humoured face. He, too, wore many ribbons and possessed also the red one of the Victoria Cross. He had a quick, sharp way of asking questions, and a somewhat "stand-off" manner with strangers though when you knew him there was no pleasanter companion or kinder-hearted friend. He possessed also an attractive manner and a cool, quiet way of taking things, which made him to a certain extent popular. He looked as though he had the constitution of a giant and as if he could stand or go through with anything. He was always perfectly self-satisfied and even when things went against him he acted as though it all was *couleur de rose* and rather a good thing for him'.[1]

The transport requirements were correspondingly huge. Very few carts were employed which was curious since the country lent itself to the use of wheeled transport. Instead, reliance was placed primarily on camels, and, to a lesser extent, on mules. Transport was, as always, the weakest feature of the British Army. In the absence of permanent transport units, it had to resort to buying animals wherever they were available. Egypt was already denuded of good quality animals by the needs of Wolseley's expedition. For Graham, camels had to be bought in Aden, Berbera and, above all, in India, as well as Egypt. India alone supplied 4000 camels, with 2000 drivers and 300 muleteers; another 600 camel drivers and muleteers were hired in Aden. Just over 1000 mules came from Gibralta, Malta and Cyprus.

In due course, the transport was organised into seven sections:

No 1   General convoys, water transport, support of expeditions –
       2,500 camels.
No 2   Base and local transport – No 7 C and T Coy (900 camels
       and 32 mules).
No 3   Lines of Communications, railway transport – No 3 C and T Coy
       (1100 camels, 90 horses, 30 mules).
No 4   Brigade of Guards – No 5 C and T Coy (600 camels).
No 5   2nd Brigade – No 12 C and T Coy (600 camels).
No 6   Hospital work – 330 camels, 230 mules.
No 7   Transport depot for replacing casualties, 17 (Field) Coy RE –
       544 camels, 235 mules, 248 horses.

In addition to this organised transport force, each British infantry battalion had 34 mules attached to it to carry reserve ammunition, pioneer tools, signalling equipment and miscellaneous items such as mess gear. The artillery and their ammunition columns had a total of 205 camels and 174 mules. Finally, and quite separately, the Indian Contingent had with it a total of 1973 mules and 150 bullock carts, mainly distributed among the regiments.

Osman Digna in old age.

The harbour at Suakin in March 1885. The ship in the centre is the *Seaham Harbour* (ship no 31). Note the paddle steamer on the left.

Suakin Island and harbour 1885.

Street in old Suakin 1885.

Arab house in old Suakin 1885, probably a merchant's.

Hadendowa warrior. Note the characteristic sickle-shaped knife worn on the arm.

Sir Gerald Graham with his staff 1885. The officer with white moustaches (centre right) is Major General Greaves, the Chief of Staff. The officer on his right, with cross belts, is the Italian military attache, Captain Gioppi.

Headquarters Camp outside Suakin 1885. The two officers on the left are standing outside the Commander Royal Engineer's tent.

Staff officers of the Adjutant General's and Quarter Master General's
Departments at Suakin 1885.

G Battery, B Brigade, Royal Horse Artillery at Suakin 1885.

Indian officers of the 9th Bengal Cavalry at Suakin 1885. They are all Sikhs except for two who appear to be Punjabi Muhammadans. Note the blue puttees, and the native shoes worn by the trumpeter.

British and Indian officers of the 15th Bengal Native Infantry (Loodhiana Sikhs).

NCOs and sepoys of the 28th Bombay Native Infantry at Suakin 1885. The rifles are Sniders and the men are wearing boots; note the cartridge loops on the blouses.

Group of NCOs at Suakin in 1885. Two are wearing the mushroom-shaped solar topis supplied from India.

Officers of the 3rd Battalion Grenadier Guards at Suakin 1885. Note the wide variety of dress, the white helmets and the very necessary fly whisks. The officer sitting cross-legged in the middle appears to be wearing golf shoes.

The hospital ship *Ganges* (ship no 20) at Suakin 1885. Note the canvas ventilation funnels.

The gunboat HMS *Dolphin* at Suakin 1885. The electric searchlight is amidships.

Standard gauge engine and waggons of the Lucas and Aird Suakin-Berber Railway. The watchtower suggests that this was taken at Handub.

Handub Camp and railway station, looking south, with Signallers' Hill on the right.

Country near Handub. Note the tall mimosa bushes or trees.

Part of the camp at Otao in April 1885.

View southwards from Otao, showing the railway in the middle distance with a construction train on it.

The West Redoubt at Suakin. Note thorn zariba and field guns which are probably Krupps.

The Quarry Fort at Suakin 1885. Note the barbed wire entanglement in the foreground.

Troopship HMS *Jumna* at Suakin 1885. Note the standard gauge railway.

Camp at Tambuk 1885, with Mounted Infantry in the foreground and the Red Sea Hills in the background.

Osman Digna at the time of his capture. The officer on the right is probably Muhammad Ahmad Bey.

View from Signallers' Hill at Handub, looking south west to the Waratab Hills. Note the wells in the foreground and the line of the railway in the middle distance.

The battalions averaged about 840 men each on landing, the strongest being the Shropshire Light Infantry with 876, but whereas the British battalions averaged about 25 officers per battalion, the Indian battalions varied between only eight and twelve; this was a well-known weakness which persisted until the end of the Indian Army. The 9th Bengal Cavalry landed 507 strong (10 officers and 497 troopers), the squadrons averaging nearly 166 men; the British squadrons averaged 124.

Although formidable in size, Graham's force was less so in terms of experience. The most experienced troops were the Indians. They were long-service soldiers and all three battalions had taken part in the Second Afghan War only five years before.

The 15th Sikhs were as fine a regiment in terms of physique, appearance and reputation as any the Indian Army could produce and for the Suakin expedition, it had been reinforced by a draft from an equally fine regiment, the 45th Sikhs. The 28th Bombay Native Infantry was composed mainly of Mahrattas from the Bombay Presidency. Although less imposing physically than the Sikhs, the Mahrattas were active, intelligent soldiers with a long military history. The 17th Bengal Native Infantry, largely composed of Hindus and Hindu Muslims from Oudh, was the least experienced of the three Indian battalions. It had seen service towards the end of the Second Afghan War but no serious fighting. Sir Frederick Roberts had inspected it before it embarked and had expressed grave doubts about its fighting qualities.[2] It was unfortunate that the Commanding Officer had taken command only as the regiment embarked at Bombay. The 9th Bengal Cavalry had not seen service since the Mutiny but it was composed of excellent material from the Punjab and Northern India – Sikhs, Dogras, Pathans and Punjabi Muhammadans. Its commander, Colonel A.P. Palmer, was a very experienced Frontier soldier and had distinguished himself in the Second Afghan War.

The Indian regiments quickly impressed spectators at Suakin with the efficiency of their arrangements, based upon long campaigning experience. Each regiment brought with it its own mule transport, and the cavalry regiment, in addition to its 192 mules, brought 245 ponies for use in collecting forage and carrying baggage. The regiments were thus able to march into action the moment they disembarked. There was a price to be paid, however, which was the large number of followers who necessarily accompanied each regiment. Nevertheless, to a dispassionate observer like Wylde, the superior efficiency of the Indian troops was manifest: 'The whole force sent from India was in fact deserving of every praise, and any casual observer must have seen how very far ahead they are in organisation to the English home authorities, and how every department immediately fell into its allotted place without any noise and confusion. The transports were cleaner, better ventilated and better organised than those from England, and any foreign nation would have been able to learn many things and taken useful hints from the management of the force that arrived from India'.[3]

The British regiments could not match this level of experience and expertise. The short-service system had largely eliminated the old, long-service soldiers. The regiments which landed at Suakin were full of young soldiers with relatively little service. More than half of the 5th Lancers and the 20th Hussars had less than 18 months service. Lieutenant Alexander Edwards, of the Royal Irish Regiment, attached to the 28th Bombay Native Infantry, had some interesting things to say after the action at Hashin: 'The cavalry really did have some fighting, the Bengal Lancers doing very well, better, I think, than the British as their small horses are so handy and they have much more control over them than these young soldiers over their big horses; at least, so it seems to me. The 5th Lancers are a good looking lot but I don't think much of the 20th Hussars, if the stories we hear in camp about them are true, but no doubt in every campaign there are always certain events that are never made public and don't get known'.[4] Many of the British units had been a long time away from active service. An illustration of their inexperience was in the field of sanitation. The Brigade Surgeon of the Indian Contingent reported that the British camps were very dirty, and that the smell from their latrines was often perceptible in the Indian camps a long distance away. In his view, the British should have employed a proper corps of sanitary sweepers, as the Indians did. Quarantine Islands was even filthier and Wolseley commented on the disgusting condition of the harbour when he arrived in May.

The New South Wales Contingent contained a sprinkling of ex-soldiers who had served in Afghanistan, Zululand, the New Zealand Wars and even the Mutiny; there were at least two men who had served in the United States Army. But, taken as a whole, the two units were raw and inexperienced.

The *Calabria*, with a condensing capacity of 250 tons, had arrived on 15 March; with the Egyptian condensing ships already there, this gave a total production capacity of distilled water of some 400 tons a day, with nearly double that capacity on its way in other ships. With the water available from the wells at Suakin, Graham was in a position to start operations.

Graham's performance in the previous year – and particularly the near-disaster and heavy casualties at Tamai – had been criticised in many quarters and it is clear that many officers regarded his present appointment with a good deal of reserve. Their doubts had not been lessened by the poor layout of the camps and the resulting inability to deal with the nightly attacks by Osman's men. While Graham appears to have been generally liked as a man, his methods of business, and particularly his secretiveness, did not inspire universal confidence. Gambier-Parry left a fairly sharp portrait: 'The first of these was a very tall, broad-shouldered man, with a certain shrewd look in his face, with a kindly manner and a soldierly bearing . . . He always seemed very brave, as if he bore on his shoulders the weight of some overpowering responsibiity and he certainly acted on the principle that silence was golden, for he told his staff nothing and, they say, consulted nobody. One of his personal staff told me that they never knew an hour beforehand when a move was going to take place and that this reserve was carried so far that they never even knew what time they were going to have their dinners . . . We all liked him because of his many attractive qualities, and above all, he was a true friend and a perfect gentleman. He might have been popular, but his somewhat cold manner and habitual reserve rather repelled any advances, and there was none of that spontaneous *bonhomie* and happy manner with his troops which, while it sacrifices nothing in discipline, wins for his commander the love of his soldiers'.[5]

De Cosson's portrait is equally sharp: 'His voice was good but his manner of speech slow and he said very little at a time, while his eyes had a placid expression which reminded one somehow of the calm gaze of an ox – a placidity that never left him, I believe, even in the moment of danger . . . his features rarely lit up and were not characterised by that bright alertness of expression which distinguishes Lord Wolseley'.[6] Many of those involved in the expedition could not see the point of it. Gordon was dead, Khartoum and virtually the whole of the Sudan was in the hands of the Mahdi, and it seemed incredible that any British Government should want to spend blood and treasure on conquering what seemed to most a barren, inhospitable desert, especially since the British occupation of Egypt was still regarded as only temporary. If the only real purpose of the expedition was to crush Osman Digna and his followers, that too seemed to many an unworthy motive. Thus Wylde wrote that 'For the life of me, I never could see what was the use of our Suakin expedition in 1885 unless it was to spend money and to make a military demonstration'.[7]Gambier-Parry recalled that 'We often used to talk, as we looked round on all these vast preparations and this great concourse of men of all sorts and conditions, on the enormous outlay of money that was being spent without stint, on the toil and sickness and death around us, and we used to wonder then what it was all for. We knew that, being soldiers, we went where we were told and did what we were told when we got there, but beyond this I do not believe there was a man in the whole of this magnificent force who could have given you any intelligible reason for which we were fighting, if indeed his ingenuity enabled him to give you any reason at all'.[8]

With the doubts about the purpose of the expedition went a good deal of sympathy for the enemy which Kipling caught accurately in his verse. The sheer courage and determination of the tribesmen, their ability to take incredible punishment and still keep coming, and their refusal to give up so long as there was a breath in their bodies, had made a deep impression on the British solider, officers and men alike. There was a distinct feeling of unhappiness that it should again be necessary to kill men who were perceived to be fighting only for their own country and faith, and who had so many of the qualities that the British admired.

There were equally some, like De Cosson, who saw the campaign as a crusade to avenge Gordon and to bring light into darkness: 'Too late, it is true, to save Gordon, we may still rescue our gallant comrades from their perilous position on the Nile and, joining hands with Wolseley, deliver a crushing blow to the power of the Mahdi . . . Is it not a new crusade to strike a death-blow to Mahdiism, that growing power embodying all the dark and ferocious bigotry which actuated the earlier followers of the Prophet when they swept in their countless hordes over Europe?'[9] But all were anxious to get on with the campaign; the sooner the fighting was over, the sooner they could leave this dusty, barren, unhealthy country (or, as Gambier-Parry put it, 'this bloodstained frying pan').

By 18 March, Graham had available some 11,500 men, 1900 horses, 1200 camels and some 2700 mules and ponies, with 3500 followers. He could make his first move. Early on Thursday 19 March, Gambier-Parry, who was sleeping after a long night's work, was woken by a friend telling him to come and see the cavalry forming up. Graham had assembled the Cavalry Brigade,[10] the Indian Infantry Brigade and the Guards Brigade south of the West Redoubt. After a short inspection, the mounted men moved out towards Hashin, some seven miles west of Suakin where Osman was reported to have a force which was mainly responsible for the nightly attacks on the camp. Graham's object, as he defined it in his orders, was to reconnoitre as far as Hashin village, examine the wells there but to avoid an engagement if possible. He accompanied the force himself in order to see the ground over which he intended to make a major advance the next day.

Hashin, a collection of some forty huts, lay at the north western foot of a small, round-topped hill known as Beehive Hill, rising a hundred feet or so out of the surrounding sandy gravel plain (Map 6). Immediately to the south of Beehive Hill was Dihilbat, the most prominent feature of the area – a large hill, shaped something like the Rock of Gibraltar and reaching a height of 828 feet above the plain. The plain around Beehive and Dihilbat was covered in dense mimosa scrub, six to eight feet high, making cavalry movement difficult and giving ample protection to the enemy. Two thousand yards east of Beehive Hill was a group of six small hills (A,B,C,D,F,G) varying in height between 360 and 530 feet. To the west of Hashin lay the spurs of the Waratab Hills, the easternmost range of the Red Sea Hills, through which the railway to Berber would need to find a way in due course.

The small group of hills east of Hashin were occupied by small parties of Osman's men but, as the cavalry approached, the 9th Bengal Cavalry leading, these hills were evacuated and the Dervishes fell back on the main body at Hashin which then moved slowly further west, one party however continuing to occupy the top of Dihilbat. Hashin village was occupied by Graham and the mounted troops at about 0940 hours, three Remington rifles and some cartridges being found.[11] There were two wells, apparently recently sunk, and the water was reported to be good.

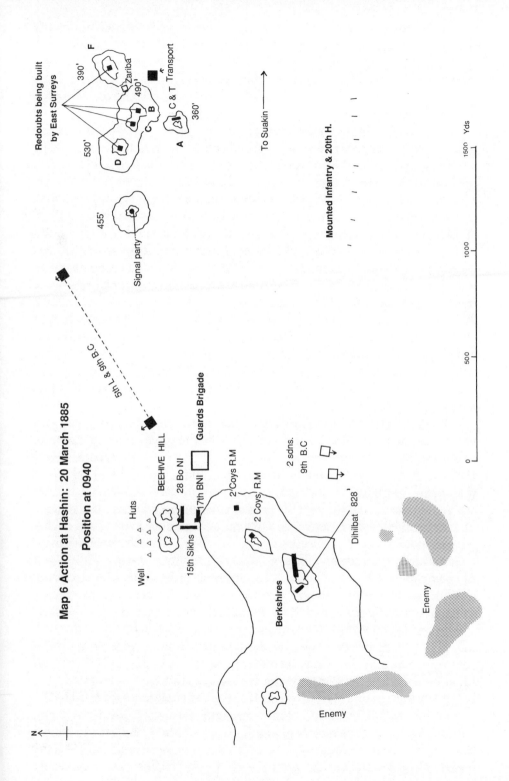

Map 6 Action at Hashin: 20 March 1885
Position at 0940

Redoubts being built
by East Surreys

F
390'
Zariba
490'
C & T Transport
360'
B
C
A
530'
D

To Suakin →

455'
Signal party

Mounted Infantry & 20th H.

0   500   1000   1500   Yds

5th L & 9th B.C

BEEHIVE HILL
Guards Brigade

Huts

Well

15th Sikhs

28 Bo NI
17th BNI

2 Coys R.M

2 Coys. R.M

Berkshires

2 sdns.
9th B.C

Dihilbat   828'

N ←

Enemy

Enemy

113

Small groups of the enemy on camels kept watch on Graham's troops and the men on Dihilbat fired from time to time. Despite the absence of major resistance, the Dervishes were always dangerous. A patrol of the 20th Hussars, approaching too close to Dihilbat, was fiercely attacked, losing a private killed and a sergeant wounded. Lieutenant Birch of the Mounted Infantry, anxious to get a better view, climbed one of the lower spurs of Dihilbat and was immediately attacked by five or six of the enemy for his pains; he was very lucky to escape with his life, although he was wounded.

Having seen all that he needed, Graham ordered the mounted troops to retire at 1015. To cover their retirement, the Horse Artillery battery took up a position on one of the small hills (A). By 1230, the mounted troops were back in camp. As they retired, the enemy re-occupied the group of small hills.

The Guards Brigade had spent the day lying down near the West Redoubt, ready to advance if required. The Indian Brigade had followed the cavalry for some three miles towards Hashin and had then halted in immediate support. It too had a peaceful day, returning before the cavalry. The whole force was back at Suakin by 1300 hours. Graham had left behind on a white stick in the middle of the village a letter to Osman, asserting that the British respected all religions and wished only to establish peaceful relations; it warned Osman, however, that unless he and his men submitted, they would be punished as they had been the year before. The letter was a rejoinder to one which Osman had sent earlier, telling the British to withdraw before they were driven into the sea.

Graham determined to repeat the operation the next day, in force, with the object of establishing fortified posts on the small hills in order to dominate Hashin and prevent any further concentration of the enemy there. Gambier-Parry spent the night near the harbour loading 13,000 gallons of water into portable tanks and barrels to be carried by 700 camels accompanying Graham's force the next day. He managed to finish just as the force assembled ready to move off. Having successfully stirred up the enemy the previous day, Graham prudently decided to use virtually his whole force – the Cavalry Brigade and all three infantry brigades, together with 17 and 24 Companies RE who would be employed in building the necessary fortifications, the RHA battery, a battery of Gardner guns and two rocket troughs or launchers manned by the Royal Artillery – in all, some 8200 men.

The cavalry moved off towards Hashin just after 0600 hours on the 20th followed fifteen minutes later by the infantry forming three sides of an enormous square. The front face of the square was formed by the 2nd Infantry Brigade, consisting of the Berkshires, the East Surreys and the Royal Marines, in line of companies of fours. The left face was formed by the Indian Infantry Brigade in column of companies, the 15th Sikhs being followed by the 17th Bengal Native Infantry, with the 28th Bombay Native Infantry bringing up the rear. The right face was formed similarly by the Guards Brigade. Inside the square were the Royal Engineer companies, some of the Madras Sappers and Miners, the Gardner battery and the rocket launchers, together with the transport. The front of the square was screened by the mounted troops, led by the 9th Bengal Cavalry, supported by G/B RHA. Because the rear face of the square was open, the fighting troops could move forward at a steady pace, unhampered by the transport.

The force reached the group of small hills east of Hashin at about 0825 and the Engineers and the East Surreys were set to work immediately constructing redoubts on Hills B, C, D and F, as well as a zariba in the low ground between B and F.

Osman's men were clearly present in force on Dihilbat and Beehive Hill, as well as on the plain to the south of Dihilbat and on the Waratab Hills further to the west. Dihilbat dominated the whole area and Graham decided therefore to seize it with the remaining two battalions of the 2nd Brigade, with the Indian battalions in immediate support and the Guards close behind in reserve. The Mounted Infantry and the 20th Hussars were deployed in a wide screen to the south of the small Hill A to protect the left and rear of the force. The 5th Lancers and the 9th Bengal Cavalry were posted to the north of Beehive Hill to protect the right of the force. To aid the 2nd Brigade troops in their assault on Dihilbat, Graham ordered G/B RHA to take up position on Beehive, from which to bring fire down on to Dihilbat. Graham with his staff took up position on Hill A and battle commenced.

Dihilbat (later called Hashin Hill) ascends gradually from north east to south west. Its slopes were very steep, even precipitous in places and the base was covered with dense mimosa thorn. The Indian Brigade took up position in the form of a three-sided square facing west in the valley some two or three hundred yards wide between Beehive and Dihilbat, with the Guards Brigade in square some two hundred yards to the east. The Berkshires, starting at 0900 hours and supported in rear by the Royal Marines battalion, quickly occupied the north eastern part of Dihilbat despite its steepness. Here they came under heavy fire from Osman's men on the summit and in positions to the right of the summit. The right half battalion of the Marines moved round to the right to bring a flanking fire to bear on the summit and aided by this the Berkshires occupied the summit at about 0930, the enemy retiring west-wards and southwards in the general direction of Tamai. It was a fine feat of arms by the Berkshires who suffered a mere handful of casualties.

G/B, trying to take up its position on Beehive Hill, had come under fire from Dihilbat Hill, and lost two horses. Finding it impossible to deploy satisfactorily on Beehive, the battery detached three guns to the west of the hill where they proceeded to shell the enemy who could be seen on the Waratab Hills to the west.

So far, all had gone well. But Osman's men were never so dangerous as in defeat. At about 0940, Colonel Ewart, seeing parties of the enemy streaming off Dihilbat and heading southwards towards Tamai, took two squadrons of the Bengal Cavalry to intercept them. As they passed along the south east face

115

of Dihilbat, they came under heavy fire from a large party of the enemy ensconced on the hillside. Ewart ordered one squadron to dismount and engage this party with their carbines. In this position, the squadron was suddenly attacked by enemy spearmen who had filtered unseen through the thick bush. Taken at a disadvantage, with their swords and lances still on their saddles, the Indian sowars fought desperately to regain their horses. Major Robertson, commanding the squadron, was attacked by two Dervishes and received a spear in his thigh while trying to save a dismounted sowar. Captain Garstain was hit by two spears, luckily without serious injury. In the thick scrub, it was impossible for the squadrons to re-form and charge and there was something of a pell-mell for a few minutes as the squadrons retired on the Guards Brigade half a mile or so to the north, with the Dervishes in close pursuit.[12] As soon as the cavalry had cleared the front of the Guards, a few volleys from the latter stopped the enemy pursuit. The two squadrons had lost heavily in the meleé – 12 sowars and seven followers killed, and two officers and 14 men wounded. The Dervishes had worked in small groups, one man distracting a trooper's attention while two or three others attacked him from behind, pulling him off his horse and stabbing him to death with knives, spears and swords.

An hour or so after this minor disaster, the 5th Lancers and the remaining two squadrons of the 9th Bengal Cavalry, stationed to the north to protect the British right flank, were engaged with large groups of the enemy coming down from the Waratab Hills and intent upon cutting in behind the right flank of the force. Although they were operating in thick bush, the 5th Lancers were highly-trained spearmen. Against them, the usual Dervish tactic of lying down and thrusting up at the horse as it passed would not work and the lances took heavy toll of those who tried it. Major Harvey, of the 5th, seeing action for the first time in 21 years' soldiering, was stabbed with a lance which the Dervish had taken off the 9th Bengal Cavalry as he charged through the enemy for the second time. Despite the lance sticking in his thigh, he managed to stay on his horse. The 5th lost five men killed and eight wounded in this brief action but the Dervish threat to the right flank was stopped.

Despite the occupation of Dihilbat, enemy opposition was increasing. By 1225, the fortifications on B, C, D, F and the zariba in between had progressed sufficiently for Graham to start his withdrawal. The Indian Brigade retired, covered by the Berkshires and the Royal Marines, and these elements of the force halted in the open ground south of Hill A. To the Guards fell the distinction of forming the rear guard. They remained in position near Beehive until 1300 hours, supported by G/B. They then moved off, taking a more southerly route than the Indians and the 2nd Brigade troops, and were continuously fired upon from the right flank by parties of the enemy concealed in the mimosa bushes. It was a trying ordeal for inexperienced troops but the discipline of the Guards pulled them through. Firing steady volleys as they went, they finally reached the concentration area south of A. The Royal Horse Artillery took up position on Hill A and opened fire on parties of the enemy who had been attacking the Guards. Nevertheless, if Osman's men had been better shots, the Guards could have been in a critical position, and Gambier-Parry, for one, thought it poor generalship.

Graham now halted his force for a couple of hours while the wounded were attended to, water distributed (half a gallon per man) and the troops had their dinners. The fortifications and the zariba were finished off and stored with water, provisions for four days and stocks of ammunition. They were then occupied by the East Surreys and the Gardner guns.

The general retirement of the force began at about 1630 hours. The gallant Berkshires and Royal Marines formed the rear guard, the post of honour, with the Guards on the right and the Indian Brigade on the left, with the transport in the centre of the square. The cavalry formed a screen round the infantry. Suakin was reached at 1815 without further loss. The wounded were immediately transferred to the base hospitals and then to the hospital ships in the harbour.

Graham had lost one officer and 28 men killed, and three officers and 36 men wounded. The 9th Bengal Cavalry lost 12 men killed and 16 wounded while the Guards lost one officer killed and 22 men wounded. Graham estimated that Osman's force had numbered about 3000 and had lost at least 250 killed, but these figures were necessarily speculative.

Graham made relatively light of the reverse suffered by the Bengal Cavalry in his official despatch of 21 March 1885 although he referred pointedly to the cavalry 'being dismounted at a most unsuitable moment'.[13] But he was furious with Ewart for the blunder and recommended privately to Wolseley that Ewart should be denied the rank of Brigadier General.[14] In his turn, Ewart protested against the statement in Graham's original despatch that both squadrons had been dismounted and on 10 May Graham formally asked for his printed despatch to be amended to read 'Colonel Ewart ordered part of one of these squadrons to dismount and fire volleys'.[15]

Much more to the point was why the operation had taken place at all. In his despatch, Graham claimed that the construction of the fortified posts was necessary in order to 'protect my right flank in the impending advance on Tamai, to obtain a post of observation near to the mountains and to assist in over-aweing the tribes'. None of these reasons holds up to serious analysis. In open country such as that round Suakin, the enemy could move freely in any direction and no single post, isolated in the middle of the desert, could conceivably stop the Dervishes from concentrating and moving wherever they wished. While the posts might have had some value for observation purposes, they could not conceivably protect 'the right flank' or materially over-awe the tribes. The speed with which the enemy re-occupied Dihilbat when Graham withdrew was clear testimony to the pointlessness of the operation.

The difficulty of keeping the posts supplied with water and food quickly became apparent although it should have been obvious from the beginning. The posts themselves were virtually impregnable. On Hills D and C, they consisted of breastworks of stone four to five feet high and some two and a half feet thick, roofed-in and protected by a ring of thorn bushes wired together, and holding 30-50 men. On Hill F, an outer rifle trench protected an inner redoubt in which two Krupp field guns from Suakin were mounted; it was held by 20 men. The remainder of the East Surreys occupied a zariba built in the valley between Hills B and F. It had been intended to link the zariba to Hills B and F but lack of labour prevented it. On 25 March, three days after the near-disaster at Tofrek, the posts near Hashin were quietly dismantled and the garrison returned to Suakin. There was simply not the effort available to run convoys to Hashin as well as to Tofrek and it was by then clear that the Hashin posts served no purpose since the real centre of gravity of the military operations lay in the direction of Tamai and along the line of the railway to Handub and Otao.

Even if there was a case for occupying a post at Hashin, why was it necessary to storm Dihilbat? And if it was necessary to turn the enemy off Dihilbat, would it not have been neater and easier to have attacked frontally with one brigade while moving the other two brigades round to the rear (west) to cut off the enemy line of retreat? These, and other questions, disturbed some officers with the force. If there was an answer to them, it was probably that Graham wanted, and expected, a full-scale attack in which he would annihilate Osman's army with his superior fire-power. This time, however, Osman did not oblige. Gambier-Parry no doubt expressed a fairly general view when he wrote of the Hashin operation 'how far the blood then shed helped us on our way at all, or furthered the object of the campaign, we were at a loss to imagine, and were never afterwards enlightened'.

There were other curious aspects of the operations round Hashin. The transport, consisting of about 1200 camels, of whom some 5-700 were carrying water, had been intended to advance inside the square. The camels carrying the water had however some two miles to go from the water depot before they could reach the main assembly point of the force near the West Redoubt and the infantry had already moved off when the camels arrived: 'It was two miles from the seashore to the point of rendezvous South of the West Redoubt and, by the time we reached it, the troops had already gone forward and were visible only as a cloud of dust advancing slowly across the plain some miles before us, with the sun playing brightly on the glancing bayonets which flashed through it here and there . . . We were now marching due west, across a broad and sandy plain dotted with mimosa trees, without guard or escort of any kind, except the few men of the Commissariat and Transport Corps who accompanied the camels'.[16] The rest of the transport ahead of the water camels had suffered the usual delays inherent in camel transport and gradually fell behind the infantry square which, of course, had no rear face.

One has therefore the picture of the transport force gradually emptying out of the rear of the square, rather like flour emptying out of an open-ended box as it is dragged along. When the infantry square halted near the small hills, the transport caught up and remained close to the hills during the whole of the action. It is clear therefore that there was room for criticism of the way in which the transport was allowed to advance with very little attention paid to its protection. If the water camels in particular had been attacked (and such an attack was well within the enemy capabilities, given the cover afforded by the scrub) then the force could have been in some fairly serious difficulties.[17] On at least one soldier, the events at Hashin had made a considerable impression. 'Those Arabs are very cruel. Even when the cavalry charge them, they throw their spears which are tied to their wrists and then lay down and cannot be reached with swords – in fact, Lances are the best to charge with. A sword is not the least bit of good with these fellows, we are only fit for scouting' wrote Private Fergusson, of the 20th Hussars, 'Those Arabs take no prisoners nor do they have mercy but cut fingers [sic] off and put them in your mouth. These men lay down and cling to the horses' heels like leeches and hamstring the horses – that is, cut the fetlocks in two and rip the horses up the belly and then cut hands or tongue or scalp off the men'.[18]

Having, as he put it, 'secured his right flank' Graham now moved against the main enemy concentration which was understood to be round Tamai, nearly 14 miles south-west of Suakin. Given the distance and the relatively short day (sunrise was just after 0600 and sunset at roughly 1800 hours) it was clear that the troops could not reach Tamai, fight, and get back to Suakin in one day. Graham therefore decided to establish two staging depots along the route to Tamai, filled with food, water and ammunition.

The way he chose initially to do this was curiously complicated. The Instructions issued on the afternoon of 21 March ordered M'Neill, with two British and three Indian battalions, a squadron of cavalry, a squadron of Mounted Infantry, together with a large transport force and four Gardner guns, to advance five miles along the Tamai road. There, two of the Indian battalions would be dropped off to construct a zariba (No 1). The two British battalions and the third Indian battalion would advance another three miles and there build a larger zariba (No 2). When this was completed, it would be garrisoned by the British battalions; the third Indian battalion would retire and occupy zariba No 1, the other two Indian battalions, with the transport and mounted troops, going back to Suakin. The transport would initially be held at zariba No 1, until it was safe for it to move on to zariba No 2. Once the depots had been built, then Graham would be ready to advance with the rest of his force and attack Tamai.

There were three noteworthy features about the force allocated to M'Neill for this task. First, he was allocated only two squadrons of mounted men, just under 200 in all, the remainder of the mounted troops, amounting to another eight squadrons, being retained at Suakin. A force of less than 200 mounted men was clearly insufficient to screen the rest of M'Neill's force. Secondly, apart from four Gardner guns manned by the Naval Brigade, there was no artillery, not even the Royal Horse Artillery battery (G/B). Thirdly, M'Neill was being saddled with a very large transport force. His instructions were to take out three days rations and water for the garrisons of the two zaribas and as much additional food and water as he could carry. No precise figures are available for the amount of transport which M'Neill ultimately took with him. The final campaign report of the Senior Commissariat Officer gave a figure of 1080 camels carrying water and supplies. In addition, each of the battalions and detachments had its own transport, and there was a number of carts. A minimum figure would therefore be 1500 transport animals of all kinds.

The orders did not reach units until late on the afternoon of 21 March, for an advance on the 22nd. Very few of the troops detailed got much sleep that night. Graham's instructions required tents to be struck and deposited with the Shropshire Light Infantry near the Right Water Fort, and heavy baggage to be taken back to the Base Depot opposite Quarantine Island. By the time that this had all been done and transport loaded with regimental supplies to be taken forward next day, there was little opportunity for sleep before Reveille sounded at about 0430. For the Commissariat and Transport Corps, it was even worse since they had the job of filling the water containers and loading up the camels, a slow process at the best of times. Few of them got any sleep at all.

When the force assembled on the morning of the 22nd, M'Neill's instructions had been significantly changed. Only one squadron of cavalry was to accompany him, and the order of construction of the two zaribas was altered. Instead of being constructed simultaneously, they were to be constructed consecutively but in reverse order. The whole force, *including* the transport, was to advance to the eight-mile point and construct zariba No 2. When that was ready and garrisoned by the two British battalions, the remainder of the force was to retire to the five mile point and there construct zariba No 1. The 15th Sikhs would be left to garrison that and the remainder of the force would then march back to Suakin. Why the Instructions were altered in this very curious way is not clear. The main effect was to require M'Neill to take the whole of the transport force with him to zariba No 2, instead of leaving it behind at zariba No 1 until it was safe to move on to zariba No 2. It was a change which was to have disastrous results. The decision to reduce the mounted troops to one squadron only of the 5th Lancers, some 110 men, is inexplicable. One squadron was hopelessly inadequate to provide a useful screen round the rest of the force. If it was considered that the country was too thick for cavalry to operate in successfully, then it would at least have been better to send a squadron of mounted infantry rather than lancers whose primary weapon was particularly useless in close country.

The force which eventually paraded near the Right Water Fort early on the morning of 22 March (Sunday) consisted therefore of one squadron of the 5th Lancers, four Gardner guns manned by the Naval Brigade, the Berkshires, the Royal Marine Light Infantry battalion, the three Indian infantry battalions, the Madras Sappers and Miners, and 24 (Field) Company, RE. Finally, there was the Telegraph Detachment of the Royal Engineers, made up of reservists from the Post Office, with its equipment, including cable laying reels, on a wagon. Again, surprisingly, there are no precise official returns but a force of some 3300 combatants, with 1500 transport animals and 500 followers, would be a reasonable estimate.

Apart from the decision to leave the Mounted Infantry squadron at home and use the 5th Lancers instead, and to take no artillery, the other noteworthy detail was the decision to use the Berkshires and the Royal Marines again. Presumably, it was Graham's intention to use the Guards Brigade and the Shropshires for the final advance on Tamai. As it turned out, the experience of the Berkshires and the Royal Marines, who had been at Suakin for several months, proved a lucky bonus for Graham and M'Neill.

The force was originally to have moved off from the Right Water Fort at 0600 hours but it appears from Graham's despatch to have moved off at about 0700 hours, a delay which had an effect on subsequent events. Graham himself accompanied the force for the first two and a half miles and then returned to Suakin. The obvious route to Tamai followed the Kassala road southwards for some six miles before branching off south westwards towards Tamai. It had been traversed the year before by Graham with a force similar in size to M'Neill's.[19] Graham seems then to have encountered no particular difficulty in marching along this track. His despatch of 15 March 1884 to Hartington records that on 11 March the artillery and infantry marched from Suakin to Baker's Zariba, a distance of some 8½ miles, in 4½ hours; the only problem was the soft sand which made dragging the Gardner guns hard work for the sailors.

The natural assumption was that M'Neill would follow the same track; indeed, the Instructions circulated on the afternoon of 21 March specifically referred to the construction of a zariba eight miles off 'on the Tamai road'. If that had been the case, however, then the obvious location for M'Neill's main depot would have been Baker's 1884 zariba. That would have saved a good deal of time and effort since what remained of the original zariba could have been utilised by M'Neill. But Baker's Zariba was not mentioned in M'Neill's orders which suggests that that route was never in Graham's mind. When Graham arrived on the morning of the 22nd to inspect M'Neill's force, he found that it had been drawn up by the Brigade Major, Lieutenant Colonel Kelly, facing south i.e. along the Kassala road. Graham immediately ordered it to be aligned towards the south west and it was in this direction that the force moved off at 0700 hours, in two large squares. The reason for that decision we will come to. The immediate effect was to plunge M'Neill's force into mimosa scrub which soon became dense, rising six to eight feet in height. Traversing such scrub in relatively small units is one thing; to traverse it in large, unwieldy squares with a very large force of transport animals was quite another. Almost immediately, the transport was in difficulties.[20] The animals were probably overloaded anyway, given the instructions to M'Neill to take as much water and stores as he could manage, and the fact that they had all had to be loaded in the dark. Forcing their way through the scrub, it was inevitable that loads would be knocked off or unsettled. Every animal which had to be re-loaded entailed delay and disorder. The whole transport force began to straggle and frequent halts had to be made in order to concentrate it and re-enclose it in the Indian Brigade square. Progress was thus abysmally slow and by 1000 hours, the force had covered only some five miles. At that rate, M'Neill would not reach the eight mile point until midday at the earliest. Allowing three or four hours for the troops to have their dinners and build the zaribas, there was clearly going to be insufficient time to build the intermediate zariba and to get the surplus troops back to Suakin before nightfall. M'Neill accordingly proposed to Graham, via the mobile telegraph with him, that he should stop at the six-mile point and form a zariba there, sending the surplus troops straight back to Suakin as soon as the zariba had been finished and garrisoned; on this basis, the troops should be back well before sunset. Graham approved.

Lieutenant Colonel Elliott Wood, of the Royal Engineers, who was guiding the force, was accordingly sent on ahead to locate a suitable open space and at about 1030 the force reached the point he had chosen, a large horseshoe-shaped clearing, with the head of the shoe facing towards Tamai.

The force had marched from Suakin in two brigade squares, the British brigade leading, with the Indian Brigade following to the right rear, with the transport inside it. The British square contained the guns, the water carts, and the spare ammunition. Alongside the British square marched the Telegraph Section with ten miles of cable mounted on drums on a wagon. The end of the cable had been joined on to the main cable in Suakin and as the column advanced, the cable was unreeled into the ruts left by the wagon wheels. There was no time properly to bury the cable so some of the detachment, following, simply kicked sand over it.[21] The Indian square contained all the transport animals and, unlike the formation at Hashin, the rear of the square was closed by the 17th Bengal Native Infantry and the Sappers and Miners.

M'Neill had been giving consideration to the deployment of the troops when they reached the site of the proposed zariba. The planned lay-out of the zariba comprised a large central enclosure, roughly 120 yards square, with smaller enclosures or redoubts at the north-eastern and south-western corners, 75 yards and 65 yards square respectively. The central enclosure would contain all the stores, with the two smaller enclosures providing protection. M'Neill's first idea was to deploy the infantry in one huge square, within which the zariba with its three enclosures could then be built.

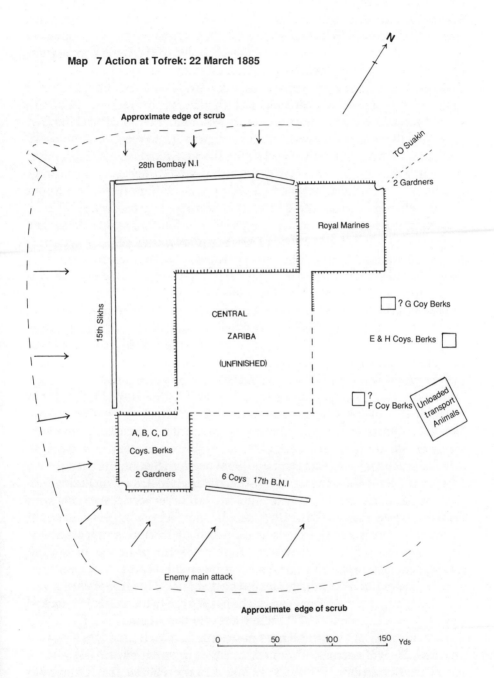

Map 7 Action at Tofrek: 22 March 1885

N

Approximate edge of scrub

TO Suakin

28th Bombay N.I

2 Gardners

Royal Marines

15th Sikhs

CENTRAL

ZARIBA

(UNFINISHED)

? G Coy Berks

E & H Coys. Berks

?
F Coy Berks

Unloaded transport Animals

A, B, C, D

Coys. Berks

2 Gardners

6 Coys   17th B.N.I

Enemy main attack

Approximate edge of scrub

0   50   100   150   Yds

123

That plan suffered from two major disadvantages. Firstly, the troops would be relatively thinly spread round a square which could hardly be less than 550 yards along each side, giving rather less than one man per yard; against the sort of onslaught to be expected, that was hardly strong enough. Secondly, the work of dragging in the necessary brushwood to make the enclosures and leading the transport animals in and out to unload meant that there would be constant gaps in the square – and the Dervishes had repeatedly shown the critical danger of leaving gaps of any kind. M'Neill's second thought was to allocate the south-west redoubt to the Royal Marines and leave them to get on with the construction while providing their own protection. That would still have left the Indian Brigade in difficulties over protecting their enclosure while at the same time allowing access to the large transport force. M'Neill reached a compromise solution; the British troops would halt in square to the east of the clearing, to provide a solid *point d'appui* in case of attack before the zariba was finished, while the Indian battalions would form three sides of a large square facing west, within which the zariba would be built. The cavalry would provide a screen of vedettes round the northern, western and southern faces, the most likely directions from which an enemy attack might come.

When the troops marched on to the selected ground, that was the deployment they took up. At this stage, the only indications of the enemy were small parties which had been sighted during the march and which had retreated before the force as it advanced. There was no obvious sign of a major attack although Tamai, only some six or seven miles ahead, was known to contain a large concentration of Osman's troops and the Dervishes were capable of covering that distance very rapidly. Information was, in fact, available to Graham that Osman was preparing to attack any force sent out from Suakin towards Tamai. The Intelligence Department had a well-ordered system of spies who came and went between Suakin and the Dervish forces with comparative ease. Moreover, the friendly tribes, including portions of the Amarar, maintained contacts with other sections serving with Osman; indeed who was 'friendly' and who 'hostile' was largely a matter of judgement. As early as 14 February, Ali Adam, of the Amarar, reported that 'If the English came out, they [the Dervishes] will not wait as before but attack them in their zariba'. The same warning was repeated on 22 February. Ten days later, an Amarar tribesman reported that 'If the troops encamp on the way to either place [Tamai or Hashin], they are to be suddenly attacked during the night'. Next day, Brewster was told that 'If a zariba is formed on the way to either of Osman Digna's positions, he has given orders to have it attacked. He will not make the mistake, which caused his losses last year, of letting the British attack him'. On 13 March, a spy reported that 'Osman has given orders that if the army leaves here [Suakin] they are to attack it before it has time to unload or settle down'. These warnings were clear and consistent; what is most significant is that Osman had grasped the fact that, once allowed to form proper square, and given reasonable fields of fire, the British troops were invincible. If they were to be overcome, they must be attacked either at night or before they had managed to form a tight square.

What is not clear is how far this accumulated information, or at least, the clear drift of it, had been communicated to M'Neill before he marched out. On the face of it, it would seem extraordinary if the tenor of this information was not generally known to the senior officers of Graham's force, even if they had not seen the detailed reports. Such information tends to spread through ordinary conversation, either in the Mess or during daily official intercourse. On the other hand, Galloway claims that M'Neill did not know until after the action on the 22nd.[22] Even more extraordinary, M'Neill appears to have been ignorant of a message which Brewster claimed to have passed to the Intelligence Staff early on the morning of the 22nd to the effect that M'Neill was to be attacked by a force of 5000 Dervishes.[23] Not surprisingly, M'Neill claimed that if he had been aware of this message he would have sent back most of his transport and advanced with a purely fighting force. One might hazard a guess that he might also have sent back for more mounted troops to give him both a better screen and a striking force for after the battle.

Returning to M'Neill's force, the position at noon (Map 7) was that the British battalions were lying down in square, their weapons piled, with sentries posted, while fatigue parties assisted the Royal Engineers in cutting bushes and constructing the zaribas, and other parties helped to unload stores. The Indian brigade formed three sides of a large square further to the west, shielding the zaribas under construction. The 28th Bombay Native Infantry, reinforced with two companies of the 17th Bengal Native Infantry, faced north where the scrub was thickest and closest. At right angles to the 28th, the 15th Sikhs faced due west while the remaining six companies of the 17th formed the third side facing south, with the end of their line in the air. The Indian battalions remained in position, their rifles in their hands, bayonets fixed, with small pickets of four or five men thrown out 150 yards ahead. The 5th Lancers, in 'Cossack posts' of four men (one man mounted on watch, three men dismounted, resting) covered a frontage of some three miles at a distance of perhaps half a mile.[24] With a force of only some 110 men, the Cossack posts were necessarily spread at very wide intervals of not less than 250-300 yards, a very wide mesh indeed in such close country. With the mimosa bushes reaching a height of six to eight feet, the cavalry pickets could neither see, nor be seen, from the main force. More importantly, they could not see except at very close range, anyone creeping towards them through the scrub. M'Neill was not oblivious to the possible danger and roughly two-thirds of his infantry – perhaps 1500-1600 – were either standing-to, with rifles in hand, or had their rifles stacked close at hand.

At 1300 hours, Major Graves, with a squadron of the 20th Hussars, arrived from Suakin. He had been sent out at 1000 hours to follow the line of the telegraph cable and to make contact with M'Neill. He reported sighting small parties of the enemy who retired before him; this confirmed M'Neill's own experience that morning. At 1330, Graves started back to Suakin with a despatch from M'Neill to Graham, reporting that the situation was all quiet, with construction and unloading proceeding well.

About 1400 hours, the north-east redoubt was virtually complete and was then occupied by the Royal Marines, with two of the Gardners. The Berkshires had had no food since 0400 and had been marching and working since then in conditions of intense heat. Their colonel, Huyshe, asked permission for the men to get their dinners, and M'Neill ordered them to receive their rations by half-battalions. As soon as the right half-battalion (A, B, C and D Companies) had fed and watered, it was marched off to occupy the south-west redoubt, with the other two Gardner guns. The left half-battalion (E, F, G and H Companies), with Huyshe, remained at the eastern end of the ground, to the south of the Royal Marines redoubt, having its dinner, with rifles piled.

The south-west redoubt was not completely finished and while some of the Berkshires stayed inside the redoubt on the alert, the remainder were outside cutting brush and dragging it in to complete the fence round the redoubt. Of the central enclosure, only the northern face and roughly three quarters of the western face had been completed; the southern and eastern faces were virtually untouched. But in the middle of the enclosure was a growing mound of stores, biscuit boxes and water barrels. As the animals were unloaded, they were led out of the enclosure and parked outside, to the east of the zariba, near the left half battalion of the Berkshires. The scene was therefore one of disciplined confusion, spread over an area roughly a quarter of a mile square. Long lines of camels were filing in and out of the central enclosure, where mixed working parties of infantry, Engineers and Transport Corps were hard at work unloading and stacking the stores and water. To the south of the position, working parties of Engineers and infantry were cutting down mimosa bushes and dragging them back to the zariba where other working parties were binding them together to form the impenetrable prickly hedge which was the hallmark of the Sudanese zariba. Over all hung thick clouds of sandy dust.[25]

By 1430, all this work was so far advanced that M'Neill felt confident enough to tell Brigadier General Hudson that he hoped to be able to release the Indian Brigade and the transport at 1500 hours to start back to Suakin. Hudson was ordered to start assembling the unloaded transport in readiness to move off, and to report back to M'Neill at 1500 hours. M'Neill then moved into the south-west redoubt, presumably to check for himself how the work there was going. Even if the central enclosure was not fully finished, M'Neill would have been justified in withdrawing the remainder of the force once the Berkshires and the Royal Marines were solidly protected in their redoubts with the Gardner guns mounted.

Apart from the small bodies of the enemy seen during the morning and by

Major Graves during his ride out to the zariba, there had been no indication that the enemy was present in strength or that he was contemplating an attack.[26] M'Neill might have been forgiven therefore for feeling that the major part of his task was nearly over. Very soon he would be in a position to start the homeward march. In reality, the storm which had engulfed Baker at El Teb and threatened to sweep away Graham at Tamai in March 1884 and the Desert Column at Abu Klea in January 1885 was about to break over M'Neill's troops. At about 1440, while M'Neill was inspecting the work on the south-west redoubt, a Lancer came galloping in to report that the enemy was gathering in front. He was closely followed by a second trooper who reported that the enemy was advancing rapidly. Close behind the second Lancer came the rest of the squadron, galloping in pell-mell. M'Neill immediately ordered the whole force to stand to its arms but within seconds the first enemy wave burst upon the 17th Bengal Native Infantry and upon the troops in the south-west redoubt.

In attempting to get a clear picture of events thereafter, it is important to bear firmly in mind that no one person was able to see the whole battle and that events did not necessarily follow a consecutive order. Many things were taking place simultaneously. The account which follows therefore is almost certainly misleading in conveying a sense of ordered events, but a completely synoptic picture is beyond the capacity of any historian. Behind the narrative, the reader must be conscious of the noise, the dust, the panic, which together produce the confusion which is the keynote of any battle, however small. And he must remember that in practice men knew only what was going on within twenty or thirty yards of them.

The Dervishes came in from the south-west and south. We know nothing of the planning on Osman's side and it may simply have been chance that the attack came in on the British force at its weakest spot. But it would probably be more realistic and fairer to give the Dervishes the credit for having scouted the position thoroughly and for having deliberately chosen the most formidable direction of attack. It is unlikely that the tactical sense that they had shown at Abu Klea, and at Tamai a year earlier, had deserted them.

The attack fell in the first instance upon the 17th Bengal Native Infantry, deployed still in line two deep, and upon the Berkshires, the Engineers of 24 Company and the naval detachment manning the two Gardner guns in the south-west redoubt. The 17th Bengal Native Infantry line was disordered and broken in places by some of the 5th Lancers galloping back straight through them. The 17th fired one irregular volley and then broke, despite the efforts of their officers to stop them. The two companies nearest to the south-west redoubt retired precipitately into that for protection and, once within its walls, fought well alongside the Berkshires. The remainder fled back through the central enclosure. Some fetched up in rear of the 28th Bombay Native Infantry. Some managed to reach the Royal Marines' redoubt and, carrying on in their panic, fled along the track to Suakin.

The dissolution within seconds of the 17th left the central enclosure, still filled with stores and transport animals, wide open to attack. Into that gap poured the enemy, hacking and stabbing with their spears, swords and knives, and driving the animals before them. One observer wrote of the scene: 'Suddenly from the bush all along the face of the zariba fronting Tamai burst out a clamour of savage cries and the next instant the whole assemblage of transport animals plunged forward. There was a multitude of roaring camels, apparently heaped one upon another, with strings of kicking and screaming mules, entangled in one moving mass. Crowds of camp-followers were carried along by the huge animal wave, crying, shouting and fighting. All these surged up to the zariba, any resistance being utterly hopeless. This mass of brutes and terrified natives swept all before it, and a scene of indescribable confusion ensued'.[27] Within the enclosure, the men of 24 Company RE, under Colonel E.P. Leach VC, and the Madras Sappers and Miners under Captain Wilkieson RE, found themselves fighting for their lives. 'For the next few minutes, we were infantry pure and simple: targets in plenty: range three to thirty yards: ammunition, not marksmanship, required' wrote Lieutenant Godby of the Royal Engineers. He was lucky; with some of his men, he managed to join up with the Berkshires outside their redoubt. Others of his comrades were less lucky. Captain Romilly, attached to the Madras Sappers and Miners, was speared through the heart by a Dervish running alongside his horse; Romilly may have been trying to save the life of a fellow-officer, Lieutenant E.M.B. Newman, who was killed by a swordsman who took off Newman's left arm and the top of his skull. Against the heavy, cruciform-hilted Sudanese swords, sharpened to a razor edge and wielded by a fanatic, the regulation sword was virtually useless; the only real defence was to shoot one's assailant before he got to close quarters.

The south-west redoubt had been entrusted to the right half battalion of Berkshires, supported by two Gardner guns manned by sailors under Lieutenant Seymour RN. Having had their dinners in the redoubt and left their weapons there, most of the Berkshires, at the moment of attack, were outside the zariba cutting brush to complete the fence. Major Dickson, of B Company, estimated that he was 250 yards from the zariba. By the time he got back, the enemy was inside the zariba, the piled rifles had been knocked over in the struggle and he was quite unable to find his own sword and revolver.[28] Lieutenant Southey, A Company, wrote in his diary that he 'went out with "A" Company to continue cutting brushwood. This would be about 2.30 p.m., I should say. I had not been out a quarter of an hour before in came the cavalry at a gallop, saying the enemy were on us, and sure enough they were close on their heels, rushing on to the "zariba" from all round. I rushed off to the "zariba" with the company who were stripped and unarmed. We got in at the same moment the enemy began to penetrate the left corner of our "zariba"'.[29] The Berkshires were clearly extremely lucky to get back at all – unarmed as they were, they were potentially easy prey for the Dervishes who excelled in hand-to-hand fighting.

While most of the south-west redoubt had a brush fence already in position, even if not fully built, the extreme south-west corner had a gap where the sailors were struggling to mount a Gardner gun. Into this gap the enemy penetrated, killing Seymour and six of his sailors. The Berkshires and the men of the 17th Native Infantry were forced back against the back (north) wall of the redoubt. M'Neill himself was inside the redoubt and he ordered Southey to take his men across to the south wall. Once they were there, the inrush of the Dervishes was halted and the work of clearing the inside of the redoubt with bullet and bayonet was quickly over: 'we formed up along half the side and fired furiously at the enemy who were emerging from the brushwood in hundreds. They went down like ninepins but bullets were flying about us and spears were thrown at us by the enemy who got up near enough. After we once got to the side of the "zariba" no more managed to get inside again'.[30] After the battle, 112 enemy bodies were counted inside the redoubt.

While the fighting was going on round the south-west redoubt, the main mass of the enemy was sweeping around to the east into the mass of animals and stores which were being unloaded in the central zariba. This was totally unprotected along its southern side to enable the transport animals to file in and out. The Dervishes, stampeding and killing the animals as they went, were thus able to advance through the central enclosure and attack the Royal Marines in the north-east redoubt. Pushing in front of them a mass of frightened animals and men – Engineers, 17th Native Infantry and Commissariat and Transport men – the Dervishes were able to force an entry into the Royal Marines stronghold. Some of the Marines, borne along on the tide of fleeing animals and men, were temporarily forced out of the redoubt. They were quickly re-formed and brought back. Colonel Way, commanding the Royal Marines, described the scene thus: 'Everything seemed to come at once, camels, transport of all kinds, including water carts, ammunition mules, 17th Native Infantry, Madras Sappers, sick-bearers, Transport Corps, cavalry and Arabs fighting in the midst. All these passed close by me and went out the other side of the zariba, carrying away with them a number of the Marines and some officers who eventually got together and returned. The dust raised by this cloud was so great that I could not see anything beyond our zariba for a minute or two, and it was impossible to say what might happen. The men behaved splendidly and stood quite still. It was about the highest test of discipline I shall ever see, as in my opinion nothing could beat it'.[31] Unlike the Berkshires, the Marines occupied a completed redoubt, with Gardner guns mounted. Most, if not all, of the Marines were inside the zariba with their rifles close at hand. Against them and the Gardner guns, the enemy made little further progress. For once, the Gardners performed reasonably well and over 400 rounds were successfully fired, causing considerable execution. In the central zariba, a small party of the Madras Sappers and Miners, fighting stubbornly, succeeded in halting the enemy rush and in protecting the rear of the 15th and the 28th.

Two elements of M'Neill's force were wholly outside the zariba and redoubts. The left half-battalion of the Berkshires, were having their dinners in the open ground south of the Marines' redoubt, where the British troops had initially been halted that morning. The men were in formation, with their arms piled close at hand. It was the work of a moment therefore to seize their weapons and to form squares.

To the south of the left half-battalion was a mass of unloaded camels already formed up in a compact, solid square, awaiting M'Neill's orders to move off back to Suakin. When the Dervishes attacked, the mass of the unarmed camel drivers fled precipitately towards Suakin, leaving the animals to stampede in all directions. Many of them fled across the field of fire of the Berkshires. It was clearly no time for half-measures and the Berkshires opened fire, killing transport animals and enemy alike. As the animals were shot down, so the Berkshires found themselves with a clear view of the enemy. Against the disciplined volleys of troops solidly formed and well in hand, the Dervishes were unable to make progress. No Dervish got to close quarters with the Berkshire square although Huyshe had a narrow escape. He was sitting his horse close to the square as it was forming when he was attacked by a gigantic Sudanese, emerging from behind a camel and armed with a spear. For a moment, the two oddly contrasted men faced each other and then, as the Arab rushed forward, Huyshe brought him down with a lucky revolver shot full in the face. The left half-battalion suffered only one minor casualty during the fight; afterwards, more than 200 bodies were counted round its position.

On the northern flank, the 28th Bombay Native Infantry and the two companies of the 17th Bengal Native Infantry stood their ground and appear not to have been seriously attacked. The 15th Sikhs, on the western flank, were attacked in great force but stood their ground equally steadfastly. At the left hand (southern) end of their line, the Sikhs were involved in the struggle round the Berkshire's redoubt. It was here that Subedar Gurjit Singh won the Indian Order of Merit for saving the life of a Berkshire private. The Subedar killed two of the Dervishes with his sword as they were closing in to kill the soldier, who had been caught outside the redoubt during the initial onslaught. The Snider rifle with which the Indian Infantry were armed fired a huge 0.577" lead bullet which was a genuine man-stopper. Even the fanaticism of the Dervishes found it difficult to withstand a well-aimed Snider volley. In consequence, the attackers did not succeed in getting to close quarters with either the Sikhs or the Bombay Infantry and both regiments suffered insignificant losses.

With the right half-battalion of the Berkshire firmly in control of the south-west redoubt, the Royal Marines solidly ensconced in the north-east redoubt and the left half-battalion of the Berkshires, the Sikhs and the Bombay Infantry standing firm, the momentum of the Dervish attack began to ebb quickly. In a daring sortie, the Adjutant of the Royal Marines battalion,

130

Captain T.F. Dunscombe, accompanied by Private Bayley, captured a Dervish standard, killing the shaykh who was carrying it with his revolver.

Twenty minutes after the attack started, M'Neill was able to order the 'Cease Fire' to be sounded.[32] The Dervishes withdrew sullenly and reluctantly, continuing to lurk in large numbers in the dense scrub surrounding the zariba. At about 1530 hours, a large gathering to the south-east of the Berkshire redoubt hinted at a renewed attack and M'Neill decided to launch a counter-attack and break up this gathering. With two companies of Marines, under their colonel, Nowell Fitzupton Way, M'Neill led the counter-attack himself, riding his grey horse. In face of the Royal Marines' fire, the gathering melted away and since it would have been too dangerous to pursue the enemy in the bush, M'Neill withdrew the small force. The enemy was even yet not disposed to disappear and it was not until about 1615 that the main body withdrew from sight; no doubt individuals and small parties remained, hovering out of sight in the bush, until even later.

NOTES

1. Gambier-Parry, op cit, p119. He records also the fact that Graham, Greaves and M'Neill were Freemasons.
2. Roberts to Lord Randolph Churchill 15 April 1885 – NAM 7101-23-97-1/CXXVII.
3. Wylde, op cit, Vol II, p90.
4. Letter dated 21 March 1885 – NAM 81111-30, f75.
5. Gambier-Parry, op cit, pp18-19. He does not identify Graham by name but the identification is clear.
6. De Cosson, op cit, p86.
7. Wylde, op cit, Vol II, p87.
8. Gambier-Parry, op cit, p55.
9. De Cosson, op cit, p5.
10. 2 sdns. 5th Lancers, 2 sdns. 20th Hussars, 9th Bengal Cavalry, the Mounted Infantry and G Battery, B Brigade, Royal Horse Artillery – about 1300 in all.
11. Given their shortage of modern weapons, Osman's men were remarkably careless about leaving rifles and ammunition behind. The same phenomenon had been observed in the 1884 campaign, notably at Tamai. Osman must be held to blame for failing to teach his men the value and effectiveness of modern weapons; if he had done so, the British would have been in serious trouble.
12. 'An officer who was with them [the cavalry] ran on foot a great part of the way, having lost his charger, at a pace he never believed himself capable of, closely chivvied by the Arabs, and was found later, sitting on a stone, quite out of breath and in a very excited condition after his race for life'. De Cosson, op cit, p98.
13. In the version of this despatch published in R.H. Vetch *The Life, Letters and Diary of Sir Gerald Graham* (London, 1901), at page 419, this phrase was omitted.
14. Adrian Preston *In Relief of Gordon. Lord Wolseley's Campaign Journal of the Khartoum Relief Expedition 1884-1885* (London, 1965), p174.
15. See *Egypt No.18 (1885) (C4598)*.
16. De Cosson, op cit, pp91-2.
17. W. Galloway *The Battle of Tofrek* (London, 1887), is very critical of Gambier-Parry's comments on this matter but the evidence from De Cosson which is quoted by Galloway in rebuttal seems to me largely to substantiate Gambier-Parry's criticisms – see Gambier-Parry, op cit, pp162-3 and De Cosson, op cit, pp91-3.

131

18. Letter dated 21 March 1885 – NAM 8809-269. Fergusson had, no doubt, also listened to the stories of other soldiers.
19. Graham's force which advanced on Tamai in March 1884 numbered about 4150, M'Neill's about 3300 but with a larger transport force.
20. Since Graham accompanied the force for some 2½ miles it is surprising that he did not grasp the difficulties facing the force. M'Neill was clearly not consulted and De Cosson overheard M'Neill complaining bitterly about the arrangements – De Cosson, op cit, p124.
21. See the account in J.B. Boon 'The Telegraph in the Firing Line' *Soldiers of the Queen*, No. 41 (June 1985). This contains an extract from the diary of one of the detachment, originally published in the *Post Office Magazine* in 1900.
22. Galloway, op cit, p42.
23. According to Galloway (op cit, p43-4), Brewster claimed this at a meeting with M'Neill, in the presence of witnesses on 1 April 1885.
24. The precise distance is not clear. Graham, in his despatch, talks of half a mile; Galloway (op cit, p55) infers a distance of 550-600 yards, while Gambier-Parry infers something much shorter. The point is important.
25. A zariba (or zareba) was made by cutting down the large mimosa bushes and laying them down with the thorny heads facing outwards. The interstices were filled in with smaller branches and, if time permitted, the whole hedge was then bound together with wire. This made an obstacle almost impossible to penetrate although the Dervishes were capable of jumping over it. The mimosa was tough and hard to cut, and the billhooks and axes supplied were often of very inferior quality and easily broken or blunted, lengthening the construction time.
26. In the account in the official *Diary of the Suakin Expedition 1885* (HMSO, 1885), M'Neill is shown as receiving warnings of an enemy presence at 1355 hours, 1400 and 1410 hours. M'Neill claimed that he received no warnings. The amended *Official Account*, dated 5 October 1885, and signed by Colonel A.S. Cameron of the Intelligence Department, makes no mention of such warnings. Since that account was issued 'to correct certain inaccuracies in the hurriedly compiled diary of the Suakin Expedition', it would seem that either no warnings were received or that M'Neill succeeded in getting the record altered.
27. Quoted in Royle, op cit, p423.
28. F. Lorraine Petre *The Royal Berkshire Regiment* (Reading, 1925), Vol I, pp328-29.
29. Petre, op cit, pp329-30.
30. Southey's account in Petre, op cit, p330.
31. Royle, op cit, p423.
32. The concensus of evidence is that the attack started at about 1450 hours and the 'Cease Fire' was sounded at about 1510, but these times cannot be guaranteed to within five minutes. The amended *Official Account* gives these times. Graham in his brief despatch of 28 March 1885 gives no precise times but estimates that the fighting was over in twenty minutes. Galloway gives the times as 1452 and 1512 but this seems spuriously precise, if only because no one in an action of this kind was likely to have had time to synchronise watches or even look at them.

9

Food for Thought

M'NEILL'S ZARIBA was only some six miles from Suakin and the sound of firing was immediately heard in the camps there. Observers listening anxiously to the early sounds of irregular firing were relieved when that was succeeded by the unmistakable sound of volley firing which showed that at least parts of M'Neill's force had retained their cohesion. Lieutenant Cotesworth, of the Mounted Infantry, escorting a convoy to Hashin, has left a particularly vivid description: 'We had just made out a large force of the enemy making in our direction . . . when we heard a shot from the other column (M'Neill), then another, then two or three in quick succession, then a spluttering of shots showing that there was no control of fire, then independent firing, then after a few minutes a few ragged volleys, then at last to our great relief, regular volleys; the men were in hand at last'. Very shortly, the effects of the Dervish attack could actually be seen in Suakin in the form of an immense dust column, mixed with smoke, which ascended over the scene of the fighting. In less than an hour, the first fugitives – probably men of the 5th Lancers who had been cut off from the infantry by the Dervish attack – had reached the outposts at Suakin. They were followed by a melancholy procession of transport camels and drivers, some of the 17th Bengal Native Infantry, who had simply kept going after the regiment had disintegrated, together with a number of British soldiers.[1]

Lieutenant Drummond-Hay, of the Coldstream Guards, had been part of the escort of a convoy taking supplies to the East Surrey Regiment in its zaribas at Hashin. The noise of the fight at Tofrek was clearly audible at a distance of perhaps eight miles. Drummond-Hay, with the convoy on the plain below Zariba Hill, could see nothing of the action because of the thick scrub between Hashin and Tofrek. But the troops manning the posts on Zariba Hill could see large numbers of the enemy clustered about in the direction of M'Neill's zariba and using one of the Krupp field guns mounted on the Hill fired some 30 rounds.[2] According to Drummond-Hay, this caused some of the Dervishes to scatter but no one at Tofrek records hearing or seeing these shells, which is perhaps not surprising, and it seems unlikely that they can have had any significant effect at that range. To those in Suakin listening anxiously to the sound of musketry from the direction of M'Neill's force, the arrival of the first fugitives an hour or so later seemed to indicate that there had been a disaster. 'What with the number of fugitives coming in, riderless horses rushing down to the sea, mules with their saddles all adrift, and many wounded stray camels here, there, and everywhere, some with one camp follower on their back, some with two' wrote Wylde, 'it looked as if our force had been wiped out, and those that were coming in were the ones that got away'.[3]Each fugivitive was, as always, sure that he was the last survivor.

Graham's immediate reaction on hearing the news of the fighting was to collect the Grenadiers and Scots Guards, together with G/B, RHA, and despatch them towards the sound of the guns. They had gone some two miles when Graham received a telegram from M'Neill, reporting that he did not need reinforcements. The troops were then brought back. Wylde had meantime established the same picture by interrogating some of the native followers.[4]

The telegraph line which the Telegraph Section had laid from Suakin to M'Neill's zariba miraculously survived the fighting unbroken. The telegraph instrument itself had been trampled on and ruined but the Section had a spare buzzer with it which was quickly connected up and the Section found itself again in direct communication with the telegraph station on Quarantine Island. Traffic flowed uneventfully until about 1900 hours when, in the midst of transmitting a despatch from the Times correspondent, the line went dead. Nothing daunted, the signallers opened communication by lamp to the Right Water Fort.[5]

Like others, the telegraphists had had an eventful half hour. The Section, with its wagon, had accompanied the British square on the outward march and had presumably stayed near the left half-battalion of the Berkshires, in the area south or south east of the Royal Marines' redoubt. When the attack came 'Lieutenant Lindsay gave the order, "Left about wheel. Charge" and we showed the enemy a clean pair of heels being about the last to get into the zariba [Royal Marines']. The opening was quickly closed by the Naval Brigade under Lieutenant Paget and we manned the side of the zariba with the Marines . . . The enemy being driven from the zariba itself now turned to those who had been cut off by the surprise and those who had been carried out by the stampeding animals. Small squares started by men standing back and gradually increasing in size fought their way in', wrote one of the Section.[6]

The scene around M'Neill's position defied easy description. 'The sight of our "zariba" and the cleared ground immediately in front was most ghastly. Dead Arabs mutilated by our close fire, heads and brains blown out, and fearfully bayoneted. Camels dead and wounded, mules and horses in same state, great pools of blood, our own dead and wounded. Oh! a very awful sight and one which I shall never forget' wrote an obviously shaken Lieutenant Southey, of A Company of the Berkshires.[7] Similar scenes existed round the Royal Marines redoubt, round the rallying ground of the left half-battalion of the Berkshires and, indeed, wherever groups of men had succeeded in standing their ground and pouring in their volleys.

As always, the Dervish wounded were as dangerous as rattlesnakes. Lieutenant G.S. Swinton, the regimental transport officer of the Berkshires, was looking for his pony after the action was over when a wounded Dervish jumped up and drove his spear into Swinton's back. The Dervish was instantly shot but Swinton died the same evening; he had been commissioned into the regiment only three years before. Both women and children were found among the enemy casualties. Given the fanatical nature of the Dervishes, no quarter was given and every wounded man found in or around the zariba was killed. There are no records of prisoners.[8]

Just before 1600 hours, Major Graves reached the scene of the action again and reported to M'Neill again. Graves had gone about two miles on his original return journey to Suakin and had just met his relief, Lieutenant Peyton, with a squadron of the 9th Bengal Cavalry, when they heard heavy firing from the direction of M'Neill's force. Graves, with both squadrons, immediately turned back towards the zariba. A mile from it, he came upon a motley crowd of camel drivers, British soldiers and 17th Bengal Native Infantry, closely pursued by Dervishes.

Graves promptly wheeled his squadron into line, facing right and charged into the enemy at right angles. As the enemy pursuit dwindled to a halt, Graves dismounted every man with a carbine and fired volleys until the pursuit was totally halted. Remounting his men and pressing forward, Graves again opened dismounted fire. The Dervishes, baulked of their prey, then retreated towards the zariba, leaving dead, wounded and a number of men shamming. As the troops passed, some fifteen of the latter jumped up and attacked the cavalry. They were all killed but not before Graves himself had had a narrow escape.

Some of the Dervishes now tried to get round Graves' left flank in order to resume pursuit of the original fugitives. Lieutenant Peyton with a troop of Bengal Cavalry was ordered back to intercept the enemy and prevent them cutting up the stragglers. This he managed to do and eventually reached Suakin with some twenty stragglers.

Graves, in the meantime, had been reinforced by another troop of the 5th Lancers from Suakin and now drove the enemy in front of him back towards the Royal Marines' zariba where they again came under fire and dispersed, not to re-assemble. Graves, having reached the scene of the action, now threw a strong cordon of cavalry round the transport and supplies, covering the whole southern face of the site. He then reported to M'Neill, who must have been greatly relieved to see him since M'Neill's own cavalry had largely dispersed. Graves had lost only one man wounded but had killed upwards of 40 of the Dervishes; moreover, under cover of his cavalry, a number of men, cut off in the fighting, had managed to get back to the cover of the zaribas. Like M'Neill's own cavalry force, Graves had found the scrub extremely difficult to negotiate and virtually impossible to charge through effectively, so he had very sensibly resorted to dismounted fire tactics. Of all the officers present that day, he stands out for his quick grasp of the situation and for his initiative. He gives the impression of having been a cool, sensible, practical officer.

The Dervishes having dispersed, M'Neill could start to tidy up the chaotic situation round his zariba. The wounded were collected into a makeshift field hospital created by stretching the walls of tents over piles of biscuit boxes to provide shelter from the sun. Lieutenant Colonel Way was despatched with two companies of Marines to round up the remaining transport animals. This proved dangerous and frustrating work. The enemy wounded remained deadly adversaries and there were still isolated parties prowling about in the scrub waiting for an opportunity to strike. Many of the camels were wounded and seemingly in a state of shock and, in the absence of their normal drivers, refused to move and gradually drifted southwards into the bush and were lost. The zaribas had to be cleared of Dervish dead and wounded (in practice, the distinction soon disappeared) and M'Neill's own dead had to be brought in and laid out for burial. Finally, the zaribas themselves had to be repaired and strengthened, and precautions taken against a night attack.

By 1800 hours, the sun had gone down and M'Neill and his troops faced a long and nerve-racking night. Inside the three zaribas (the central one being occupied by the Indian infantry regiments), the troops lay down in ranks two deep, clutching the weapons; one rank slept for two hours while the other rank remained on the alert. Talking and lights were not permitted and everyone waited tensely for the first indications of a night attack. A false alarm early in the night resulted in a massive fusillade by all the troops, confirming only that nerves were tightly stretched. Given the terrifying nature of their daylight attacks, a night attack by the Dervishes was clearly something very much to be feared by any troops and it is perhaps surprising that Osman never resorted to a major night attack during either of Graham's campaigns; he might conceivably have had a devastating success.

The sun rose next morning (23 March) just after 0600 hours and the British dead were then buried in large graves.[9] M'Neill's losses had been severe. Counting the missing as dead – a reasonable assumption in these circumstances – he had lost 141 killed and 155 wounded together with 157 followers killed and 19 wounded.[10] He had also lost 501 camels, roughly a third of his transport force. The heaviest losses had fallen inevitably upon the 17th Native Infantry which had lost its Commanding Officer and over 50 men killed. The Berkshires had lost one officer and 22 men killed and 30 wounded. The Royal Marines had escaped very lightly, due to the fact that they were all safely inside their completed zariba when the fighting started; conversely, the Royal Engineers and the Commissariat and Transport Corps, who had been caught in and around the uncompleted central zariba, had suffered relatively very heavily. The Engineers lost two officers and 13 men killed, and one officer and four men wounded; the Commissariat and Transport Corps lost a total of 12 men killed or wounded.

Five years before, in July 1880, a British force, including the 66th Foot (subsequently the 2nd Battalion of the Berkshire Regiment) had been overwhelmed at Maiwand in Afghanistan. Two survivors of that force were present during M'Neill's fight – Colonel E.P. Leach VC, commanding 24 Company RE, and Captain Lynch, commanding G Company of the Berkshires. One can only imagine their thoughts when the full fury of the Dervish attack hit M'Neill's force.[11]

Proportionately and absolutely, the action on 22 March was the most costly of Graham's two campaigns. Out of a force of some 3000, M'Neill had lost roughly 10 per cent. Such a loss was bound to arouse criticism both within and without Graham's expeditionary force. A good deal of ink has been spilled subsequently on the question of whether M'Neill had been surprised. As we have seen, M'Neill was firm in his denials that he had ever received any clear warning that he was likely to be attacked, and that the intelligence on this point which Graham had received had not been passed on to him. But even in the absence of any specific warning, it was always possible that the Dervishes would attack and M'Neill had maintained a reasonable state of vigilance. Throughout the day, he had kept at least two thirds of his troops under arms and had maintained a screen of cavalry lookouts as well as infantry sentries posted well in advance of their lines. He can therefore be acquitted of having been taken totally by surprise. Where he was clearly taken unawares was in the speed and ferocity of the Dervish onslaught when it came, and certain of his own dispositions contributed to his difficulties. It is not clear why he had not insisted on a larger cavalry force to give him a better, more extended screen. In the thick bush, the wide intervals between his cavalry vedettes gave the Dervishes complete liberty to penetrate in force before they were spotted.[12] Secondly, it was a mistake to leave the 17th Native Infantry with their left flank in the air. Even allowing for the fact that a large gap had to be left for the transport animals to file in and out of the central zariba to deposit their loads, it would surely have been better if the left half-battalion of the Berkshires had been used to prolong the infantry screen along the southern side of the encampment, linking up with the Royal Marines zariba, exactly as had been done with the 15th and 28th Native Infantry on the west and north. As it was, the left half-battalion of the Berkshires was caught out in the open and although it did not suffer any serious casualties, it was equally able to contribute little to the defence of the rest of the camp. Thirdly, it was a mistake to allow the right half-battalion of the Berkshires to leave their weapons so far away while they were engaged in cutting scrub. The Indian regiments appear to have taken their rifles with them wherever they went and Graham, in his despatch, considered that the British troops should have done the same.

M'Neill and Graham have also been criticised for the absence of any artillery with the force. There were three batteries available in Suakin and there was no obvious reason why some guns should not have been taken along.

What is debatable is whether the presence of artillery would have made any real difference. Effective use of artillery depends upon the presence of reasonably open fields of fire and the heavy thorn scrub which approached so close to the encampment gave very little opportunity to artillery to find targets. Once the attack had developed, artillery would have found it difficult to fire without risking hitting its own troops and transport. Moreover, artillery required infantry protection otherwise it could quickly become a liability. It seems doubtful therefore whether the absence of artillery was of great importance although perhaps the principle of including guns in any force sent out ought not to have been breached.

What seems undeniable is that it was a mistake to send out so many camels with such a relatively small force. At Hashin, Graham had had some 1400 camels accompanying a force of 8000, which included all available cavalry; M'Neill had had the same number of camels accompanying a force of some 3300. We have seen the reason for taking so many camels and no doubt if M'Neill had managed to complete his operation without a serious fight no criticism would have been raised about the composition of his force. But in retrospect it would certainly seem better to have sent out M'Neill to establish a fortified staging point before sending out the mass of transport. Severe though M'Neill's losses were and critical as the fight had been, one shudders at the thought of what might have happened if Osman had attacked the three Indian battalions with the transport on their return journey. Altogether, the operation had been poorly conceived and had come within an ace of disaster. Only the dogged courage and discipline of the majority of the troops had pulled Graham and M'Neill through. On the Dervish side, the attack had been well-conceived and deserved success. Whether by luck or good judgement, the attack had come in at a moment when the British force was particularly vulnerable, with one supporting zariba not finished, the British infantry dispersed and a good deal of confusion and dust as the transport animals were unloaded in the centre.

Nevertheless Osman's losses had been enormous. Graham's first despatch of March 1885 put Osman's force at not less than 2000, of whom an estimated 1000 had been killed. The amended official account compiled by the Intelligence Branch in October 1885 put the attacking force at about 5000, of whom 1500 had been killed; 1100 bodies had been counted and buried, and many more were thought to have been concealed in the scrub. Osman's surviving papers alas! do not contain any account of this fight so it is impossible to be sure of these figures. On balance, it seems very probable that Osman lost nearly 1500 men killed (there were no prisoners) out of a force which cannot have exceeded 5000 and may have been fewer.[13] These were very heavy casualties indeed, given that Osman's total potential strength from among the tribes could hardly have exceeded 7000. Moreover, these losses had to be added to the very heavy losses incurred by Osman at El Teb and Tamai the year before. Osman and his adherents were in no sense finished;

indeed, when Graham and his force left Suakin only a few weeks later, Osman remained master of the field and it would be years, and many fights, later before the British could be said to be in control of the Eastern Sudan. But it may well be right, as Graham claimed, that the losses sustained at Tofrek, taken in conjunction with those sustained earlier, were such as effectively to break the back of the Dervish threat. They remained extremely dangerous and the British remained effective masters only of a relatively tiny area of country immediately round Suakin. Even Sinkat and Tokar, the original objects of the British intervention, remained in Osman's hands. But never again was he able to engage the British with as large a force as he had been able to deploy at El Teb, Tamai and Tofrek. In an attritional sense, Tofrek might be counted a British victory.[14]

But M'Neill (and Graham) had undoubtedly had a very narrow escape indeed and the question has to be asked as to whether this could have been avoided. Clearly, the difficulties in which M'Neill's force ultimately found itself were due largely to the dense scrub surrounding the zariba site. That could certainly have been avoided if Graham had elected to make his advance along the established track to Tamai which he had used in March 1884. For the first six miles, that track formed part of the road to Kassala, traversing an open sandy plain, covered with patches of stunted mimosa scrub but presenting no difficulty. F.L. James, who had traversed this road in 1881, found himself, four miles from Suakin, crossing rich green grass covered with dwarf mimosa in flower. Six miles from Suakin, the track to Tamai diverges and after another three miles reaches the zariba established by Baker in 1884. When Baker had established it, the usual thorn fence had been reinforced by a continuous mound of earth which gave complete protection against rifle fire. While no doubt the thorn fences had disappeared by March 1885, the remains of the earthworks must still have been there and it is a reasonable assumption that the restoration and repair of Baker's zariba would have been a quicker and easier task than constructing a new one at Tofrek. It would also have been safer since Baker's zariba lay in relatively open country which offered much less protection to an attacker.

Yet a further indictment of Graham's choice of route lies in the fact that it seems not to have been properly reconnoitred in advance. If it had been, M'Neill would have known the difficulties and would have appreciated that the timetable which had been sent him was incapable of achievement.

Graham's explanation for the choice of route was that it provided a line of advance against both Tamai and Tamanieb. That seems in retrospect a faulty argument. Tamanieb lay some eleven miles due west of Tamai, deep in the hills. It could not sensibly be reached via Tamai because that would have involved traversing extremely difficult, hilly country, seamed with deep ravines or khors. Instead it could be reached by a route from Suakin which again Graham had traversed without major difficult in 1884. It still had the remnants of the zaribas that he had built then. Tofrek lay several miles south of the direct route to Tamanieb. There was a balance to be struck between establishing a new zariba in unknown, scrub jungle which could be used as a base for moving on either Tamai or Tamanieb and using two known routes and existing zaribas. Since Tamai was by all intelligence a more important base for Osman than Tamanieb and a successful attack on Tamai might obviate the need for an expedition to Tamanieb, it can only be concluded that Graham made an error of judgement. What the views of Greaves and the Staff were, or indeed whether they were ever consulted, is not clear.

Graham was predictably unhappy about the action and the casualties, and there are some reports that he spoke angrily to M'Neill when he met him the next day. In his official despatch of 28 March, he wrote 'I do not consider however on full consideration that sufficient caution was exercised under the special circumstances. The density of bush round the zariba is so great that even mounted men are unable to see beyond a very short distance. It was not possible therefore to obtain a long warning of the approach of the enemy. I consider that the working parties cutting bush were not in all cases suffi- ciently covered and that these working parties should certainly have had their arms slung'.

The fine performance of the troops was recognised by the subsequent award of a bar to the Egyptian Medal; the Berkshires subsequently received the title 'Royal' for their particular performance although in strict honesty it is not readily apparent that their performance differed in quality from that of the Sikhs, the Bombay Native Infantry or the Royal Marines.

NOTES

1. It is not clear who these soldiers were. Some Royal Marines had been forced out of their redoubt by the initial Dervish onslaught, and some of the left half-battalion of the Berk- shires had been caught in the open before squares could be formed. But it seems likely that these British stragglers were men of the 5th Lancers, and men from the Royal Engi- neers and Commissariat and Transport Corps who had been working in and around the central zariba and had found themselves defenceless when the 17th Native Infantry collapsed.
2. Drummond-Hay, diary for 22 March 1885.
3. Wylde, op cit, Vol II, pp106-7.
4. Ibid, p107.
5. Boon, op cit, p3.
6. Ibid, p4.
7. Petre, op cit, p330.
8. De Cosson, for one, was horrified by the practice of killing the enemy wounded, although he must have heard stories of the practice in the 1884 campaign. With considerable moral courage, he raised the matter with Graham who replied 'Thank you; it is a practice I have the greatest objection to, and I shall see that it is put a stop to in the future' (De Cosson, op cit, p223). His reaction is curious since he was well aware of what had gone on in 1884 (see page 71 above). There is no record of him having done anything in response to De Cosson's protest.
9. The 15th Sikhs burned their dead on the morning of 23 May immediately prior to accom-

panying Graham back to Suakin. The 17th and 28th, being Hindu regiments, would also have burned their dead but I have not come across a reference to this. Presumably it was done at the same time as the 15th Sikhs.

10. British: 6 officers and 72 others ranks killed or missing; 3 officers and 60 other ranks wounded. Indian: 2 officers and 61 other ranks killed or missing; 2 officers and 90 other ranks wounded.

11. Another Maiwand survivor, Lieutenant Geogeghan, of the 3rd Bombay Light Cavalry, was with the Indian Contingent but it is not clear whether he was at Tofrek.

12. When Wolseley visited the scene of the action, in May, he was critical of the fact that M'Neill had only one mounted squadron with him; he considered that Graham should have sent out all available mounted troops. He also thought that M'Neill should have placed his vedettes at least two miles in advance instead of a thousand yards (Preston, op cit, p209). It also seems an oversight not to have sent the Balloon Section, given the difficulty of seeing any distance through the scrub.

13. On this occasion, the Hadendowa had shaved their heads because Osman had assured them that no harm could come to them if they did so – Petre, op cit, p332.

14. Compare Galloway's conclusion:

'Within twenty minutes from the commencement of this most murderous fight, within the half-mile radius surrounding the zariba at Tofrek, thoroughly crushed and beaten in the dust lay the flower of Osman Digna's following, the heart of the rebellion in the Eastern Sudan, a mass of mortality, to be burned, buried out of sight, or devoured by wild animals, but never again to lift sword or spear, to slake an insatiate thirst in the blood of the stranger, or respond to the wild appeals of an intolerant fanaticism.' There speaks the authentic voice of Victorian imperialism!

10

The End of the First Phase

THE DAY after M'Neill's action, Graham himself took out a convoy of 1200 camels to the zariba, escorted by the Guards Brigade, the 9th Bengal Cavalry and the Mounted Infantry, together with No 1 Bearer Company – in all, some 2550 men, not far short of M'Neill's own strength.

'It was a very tedious job' wrote Drummond-Hay 'as we formed the rear face of the square and the native camel drivers are so lazy they lag and throw out the whole formation, though in addition to this the thick bush, through which we had to make our way, would have rendered it almost an impossibility to keep the square unbroken'.[1] The convoy reached the zariba at about 11.30, the last mile being, as Drummond-Hay put it 'not particulaly lovely; dead camels, mules and native drivers, with a sprinkling of Arabs, all in the first stages of decomposition lay about in all directions'.[2]

For the first time, Graham could appreciate at first-hand the circumstances of the action. He was inclined to be irascible with M'Neill, not surprisingly since the nature of the action and the heavy losses were bound to reflect on Graham himself. It may well be also that Graham was sensitive over the choice of route and the paucity of mounted troops accompanying M'Neill. Nevertheless, in a telegram of the same day to Wolseley, Graham expressed the view that M'Neill had done everything possible in the circumstances.

The disposal of the bodies of Arabs and animals was an obviously pressing task and, while Graham conferred with M'Neill, the troops were busy killing the wounded animals which were limping about in all directions and dragging all bodies away from the zariba and covering them with sand. The next day, an attempt was made to burn them with brushwood, without much success; two days later, Drummond-Hay recorded lying awake and listening to the soldiers retching as each puff of air brought the foul smell of decomposing bodies.

Leaving the Coldstream and Scots Guards with M'Neill, Graham returned to Suakin on the afternoon of 23 March, bringing with him the surviving wounded and the transport animals, escorted by the Grenadiers and the three Indian battalions. It was, by all accounts, a fairly disorganised affair. The huge quantity of transport animals slowed the pace of the force until it became doubtful if they could reach Suakin before dark. An attempt to force the pace increased the confusions, with camel loads being shed in every direction and all cohesion being lost. Gambier-Parry compared it to the retreat of a beaten rabble.

142

So many stores had been destroyed in the fight on the 22nd that yet another large convoy of 425 camels and 18 carts had to be despatched from Suakin on 24 March. It was escorted by the 15th Sikhs, the 28th Bombay Native Infantry, the Madras Sappers and Miners, a squadron of the 9th Bengal Cavalry and a squadron of the 20th Hussars – in all about 1500 men. The convoy encountered no opposition and halted roughly three miles from Suakin, where it was met by the Coldstream Guards and the Royal Marines. The latter battalions then took over the convoy, the Indian battalions returning to Suakin. The Guards and the Marines had been fired on at long range on their outward journey, losing two men injured. On their return journey to the zariba with the transport convoy, the two battalions were attacked in considerable force. 'We had not gone far, when all of a sudden the bush seemed to become alive with Arabs, all making straight for the square with their heads down and their shields up, brandishing their weapons but apparently without any organisation in their movements. Of course, we halted at once, and turning outwards, opened fire, so heavy was their loss that in a few moments not a man seemed to be left alive; but as soon as we ceased fire and recommenced our march Arabs were seen slinking off in all directions from behind bushes, mounds and banks, where they had hidden when they found our reception of them turned out to be too warm for their liking; several of the apparently dead bodies also got up and disappeared into the surrounding bush at the same time, very much to our astonishment'.[3] Drummond-Hay was amazed at the fanatical courage of the Dervishes: 'The marvellous courage of the Arabs was the object of everyone's admiration. Many of them were seen to be hit time after time but on they came just the same, the only sign being a convulsive jerk of the body and a bit of stagger. The only thing that stopped them was a bullet in the head or heart or a broken leg'.[4]

In order to tighten up the square formation to resist the attack, it had been necessary to leave outside 117 camels and their loads. With the remainder, the two battalions resumed their march, throwing out a thin screen of skirmishers to fire on any Arabs who showed themselves.

The attacking force had been spotted from M'Neill's zariba earlier and preparations had been made to despatch the Scots Guards to assist the convoy escort but in the event they were not really needed. In this brisk little action, the two battalions had one man killed and 23 wounded; Osman's losses are unknown.

On 25 March, yet another convoy of 500 camels and seven carts, escorted by the Grenadier Guards and the three Indian battalions – some 2250 men – was sent out to the zariba. It was not attacked either going out or coming back and the operation was significant only because it was accompanied by the Balloon Detachment of the Royal Engineers. It was the first time that the balloon had been used at Suakin and it seems to have functioned perfectly successfully.[5] The balloon had been filled with compressed hydrogen from cylinders near the Right Water Fort. Lieutenant Mackenzie had then gone up in the basket to a height of 300-400 feet and, with the balloon being towed from a wagon in the centre of the square, had accompanied the force to the zariba. Mackenzie reported that, seen from a height above, the scrub was relatively open; he was able to see the Dervish camel patrols near Hashin, another body of them near the sea shore, south of Suakin, and yet another retiring towards Tamai. Messages on pieces of paper were passed down a rope.[6]

The same day (25 March) the zaribas at Hashin, which had been occupied by the East Surreys were quietly abandoned and the troops returned to Suakin. The work of running convoys to Hashin and to M'Neill was too heavy for the force available and the retirement from Hashin underlined the weakness of Graham's case for originally occupying it. There was no evidence that it had played any significant part in preventing Osman's forces from concentrating against M'Neill.

On the 26th, yet another large convoy set out for Tofrek, with 580 camels, of which 480 were carrying water (9000 gallons). It was escorted by virtually all the fighting troops in Suakin – a squadron each from the three cavalry regiments, the Shropshires, the East Surreys, the Grenadier Guards, the 15th Sikhs and the 28th Bombay Native Infantry. (Not surprisingly, the 17th Bengal Native Infantry was relegated to garrison duties in Suakin for the rest of the campaign.)

The cavalry moved out just before 0630 but the infantry and transport not until an hour later. Progress was painfully slow, averaging only 1¼ miles an hour. The assembly of the convoy could not be hidden from the enemy who may well have known the night before, anyway, since there was no hindrance to natives coming and going from Suakin and the collection of water and camels could not be disguised. It soon became clear that Osman's men intended to oppose the convoy this time. At 0815, the cavalry came under fire from the scrub. Three quarters of an hour later, Graham and the infantry found themselves in very thick bush with the Dervishes swarming round them in large numbers. The square was halted to allow the East Surreys to clear their front with volleys. A body of some 30 Arabs attacking the East Surreys was shot down to a man but large numbers remained round the square, firing into it and preventing its movement. It was not until nearly 1100 that the situation was relieved by a section of two guns of the Horse Artillery battery which Graham had sent for from Suakin opening fire from the right rear of the square and clearing the bush along the front of the East Surreys. Graham was then able to start moving forward slowly and at 1200 hours he was met by M'Neill, with the Coldstream Guards, a mile from the zariba. It had been a disturbed night for M'Neill's force. A 'panic' had developed and the Coldstream found themselves under fire from the Berkshires, luckily without casualties.

Matters now went smoothly with Graham's convoy. The Grenadiers were

144

left outside the immediate area of the zariba while the rest of the convoy went on into the zariba and the camels were unloaded. The two Horse Artillery guns were left with M'Neill and Graham began his march back at about 1330 hours, picking up the Grenadiers as he went; he was back at Suakin by 1800 hours. It had been a very trying day of great heat and dust but, apart from two cases of sunstroke, the only casualty had been one man wounded by a spear. Osman's losses could not be ascertained but may have been between 30 and 50 killed. He was still clearly full of fight although more careful about attacking a square openly. The size of the force which had to be employed to escort fewer than 600 camels and the use of the equivalent of a full regiment of cavalry was an indication of the effect that the action on the 22nd had had. It was also the first time that artillery had been used to support M'Neill, a fact which had caused a good deal of criticism since it was generally believed among the troops that while the Dervishes did not fear bullets, they had a terror of shells. As Drummond-Hay put it acidly 'It was pretty universally considered a case of locking the stable door after the steed had been stolen'.

Friday 27 March was something of a day of rest for the troops in Suakin since no convoy was run that day. Graham took the opportunity to issue a tactical instruction based on the experience of the Coldstream Guards on the 24th; in future, when moving across country in square, each battalion was to detach a small party of ten marksmen to move just outside the square with orders to reply to the enemy's fire whenever encountered. At the zariba, Arab sniping persisted all day until in the afternoon the two Horse Artillery guns opened fire and dispersed the Dervish marksmen.

Graham now had virtually his full force to hand except for the Australian contingent. He had in total some 12,000 men, 7400 native followers and 8500 animals. Sickness remained at a fairly low level; on the 27th, for example, he had 278 British and 91 Indian troops in hospital, a sick rate of three per cent. But he still had nearly 200 wounded.

On the 28th, yet another large convoy of 800 camels and 33 carts, carrying 16,000 gallons of water, escorted by 4300 men and two guns, went out. Day-time temperatures were now close to 100°F even in the shade and still close to 80°F at night so the work was fatiguing but this time there was no opposition. Graham took the opportunity to bring back the Royal Marines, and the Coldstream, leaving behind the Grenadiers. The Berkshires, how-ever, were left to soldier on at the zariba.

The last major element of Graham's forces – the New South Wales Contingent minus its artillery – arrived to a very warm welcome on Sunday 29th March. The motives which had led to the offer of a New South Wales contingent have been analysed and discussed at length by Australian historians. Public emotion over the death of Gordon, inter-state rivalry, a fear of French and German imperalism in the Pacific, military ambition among New South Wales' officers – all played a part in an offer which legally the NSW Government was not entitled to make since it was not empowered to enlist soldiers for service overseas. (An indemnifying Act had to be passed on 17th March 1885, *after* the contingent had actually sailed.) What had clinched the offer for the Government in London was the apparent availability of formed and equipped units. In practice, only the artillery battery actually existed, as part of the State's militia forces; the infantry battalion had to be recruited from volunteers although only men with militia or regular service, of whom there was no shortages, were enlisted. Moreover, while it was true that the contingent could be equipped from Australia, in practice it had largely to be re-equipped from England. The 16-pounder guns of the artillery battery were considered too heavy for the Sudan sands by the War Office and the battery was re-equipped with 9-pounder, rifled, muzzle loading guns (of three inch calibre) when it reached Suakin. Similarly, khaki uniforms were awaiting the contingent at Suakin to replace the heavy scarlet and blue serge in which the Australians arrived. There is some evidence also that the Alexander-Henry rifles may have been replaced by the lighter and more efficient Martini-Henry which was standard in the British Army.[7]

Nevertheless, the organisation and despatch of the contingent was a remarkable piece of work. Less than three weeks after the British Government had accepted the NSW offer, the contingent embarked at Sydney in the *Iberia* and *Australasian*, and within six weeks it was in action.

The physique and appearance of the Australians made an immediate impression; Graham noted 'many gentlemen and retired officers in their ranks'. The infantry, once fitted out in khaki, could be used immediately although it was perhaps fortunate that they did not have to encounter Osman's men in full fury. The artillery, which arrived on 30 March, needed time, however, to get used to their new guns and to train their horses.

Otherwise, 29 March, which was appropriately Palm Sunday, passed quietly. No convoy was run and Drummond-Hay noted with gratitude that his battalion was able to have a swim in the sea 'of which one and all stood sadly in need'. It needs little in the way of imagination to visualize the condition of troops who had been living out in the open for nearly a week on a gallon of water a day in temperatures reaching 100°F.

Graham had originally intended to make his long-foreshadowed advance on Tamai on 30 March but this was now postponed until 1 April, which was duly noted by members of the expedition as April Fools' Day. It was further postponed until the 2nd, presumably to allow the Australians to take part. It meant, however, that yet another water convoy had to be run to the garrison at Tofrek. Nine hundred camels and 23 carts carrying 18,000 gallons of water, and escorted by virtually the whole of Graham's force, except for the Australians – nearly 4600 men, under Hudson – left at about 0630 and encountered no opposition. In view of Graham's impending advance, the zariba itself was now altered and greatly reduced in size to enable it to be held by one battalion. The work was done by Colonel Leach VC and 24 Company RE. The original south west redoubt, held so gallantly by the Berkshires on 22 March, was reduced in size to a square with 45 yard sides, with a redoubt in the north-west and south-east angles. It was protected by an earth bank all round, solidly revetted with sandbags and biscuit boxes filled with sand. In this redoubt, the water depot and commissariat stores were placed, with the actual stores of water immediately outside. The central square was also reduced in size and similarly protected with redoubts on three corners. Two of these redoubts had the added protection of a ditch and a thorn hedge held together with wire. This central square was designed to accommodate transport animals and horses, and it was split diagonally by a traverse made of hay bales nine feet high. This was intended to delay and split up attackers if they should manage to penetrate the square as they had done previously. The square also contained a signal station.

The remaining elements of the New South Wales artillery battery disembarked on the 31st and Graham no longer had any excuse for delay. Unfortunately, it now began to look as though his target – Osman's main forces – was slipping away. It was reported that Osman had left Tamai and Hashin and withdrawn his troops into the hills. Graham despatched a force of some 240 mounted infantry and cavalry on 31 March to reconnoitre Tamai and another patrol of 5th Lancers and Bengal Cavalry to reconnoitre Hashin. The patrol reconnoitring Hashin reported back the same evening; it had been fired on and Hashin appeared to be occupied in strength. The force reconnoitring Tamai had left only at 1700 hours and spent the night at M'Neill's zariba. It reconnoitred Tamai early on the morning of 1 April and reported that it was held by some 5-6000 of Osman's men. On receipt of this encouraging news, Graham issued orders the same afternoon for the advance on Tamai to start the following morning (2 April) at 0300 hours. Tents were packed up the same afternoon so that the troops spent a fairly cold, as well as a brief, night in the open.

Camels were being loaded shortly after midnight and reveille sounded at 0200 hours. Graham was taking most of the fighting troops in Suakin except for the unfortunate 17th Bengal Native Infantry who could no longer be trusted in action. In all, his force amounted to about 7000 men, escorting 1639 camels and 930 mules.[8]

The force paraded near the Left Water Fort at 0300 but it was pitch dark and it took an hour or so to get the troops and the transport into formation. The square (or rectangle) when finally formed had a frontage of 200 yards and side of 500 yards. It followed what had now become traditional lines. Three companies of the Coldstream formed the front face; the right side was formed by the Scots Guards, the East Surreys and the 28th Bombay Native Infantry while the left side was formed by the remaining five companies of the Coldstream, the Royal Marines battalion and the Shropshires. The rear face was entrusted to the 15th Sikhs. The four double-companies of the NSW battalion were in reserve inside the square, split between the left and right sides, but, as the square began to straggle and elongate, the Australians were brought into the sides to fill developing gaps. Inside the square were the guns, Graham and his staff, the Royal Engineers and Madras Sapper and Miners, the field hospitals, and all the transport in columns. The men carried one day's rations and water on them, with another two days' provisions in brigade transport.

The square moved off at some time after 0400 and once it was on the move it was joined by the cavalry brigade and G/B, RHA who had paraded separately and earlier. Two squadrons of the 9th Bengal Cavalry covered the front of the square, two squadrons of the 5th Lancers covered the right flank and rear and two squadrons of the 20th Hussars covered the left flank and rear; G/B moved inside the square immediately in rear of the front face, ready to move out and deploy in the open.

Progress was, as always, slow – just over a mile an hour. Indeed, with the infantry spread over more than 20 acres and the pace necessarily regulated by the slowest, it is perhaps a wonder that the formation got along at all. Frequent stops had to be made to re-adjust or shift the loads on the transport animals. The day was hot and very dusty, and the prickly scrub impeded individual progress. M'Neill's (or, as it was now known, No 1) zariba was reached at about 0900 and the troops halted for an hour to eat breakfast (mainly hard biscuit and water) and get a rest. It had been a tough introduction for the Australians, after weeks cooped up on board ship, but only three men of the contingent fell out. At M'Neill's zariba, they faced yet another sobering experience: 'We had to walk over dead bodies lying in all directions' wrote Private Walters. 'Some had been only partly buried, legs and arms showing up through the ground everywhere, the stench being intolerable.'[9] Graham detached the Bombay Infantry to garrison the zariba and added the Grenadiers, the Berkshires, 24 Company RE and two of the four Gardner guns manned by the Royal Navy to his force, together with the mounted force which had conducted the reconnaissance to Tamai the previous day. His force numbered over 8600 fighting men, a force nearly twice as large as the total of his expedition in 1884.

The Balloon Detachment now inflated its balloon and sent it up to a height of 400 feet with the detachment commander, Major Templer, in the basket, and Graham re-commenced his march towards Tamai at about 1015. To avoid the worst scrub, the square headed south south-west towards the normal track to Tamai and then gradually changed direction to the west.[10] From the balloon, Major Templer was able to report parties of the enemy some miles ahead but unfortunately the wind got up and the balloon had to be lowered and packed away on its wagon. At 1215, when the main force was some three miles beyond No 1 zariba, the mounted troops reported substantial parties of the enemy, both mounted and on foot, apparently advancing to the attack. The force halted at 1245 but the enemy did not come on. The

148

square moved on until 1400 hours when it halted some 3 miles from the Tesela Hills, roughly 1½ miles north east of Tamai and apparently held in strength. Graham accordingly despatched the Mounted Infantry and one squadron of the Bengal Cavalry to reconnoitre the hills on which he expected to find strong opposition. But, skilfully pressurised on both flanks by the Bengal squadron, supported by the Mounted Infantry, Osman's men retired on Tamai. The hills were occupied by the reconnaissance force at about 1500 hours and heliographic communication opened with Graham and with Suakin, some 23 miles away.

The Mounted Infantry was now ordered to push on and, if possible, occupy New Tamai and the wells in the Khor Ghob just beyond (Map 5). But it was fired on from various positions around Tamai and fell back prudently on the Tesela Hills, from where, with the rest of the cavalry, it was ordered back to No 1 zariba for the night. The rough, rocky ground around Tesela and Tamai was no place for cavalry at night.

Graham occupied the Tesela Hills with the rest of his force at 1700 hours, just as dusk was about to fall. The hills themselves rise about a hundred feet above the surrounding plain and consequently gave excellent views over the Tamai and the country to the west. The hills runs in two parallel lines, north-east and south-west, with a valley or extended saddle some 300 yards wide dividing them. The main bulk of the troops formed a square zariba in the valley while four companies of the Grenadiers occupied the hill on the southern side nearest to Tamai, and three companies of the Scots Guards and a company of the NSW battalion occupied a hill on the northern side, with two guns of G/B. The Shropshires, with another two guns of G/B, occupied a hill on the southern side directly overlooking the zariba while the East Surreys occupied a hill to the north guarding the track back to No 1 zariba. With the hills thus strongly picketed and the zariba in the valley enclosed in a thorn hedge, Graham and his men settled down for the night. 'The picture was a grand one' wrote another Australian. 'The camp of so many thousand men occupying the heights [sic] between the rugged hills, crowned by armed men standing out clearly against the skyline, the camp fires flickering their light on the groups around, the lines of horses and mules picketed in the midst of the camp, of ungainly-looking camels, some crouched down at rest and others being unloaded, and roaring angrily at their black, weird-looking attendants, but patient withal; and the wild, rugged scenery, bare of vegetation except the stunted, prickly mimosa and a few tufts of coarse grass, made an impression on my mind which I shall not forget.'[11] They did not have an entirely peaceful night. At about 0100 hours a fusillade of shots was fired into the zariba and the troops stood to their arms. A volley from the Grenadiers and some shells from G/B quietened matters down although one man was killed and two wounded.[12]

Graham was now on ground which he had reason to remember. In March 1884, he had camped half a mile to the south-west, roughly between his present position and the wide, deep ravine of the Khor Ghob, and he was about to traverse the ground on which he had so nearly suffered disaster a year before. Reveille was sounded at 0430 on 3 March 1885 (Good Friday). M'Neill, with the East Surreys and Shropshires, was left to guard the zariba and the transport.[13] The remainder of the force formed up in a new formation.

The 2nd Brigade under Hudson formed up in three sides of a square, the Berkshires in line forming the front face, the Royal Marines in column forming the right side and the 15th Sikhs similarly forming the left side. Immediately behind the open rear of this square, the Guards Brigade with the Australians was assembled in two parallel columns. G/B, RHA was positioned to the right rear of the Guards, the four mountain guns of 5/1, RA were immediately behind the right-hand company of the Berkshires and the rocket launchers behind the centre company. Finally, the Madras Sappers and Miners and the Bearer Company of the Hospital Corps was behind the left company of the Berkshires. The cavalry arrived from No 1 zariba at 0720. The 5th Lancers covered the right flank of the infantry, one squadron of the Bengal Cavalry and the Mounted Infantry covered the immediate right front of the 2nd Brigade, the 20th Hussars covered the left front and side and the remainder of the 9th Bengal Cavalry covered the rear of the Guards Brigade.

In this somewhat curious formation, the force moved off at 0800 hours. Graham intended to occupy New Tamai village and its water supply, which had long been Osman Digna's principal HQ, and, in the process, he hoped to draw Osman's troops into a decisive fight, preferably on reasonably open ground to get maximum advantage from the disciplined fire-power of his own troops. But, of course, Osman had gone, as Graham had already been warned by his Intelligence Department. Through his spies and through Graham's fairly obvious and ponderous preparations, Osman had clearly known Graham's intentions for some days. The bulk of his men and all his rifles and ammunition had been dispersed into the hills where Graham's infantry could not follow them. The huts forming New Tamai lay in between successive rocky ridges between the Tesela Hills and the Khor Ghob. In face of rifle fire from the south of Khor Ghob, the mounted troops and the infantry pressed on and by 0930 had occupied New Tamai and reached the near edge of the Khor Ghob. The difficult nature of the country made this essentially an infantry operation from now on. Hudson and the 2nd Brigade were directed across the Khor which at this point was some 100 feet deep and a quarter of a mile wide. The Brigade halted once it had reached the far side of the ravine and opened fire on the enemy marksmen whenever and wherever they could be seen. The Scots Guards halted in the bed of the ravine and opened fire on the enemy up the ravine to their right; the Coldstream and the Australians remained on the north side of the Khor.

It was clearly impossible for Graham's force to follow Osman into the hills; the infantry were simply not the equals of the Dervishes in mobility or in endurance on small supplies of water. The huts which constituted New Tamai were burned, including, it was thought, Osman's own residence and a considerable quantity of ammunition (but no rifles) was destroyed. At 1020, Graham gave the order to retire and by 1040 both brigades were concentrated on the Suakin side of the Khor. By noon, the whole force was back at its overnight position in the Tesela Hills. M'Neill had already assembled the transport and after giving the men time to rest and eat, the whole force began its return march to Suakin. The Horse Artillery and two squadrons of the Bengal Cavalry went straight on to Suakin the same day. The remainder of the force halted overnight at No 1 zariba and reached Suakin the next day (4 April).

It had been a massive, expensive and, ultimately pointless promenade. Graham's casualties were only one man killed and 15 wounded (including three Australians, slightly), plus five transport animals. The troops had undergone a good deal of hardship, being on the march for 16 hours on 2 April and for 13½ on the 3rd, and covering distances of 12-13 miles a day in bush and deep sand. It was not their fault that the Dervishes had refused to stand and fight, and had easily evaded Graham's well-telegraphed punch. It is possible, as Wylde suggested, that if the troops had gone on and attacked Tamai on 23 March, immediately after the fight at the Tofrek zariba, Osman's men might have stood and fought, giving Graham the opportunity he had counted on. In his formal despatch of 8 April to the Secretary of State, Graham took the view that the operations at Tamai had had a salutary effect in showing the tribes that Osman's power did not exist and thus detaching some of the waverers. That may well have been true. Equally, the operations showed that Osman's new tactics of not standing to fight were working and that, if he chose his ground carefully, he could not be reached by Graham. Drummond-Hay, who by this time was disillusioned with Graham, commented sarcastically in his diary that 'The forces opposed to each other in this glorious battle were about ten Arabs (really no more) on the one side and 6000 of Great Britain's best troops on the other . . . The enemy's loss is known to be one, though whether he was killed or only wounded nobody knows.'[14]

After a day's rest, a brigade under M'Neill went out to the Tofrek zariba on Monday 6 April, destroyed the defences and brought back all the stores and the garrison (28th Bombay Native Infantry). Operations in the direction of Tamai to the south-west were now finished and efforts were now concentrated to the north-west, on the line of the railway.

NOTES

1. Drummond-Hay, op cit, p26.
2. Ibid, p26.
3. Ibid, p28.
4. Ibid, p29.

5. A balloon had been used successfully on Sir Charles Warren's Bechuanaland Expedition in 1884. The present detachment, 13 strong, left England on 19 February and reached Suakin on 7 March 1885.
6. See 'Balloon work in the Soudan' *Royal Engineers Journal* Vol XV (1885), p114. When Osman was asked by his men what the balloon was, he replied astutely that it was the Prophet's coffin, suspended between earth and heaven, and therefore a sure sign of victory.
7. On the equipment of the NSW Contingent, see Peter Stanley (ed.) *But Little Glory* (Canberra, 1985).
8. Cavalry: 5th Lancers, 20th Hussars, 9th Bengal Cavalry. Infantry: Coldstream Guards, Scots Guards, East Surreys, Shropshires, Royal Marines, NSW Infantry Battalion. Artillery: G/B RHA, 4 mountain guns 5/1 RA, rocket troop and 4 Gardner guns 6/1 RA. Corps troops: F Coy Madras Sappers and Miners, Balloon Detachment RE, elements of Army Medical Corps and Commissariat and Transport Corps.
9. Letter 9 May 1885, printed in *Sabretache* (July 1967).
10. A commentary on Graham's choice of route on 22 March.
11. Letter from Private Cope, printed in *Sydney Morning Herald* 4 June 1885.
12. According to a letter from Private Mulready, of the New South Wales Battalion, the dead man (from the East Surreys) had gone out to round up a straying mule and was shot by a sentry when he apparently failed to answer the challenge.
13. The Shropshires were once again not used in action. Graham seems to have relied on certain regiments, such as the Berkshires, the Royal Marines and the 9th Bengal Cavalry, who took a disproportionate share of the work.
14. Drummond-Hay, op cit, p73.

11

The Railway and Beyond

IN HIS ORIGINAL Instructions, Graham's second object, after the destruction of Osman's power, was defined as the construction of a railway from Suakin to Berber. With Osman safely out of his reach and with little chance of bringing him to pitched battle, Graham had no option but to concentrate exclusively on the railway.

We have already seen the genesis of this railway and, in particular, Wolseley's luke-warm reaction to it. The fact was that the railway only made sense at this time if it was intended to mount a serious campaign against the Mahdi and to re-occupy the Sudan. At the height of the Second Afghan War, in the winter of 1879-80, the Indian Government had succeeded in laying 133 miles of track in 101 days. That was across a flat, waterless desert, with very little earth work required, and without opposition. Even on that basis, a railway to Berber 240 miles from Suakin would have taken six months; in practice, the need to push the line through the difficult Red Sea Hills in face of opposition from the hostile tribes meant that the railway could hardly take less than a year and could easily take longer if the route through the Hills, still unsurveyed, proved more difficult than supposed. Moreover, unless Berber had already been taken by an expedition up the Nile, the arrival of the railhead at Berber would involve a very hazardous military operation indeed.

Nevertheless, the Government had decided to proceed and, initially, matters moved with great rapidity. Agreement had been reached with the civilian contractors (Lucas and Aird) on 15 February. The first ships carrying railway construction material left England at the end of February; the first 100 railway labourers left London on 26 February on the cargo ship *Osprey* (No 33) and reached Suakin on 15 March. By the time the contract was formally signed on 6 March, a steady stream of ships carrying railway materials was on its way to Suakin.

There was a strong body of military opinion which had wanted a metre-gauge railway, to be built by the Indian railway authorities. It was generally considered that a metre-gauge railway would be quicker to build than a standard gauge line, and India, which was still in the middle of its railway expansion, possessed ample reserves of labour and practical experience and, it was believed, materials and rolling stock. Whether in practice, a metre-gauge would have been quicker is perhaps arguable since the real brake on progress was the military threat from Osman, rather than the physical difficulties of laying the line. What is much less open to argument is that, in the hands of experienced Indian officers using Indian labour, progress would have been a good deal more rapid. In the event, India was found not to have available the expected stocks of metre-gauge material and equipment whereas there were stocks of standard-gauge material readily available from private sources in England. This in itself tipped the balance in favour of using a private contractor used to standard-gauge construction.

There remained the issue of overall control and direction. Again, there was much to be said for single, unified control in the hands of a suitable Royal Engineer officer, using Lucas and Aird simply as agents to provide expertise and to arrange the purchase and supply of material. The actual arrangements were an unhappy compromise. Graham was to have the overall direction of the line but the contractor was to be responsible for the actual detail and execution (and subsequent operation), taking over responsibility from the Royal Engineers also for the 18-inch network already being laid round the harbour area.

The railway was to be built in fifty mile sections, but no estimate for the time it would take could be made because, as a Government spokesman had admitted in the House of Commons 'the line cannot be surveyed as long as the enemy is in possession of it'.[1]

Initially, at least, no one could complain about the speed with which the contractor set about the task. A force of 750 British workmen was recruited, on the basis of free rations and accommodation, a free outfit of clothes and necessaries[2] plus pay of twelve shillings a day (exactly twelve times the pay of the British soldier); at a time when labouring wages in England averaged twenty one shillings a week, it was almost a fortune. Lucas and Aird's directing staff, including a traffic manager, left England on 20 February and as we have seen, the first party of labourers and the first batches of materials left a week later.

There was no overall lack of material available in England but equally there was no time to pick or choose or to ensure uniformity. Thus Lucas and Aird were in practice confined to buying up job lots wherever they could be found. There was a strong suspicion that some of it was ancient material from the old Hull and Barnsley Railway and that other bits of it had been grubbed up from the Tilbury docks. Inevitably, there were complaints about it when it arrived; rails were of different sizes and weights, square fish bolts were sent out for round-holed fish plates, the rolling stock was a motley collection of good and bad, with some of the engines patently unequal to the task.

Much more important in some ways was the shortage of local labour. The contractors had assumed that cheap native labour would be available in ample quantity for the unskilled work of cutting down the scrub, removing stones and boulders and generally preparing the ground for the laying of the track. In actual fact, there was virtually no such labour available since many of the tribesmen who might have been prepared to work were either supporting Osman or maintaining a watchful position of neutrality. Hundreds of Indian labourers had to be drafted in and an increasing amount of work was done by the troops themselves.

Construction of the 4′ 8½″ standard-gauge railway began on 13 March with the laying of a set of double points and a length of line on Quarantine Island. By the 20th, the line had crossed the causeway and reached the outer line of the fortifications. Construction now came to a virtual halt because Graham was pre-occupied with the advance on Tamai and could not spare a strong enough force to push out towards Handub, whither the railway line was headed. It was perhaps just as well from some points of view because Lucas and Aird's operations were not meeting with universal approval. Some of it was not the contractor's fault. The huge and growing size of Graham's expedition had created enormous problems in the unloading, storage and distribution of supplies. Railway materials of all descriptions were pouring into the jetties on Quarantine Island where they jostled for space with all the other thousands of tons of stores which were flooding in. The materials were of all shapes and sizes and shipped higgledy-piggledy so that finding the right fishplates and bolts for the right rails etc. consumed enormous quantities of time and patience. When the materials were ready to be moved forward, there was a shortage of transport. Lengths of rail could not easily be moved on camels and the 18-inch network was unable to carry really heavy loads. Recourse had to be made to using the Army's carts and wagons but these were not always available. But, equally, the contractor's own working schedule was not exactly urgent. Work normally started at 0615, in the cool of the day, but the navvies broke off for breakfast at 0830. Lunch was from 1200 to 1400 hours and little work could be done in the afternoon because of the heat. Long periods were spent waiting for the right materials to arrive from the docks.

The Army was inclined to be critical of the British workmen who were alleged to be lazy and always grumbling. Drunkenness and brawling were regarded as other failings, and some men were thought deliberately to have caused trouble in order to get sent home. Some of this was undoubtedly true – among the 750 men ultimately sent out, it would have been remarkable if there were not a number of bad pennies, and drunkenness and fighting were commonplace in Victorian working society. But much of it, no doubt, reflected the Army's irritation at the enormous disparity in rates of pay and conditions between the workmen and the soldiers. On the one hand were the ordinary private soldiers earning a shilling a day before stoppages, bound by tight discipline and enduring all the privations and dangers; on the other side, coming from the same social background, were the railway labourers, earning twelve times as much, living in rather better conditions (particularly in Suakin), bearing little of the danger and none of the discipline. It is small wonder therefore that the Army authorities looked upon the bulk of the British labour force as lazy, incompetent and generally useless; an exception was made for the engine drivers who were regarded as efficient and hard-working.

At the root of the whole problem lay the division of responsibility. Graham had been charged with the overall direction of the enterprise; under him, the day-to-day responsibility fell on Brigadier General C.B. Ewart in charge of the Lines of Communication.[3]But the contractor was responsible for the actual ordering and shipping of material and for the construction and operation of the line. It was a situation designed to foster misunderstanding and friction, especially given the fact that the Royal Engineers officers, of whom Ewart was one, made no secret of the fact that they believed that construction of the railway should have been entrusted to their Corps in the first place. In practice, there was no way in which the Army could avoid taking a large share in the detailed work of construction. When the materials arrived at Suakin, they had to be disembarked and stored by native coolies working under Army direction. Transport of the materials to the railhead had to be done in Army transport until the line had been constructed far enough to allow working trains to be used. The ground had to be cleared of scrub and rocks and levelled by Army sappers and native labour employed by the Army and, above all, the Army had to provide the necessary covering parties to protect the workmen as they toiled. When the 10 (Railway) Company, RE landed on 7 April, it took over responsibility for surveying and marking out the line of the railway, while the rest of the Company worked on the 18-inch network at base. Yet the detailed running of the trains and their precise cargoes was in the hands of Lucas and Aird's traffic manager, J.S. Forbes. Until a telegraph system could be installed, which should have been a first priority, it was not possible to run a proper block-working system and trains coming from Suakin frequently found themselves confronted by a train coming back from railhead, and vice versa.

When fully developed, the construction routine was as follows. First went a survey party of 10 Company RE under Captains Kunhardt and St Clair, escorted by a strong party of cavalry and infantry. They surveyed and marked the line of the railway, as they went; since they had no maps of the country, they followed the general line of the Suakin to Berber camel road. Behind them came working parties of infantry clearing a 100 yard swathe through the brush to provide room for construction and to clear away potential enemy snipers. Behind them came the bankhead party of Sudanese and Indian labourers under Royal Engineer officers who levelled and prepared the roadbed. Finally came the railhead party, composed of British navvies and native labourers, who laid and fastened the rails. Apart from operating the trains, virtually the only work done by Lucas and Aird's men was in fastening down (or spiking) the rails to the sleepers.

Under divided control and Graham's pre-occupation with Tamai, progress was painfully slow. Original estimates of progress – 25 miles a week – were ludicrously over-confident. By 22 March, when work stopped pending the outcome of the Tamai expedition, only 2½ miles of standard gauge railway had been laid, reaching barely as far as the West Redoubt. Work then stopped until 6 April, much to De Cosson's indignation; he believed that if the work had been continued, Otao could have been reached by 6 April.[4]

Finally, on 6 April, Graham was ready to pursue operations in furtherance of the railway. While M'Neill evacuated his original zariba and brought the stores back to Suakin, a force under Major General Fremantle[5] moved out to the site of what was to become No 1 Station, some four miles beyond the West Redoubt; the next day (7th) it was joined by the Scots Guards. Two zaribas were built, one for the troops and one for the animals, each flanked with a stout, stone redoubt.

The engineers built a wooden observation tower (or crow's nest) for lookout and signalling purposes. Osman's men were keenly interested in this advance and the first attempt to use the crow's nest for signalling by lamp was greeted with a fusillade which quickly put an end to any attempt at signalling. The inexperienced NSW battalion fired off several hundred uncontrolled rounds before repeated soundings of the 'Cease Fire' brought some order.

On the 8th, the force at No 1 Station was joined temporarily by a squadron of the Bengal Cavalry, a company of the Mounted Infantry, and some details, and the whole force minus the Scots Guards then advanced to Handub, accompanied by some 25 friendly Fadlab (Amarar) tribesmen. Handub, some six miles beyond No 1 Station and 10 miles from Suakin, was occupied at 1100 hours and work began immediately to erect a zariba while the transport animals, escorted by the Bengal Cavalry, returned to Suakin.

Private Fergusson of the 20th Hussars, who was with this force, had an even more impressive experience than at Hashin: 'I was out as right flanker when two of the rebels ran from behind a bush and threw a spear at me but missed me and struck the nose bag which was half full of corn hanging by the side of the horse, so I lifted my carbine which we carry loaded always when out in small parties, and fired at the fellow that still had a spear and hit him in the breast and he fell while the Arab without any spear drew his dagger and I did not have time to load my carbine again but brought the butt down on the top of his head and stunned him and drew my sword and finished the two but I have hurt my wrist swinging the carbine'.[6] Fergusson was clearly a pretty cool customer. The railway was now creeping forward, railhead reaching No 1 Station on the 11th, where a stout stone blockhouse was now built. Graham inspected the line for the first time on the 11th; with the immediate threat from Osman removed and more than 12,000 troops available, now was the time to push on with the railway. By the 13th, the line was going forward at a rate of a mile a day. It was not a very remarkable rate of progress in the circumstances and a long way short of the 25 miles a week which had been confidently predicted earlier. Moreover, the difficult part of the operation – carrying the line up through the hills – still lay ahead. At this rate, it would take at least another eight months to reach Berber, even if Osman decided not to interfere. The Arabs had not hitherto seen a railway and were ignorant of its capabilities. Nevertheless, Osman was not slow to perceive that the line was a threat; what he had not worked out was how best to attack it. Spasmodic attempts were made to cut the telegraph line and to burn sleepers, and volleys were fired at the blockhouse at No 1 Station at night but no concerted attempt was made to attack the railhead which was indeed strongly protected by troops. Osman's best tactic would probably have been merely to threaten an attack since this would almost inevitably have stopped work until the threat was removed. Delaying tactics of this kind would have slowed progress to a crawl. Nevertheless, it must be recognised that the odds were shifting against the Dervishes. Graham's large and still growing force, his tardy recognition of the value of mobility (symbolised by the decision to form a Camel Corps on 16 April), the constant clearance of scrub and the care which was now applied to fortifying every position meant that the opportunities for Dervish attack were steadily reducing. There remained, however, the option of a major night attack and it is curious that Osman never resorted to it. Such an attack would have gone far to nullify the crushing superiority of the British fire power and, reduced to a meleé in the dark, the odds must have been on Osman's men.

In fact, the work of stopping Graham and the railway was being done for Osman without his knowing it. The British Government, under Gladstone, was tired of the costly commitment in the Sudan. It had never had any desire to assume control of a huge, impoverished territory whose only asset appeared to be sand in unlimited quantities. In the immediate aftermath of Gordon's death, there was little it could do to oppose the tidal wave of public emotion. But Gordon had now been dead nearly four months and there was no prospect of a decisive advance on Khartoum until the autumn. Even Wolseley was losing interest, discouraged by the overwhelming disaster of failing to save Gordon. Moreover, there was beginning to loom up a confrontation with Russia on the northern border of Afghanistan, which the Government was morally bound to protect. On 13 April, Hartington signalled Wolseley, suggesting the possibility of a gradual withdrawal from Suakin.

For the moment, matters went on apace there. At Handub, Fremantle with a force of some 1500 men, including the Coldstream Guards and the Australian battalion, occupied a strong zariba at the foot of a 200 foot hill which was crowned with a stone redoubt held by a company of infantry and two mountain guns of 5/1, RA. A smaller hill, 600 yards to the south, was held by another company to provide protection and warning against an advance from the direction of Deberet and Tamai. During the daytime, cavalry patrols scouted as far as the foot of the hills 15 miles or so ahead.

For the troops at Handub, as elsewhere, there was little in the way of diversion to relieve the wearisome monotony of picket duty and clearing scrub. For the officers, there was a fairly constant stream of visitors, some less welcome than others. Drummond-Hay noted the presence in the Coldstream Mess one evening of three newspaper correspondents, two officers from 5/1 RA and a couple of other casual visitors.[7] Inevitably, the mess was able to provide the whisky and champagne without which no British battalion ever seemed to travel. There was opportunity for some shooting of gazelle and antelope and sand grouse. For the rank and file, there was probably little amusement other than smoking the short clay pipes which were the peculiar hallmark of the British soldier. Drummond-Hay recorded one minor diversion during Church Parade on 12 April when 'the poor parson began to wobble on his legs; his voice grew more and more feeble and shaky and his complexion assumed a greenish hue'. If he was not succumbing to dysentery, he was probably going down with heat exhaustion which was now a major cause of sickness.

Graham's force had on the whole kept remarkably fit and healthy. Throughout March, the number of British sick had rarely exceeded 200 while the Indian contingent had averaged between 70 and 80, an overall sickness rate of about two and a half per cent. But temperatures had been steadily increasing. At the beginning of March, when the official Diary began to record the weather, daytime temperatures averaged about 80°F. By the beginning of April, day temperatures of 90°F in the shade were becoming normal and there was not a great deal of relief at night. Drummond-Hay recorded being bitterly cold at night on 8 April when the day temperature of 89°F dropped to 47°F but that would seem to have been exceptional; by the middle of April, the night-time temperature at HQ at Suakin was ranging between 70° and 80°F. Not surprisingly, sickness among the British troops was going up. On 30 March, the number of sick in hospital, mainly from heat exhaustion, exceeded 300 for the first time, although the Indian rate remained roughly the same. By the middle of April, the British sick exceeded 350 and the overall rate for the force was four per cent, still by no means severe, although it represented a rate among the British of roughly six per cent. Boredom and morale were, as always, a major factor. The greatest number of sick recorded (905) was reached on 13 May when the dispersal of the force was just about to begin. The sickness rate for the Indian contingent, as might be expected, was consistently very much lower than among the British, undoubtedly reflecting *inter alia* the greater maturity and service of the Indian soldiers, as well as their better camp arrangements, including the use of sweepers to clean the latrines daily.

By 16 April, progress was beginning to be noticeable. Railhead was beyond Handub which was now dubbed No 1 Station on the line, the previous No 1 Station becoming No 1 Post. Railhead was in telegraphic contact with HQ at Suakin and matters were sufficiently settled for part of the stationary Field Hospital at Suakin to proceed to Handub. At Suakin, the base was re-organised so that all the camps lay along the railway, between Quarantine Island and the West Redoubt, with HQ and the British troops north of the line and the Indian Contingent (minus the Bengal Cavalry which was brigaded with the rest of the Cavalry Brigade) south of it. Each camp was linked, either by standard- or 18 inch-gauge railway, with Quarantine Island, greatly easing the daily movement of stores and water. Further along the line the carrying capacity of the trains was still monopolised by the carriage of railway materials and the troops at Handub were supplied by a daily convoy from Suakin, which was escorted as far as No 1 Post by a squadron of cavalry and from thence on by cavalry or mounted infantry sent down from Handub.

The distribution of the troops in the middle of April reflected the changed situation. At the head of the railway, beyond Handub, there was a force of 1460, made up of the East Surreys, the Shropshires and the Madras Sappers and Miners, with No 1 Field Hospital. At Handub itself, there was a force of nearly 2500, including the Coldstream and Scots Guards, a squadron of the 5th Lancers, a company of Mounted Infantry, four guns of 5/1 RA, the NSW infantry battalion, 17 (Field) Company RE, with No 4 Field Hospital (part of the Stationary Field Hospital for the native, mainly Indian, followers). No 1 Post was held by a company of the Berkshires. The remainder of the force (roughly 8000 in total) was still at Base at Suakin.

Graham was preparing to push on. Visiting the Coldstream Guards at Handub on 10 April, he had expressed the slightly surprising view that the enemy was totally demoralised 'and that he expected the "friendlies" to come flocking in daily'. The Coldstream officers seem to have been properly sceptical and, indeed, the floods of 'friendlies' did not materialise. Nevertheless, on 13 April, a party of 100 Mounted Infantry and 5th Lancers under Captain Briggs of the Mounted Infantry, and accompanied by a force of 170 'friendlies', reconnoitred Otao, 10 miles ahead from Handub. It encountered no opposition and came back with useful information about the water supply there and about the best route thence for the railway. Otao wells were found to be 480 feet higher than the wells at Handub, but the rise was extremely gradual; for most of the way, it was a hard, gravelly plain, with scattered scrub, and occasional groups of red, white and black rocks, mainly sandstone and ironstone.

On 15 April, the intrepid Briggs, with 73 Mounted Infantry and Lancers, plus 150 Amarar friendlies under Muhammad Ali Bey, reconnoitred southwards from Handub towards Hashin and beyond. Briggs and the mounted men passed through Hashin and then swung westwards through Deberet (three miles west of Hashin) and then south west for another four miles where they linked up with the friendlies under Muhammad Ali Bey who, accompanied by Captain Molyneux and Mr Brewster of the Intelligence Department, had taken a more southerly route from Handub and had reconnoitred as far as Obani, 10 miles west of Hashin. This time, the reconnaissance party intercepted a large flock of sheep and goats which had been collected to supply Osman at Tamai and was guarded by some of his men. In all, 16 men, 18 women and children, and 900 sheep and cattle were captured, without opposition, which went some way to justifying Graham's assessment. The fact that on the next day a convoy of more than 900 camels and mules could be taken up to Handub escorted by only one squadron of the 9th Bengal Cavalry strengthened his view. It was all a very far cry from the tense situation only three weeks or so before. It was becoming clear that Osman was not going to risk another costly stand-up fight. Equally, it was clear that he was safe in the hills from the plodding British infantry.

Graham had realised earlier the need for greater mobility and 500 riding camels had been ordered from India. On 16 April he issued orders for the formation of a Camel Corps, to consist of four British companies of two officers and 90 men, and one company of 100 Indian infantry, together with 200 native drivers to look after the camels. The British companies were formed, from volunteers as far as possible, as follows:

No 1 Company   –   Guards
No 2 Company   –   Royal Engineers, East Surreys and Royal Marines Light Infantry
No 3 Company   –   Berkshires and New South Wales Contingent
No 4 Company   –   Shropshire Light Infantry

The Corps was to be commanded by Major James, of the Scots Greys. Each camel took two men and the total weight per camel was about 418 pounds. The Corps was formed with a minimum of expenditure. Apart from saddlery, the only expense seems to have been in providing each man with a whip, a solar topi, a pair of Bedford cord breeches, a pair of puttees, and an ammunition bandolier.

Otao was occupied on 16 April by the Scots Guards and 17 Company RE, with two guns of 5/1 RA. In turn, the troops remaining at Handub were reinforced from Suakin by the remaining four guns of 5/1 RA, the New South Wales Artillery Battery and the 2nd Company Mounted Infantry.

Reinforcements had continued to trickle in but by the middle of April Graham's force had just about reached its maximum size – approximately 12,750 fighting men, with 9700 followers and over 10,000 animals. Luckily the water supply system had also reached its maximum efficiency. The decision had wisely been taken right at the beginning that the troops should use only condensed water, leaving the water from the wells round Suakin to be used for watering the animals of the force. Four Egyptian vessels – the *Tor*, *Mukbar Gaffariyeh* and *Deb-el-Bahr*,[8] fitted with over-the-side condensers, were moored at or near Quarantine and Suakin Islands, backed up by two horizontal boilers on Suakin Island. From the piers where these ships were moored the water was taken, initially by animal transport but in due course by 400 gallon tanks mounted on trolleys along the 18 inch-gauge network, to two supply depots – one near the Sandbag Redoubt for the 1st Brigade and the other near H Redoubt for the 2nd and Cavalry Brigades. From these two depots, the individual units drew their supplies in regimental water carts, on a scale of two gallons per man per day, with one gallon for the native followers and six gallons for hospital patients; working parties received in addition 1½ pints per man at the end of each shift. The Indian Contingent drew its water directly from the *Tor* which was moored to a pier close to the Foula Redoubt on the south side of the harbour.

In addition to the four Egyptian ships, another six British condenser ships were moored in the harbour and the water they produced was transported by lighter to the various piers for transport to the two supply depots. When the Indian Contingent moved in April to a position near the rest of the force, along the line of the standard gauge railway, it too drew its water from the supply depots. For operations in the field and to supply the various advanced zaribas, camel convoys carrying barrels, tins, skins and rubber bags were used; they were filled at No 5 Pier in the north-west corner of the harbour where the *Deb-el-Bahr* was moored.

As the railway to Berber progressed, plans were made to lay a four-inch main along the line, through which water would be pumped by an 8 horse-power engine installed by Lucas and Aird. Until this was ready, water was trundled along the line in tanks mounted on ballast trucks and filled at the Ferry Pier on Quarantine Island.

For the animals, a party of 40 native well-sinkers had been hard at work under a Royal Engineer officer, eventually sinking more than 50 wells around Suakin and at the advanced posts. The water was suitable for watering animals and for washing purposes – and was, of course, drunk without difficulty by the Sudanese! From the wells the water was drawn up by mechanical pumps of various kinds, as well as by native labour using skins. The low sickness rate generally among both men and animals showed that the water arrangements had been well planned.

Taking the week ending 18 April as representing the condensing arrangements at their peak, the 10 condensing ships and the shore boilers produced between them approximately 860,000 gallons for an expenditure of 608 tons of coal (roughly 1400 gallons per ton of coal).[9] At the end of the week, there was some 1,200,000 gallons in store, equal to about 30 days consumption. It is clear therefore that condensing capacity was well in excess of requirements although it was argued that the excess capacity would have been necessary if Graham's operations towards Berber had been carried out as originally envisaged.

The medical arrangements themselves had been, by Victorian standards, relatively lavish. In addition to the regiments' own doctors, some 50 medical officers were sent out from England to man the various hospitals. For the British troops, one Field Hospital was attached to each Brigade and moved with it on active operations. A fourth Field Hospital remained in the base at

Suakin, together with a supplementary Auxiliary Hospital located on Quarantine Island. There was also a Stationary Field Hospital, part of which moved to Handub in April where it was used mainly as a collecting point for sick and wounded prior to their going back to Suakin. Finally, there was the hospital ship *Ganges* which took the more serious cases of sickness and wounds, many of whom were then evacuated back to Suez and England; the *Bulimba* was used as a hospital ship prior to the arrival of the *Ganges* and remained in use thereafter for minor cases since it was as well-equipped. To transport the sick and wounded on land there were two Bearer Companies. No 1 Bearer Company, equipped with wagons and dandies, was attached to the Guards Brigade; the wagons, in particular, proved to be extremely useful. No 2 Bearer Company had no wagons but was equipped with mule litters and dandies and was attached to the Cavalry Brigade. Although commanded by British officers and containing some British other ranks, the Bearer Companies were mainly composed of Indian bearers.

The arrangements for the Indian Contingent were equally comprehensive. Originally, there were to be two Field Hospitals and a General or Base Hospital. In practice, the *Czarewitch* was hastily converted as a hospital ship of 125 beds and became in effect the General Hospital. On shore, part of No 1 Field Hospital was used in the mobile role to accompany the units on active operations while the remainder of No 1 Field Hospital, together with No 2 Field Hospital was moved into Fort Euryalus and became a Stationary Field Hospital. Each Field Hospital was supported by a proportion of litters and dandies. Finally, there were two Field Hospitals for the native followers of the whole Force. The Indian hospitals had been provided on the basis of a sick rate of twelve per cent among the troops; in practice the sick rate averaged about three per cent and never exceeded seven per cent. In this campaign, the Indian soldiers were probably as well looked after as they had ever been.

Medical science had made two major advances since the Crimean War. Lister had pioneered the use of antiseptics, and chloroform had come into general use as an anaesthetic. Surgery could now be performed with much greater safety and with much less suffering and shock to the patient. Gangrene remained a horrifying problem in many parts of the world – there was then no cure for it except radical surgery if circumstances permitted. But in the very hot dry atmosphere of the Sudan, gangrene was very much less prevalent than, for example, in India or even north-west Europe. In consequence, the wounded in Graham's force stood a very good chance of recovery. Among the Indian Contingent, for example, there were only two deaths among the wounded in the hospitals, of which one was a fractured skull.

Disease was a different problem. Bacteriology was only in its infancy and the cause of most major diseases was still unknown. In the absence of any clear understanding of the precise causes of diseases, treatment and prevention could only be pragmatic. As late as the Boer War, typhoid (enteric) fever was not fully understood – in particular, its relation to contaminated water; similarly with various forms of dysentery. In 1885, the use of distilled (or condensed) water by the troops enormously reduced the incidence of disease and there were remarkably few fatalities by comparison, for example, with the Second Afghan War only five years before. In the Indian Contingent, there were only four deaths from disease, of which two were from dysentery. In Graham's force as a whole, the major causes of sickness were dysentery, heat-stroke and nervous exhaustion, largely caused by the heat. As the temperature went up, typhoid fever began to appear. Among the New South Wales Contingent of 770, there were eight deaths from disease – two at Suakin, four on the voyage home and two after landing in Australia; all were from either dysentery or typhoid. Much the same picture could be obtained from the British troops as a whole.

Huge numbers of animals accompanied Graham's expedition. Accurate figures are extremely difficult to arrive at, but mules and ponies exceeded 3500, horses 2400 and camels at least 7000 and possibly more. To look after these, nine veterinary surgeons were sent out from England and India. A special depot was set up in Suakin to look after the horses in order to ensure that the mounted troops were kept at as nearly full strength as possible. Because of the incidence of skin disease – particularly parasitic mange – among the camels arriving at Suakin, a special quarantine depot was set aside for camels. Very large numbers of animals were treated for disease but casualties were fairly low.[10]

Food, of course, played as important a part as water in the health of the troops. As we have seen, the ration scales for the British soldiers were, on the face of it, generous and well-balanced and, even allowing for the problem of handling fresh meat in such a climate, they certainly sufficed to keep the troops well-fed and healthy all the time that they were in camp at Suakin. The problems arose when the troops were employed at any distance. Then the troops were quickly reduced to a monotonous diet of hard biscuit, preserved meat and tea. The preserved meat used in the early stages was principally corned beef which was universally loathed, partly because its preservation involved the use of a large amount of salt which made the men thirsty but partly because, in Sudan temperatures, the contents of the tins were quickly reduced to a liquid porridge. The preserved fresh meat which was subsequently issued was a great improvement. Even so, the rations were universally blamed for the dysentery which was the main cause of sickness. Many men, according to Gambier-Parry, threw their rations of corned beef away rather than increase their thirst by eating it; he could not understand why fresh meat could not have been sent out to the troops in the field, either on the hoof or already slaughtered since the ships at Suakin produced large quantities of ice and the troops were rarely more than 12 miles from the port. He also wondered why lime juice was not issued more plentifully. In fact, according to the ration scales, half an ounce of lime juice should have been issued whenever tinned meat was issued. As always, the Indian troops seem to have been less well-fed than their British counterparts – much less well indeed than they should have been. Exactly the same criticisms of the feeding of the native troops had been made after the conclusion of the Second Afghan War five years before. Although Graham's Final Despatch claims that there had been no complaints about the Indian ration supplies, elsewhere in his Despatch there is a tell-tale reference to cases of scurvy among the 15th Sikhs and 17th Native Infantry which had to be hastily dealt with by increasing the issue of rum, sugar and lime juice. The native labourers fared even worse, living off rations of one pound of rice or flour a day, supplemented by quantities of dates and minute rations of sugar, salt and coffee.

Although by now Graham must have strongly suspected that the days of the expedition were numbered, he had no real option but to push forward. On 17 April, Fremantle, with half a battalion of the Coldstream Guards and a squadron of the 5th Lancers, was moved forward to Otao and Graham issued orders for a major reconnaissance next day of Hashin, Deberet and the Khor Abent (running south west from Deberet). At 0500 on the 18th, Hudson with G/B RHA, three squadrons of 9th Bengal Cavalry, two squadrons 20th Hussars, 50 Mounted Infantry and the 15th Sikhs moved off from the assembly point near the West Redoubt, reaching Hashin at 0745 hours and Deberet at 0900 hours. Half an hour later, the leading scouts of the Bengal Cavalry made contact with a force from Handub under Fremantle consisting of four companies of the NSW battalion, a section of two mountain guns of 5/1 RA and half a company of Mounted Infantry. Simultaneously, heliographic contact was made with a small force which had advanced from Otao, consisting of half a battalion of the Scots Guards and a company of Mounted Infantry. The reconnaissance had really covered only the same ground as had already been covered by Briggs on the 15th and Graham had seen no sign of Osman's men although the Otao party had seen some Dervishes who had rapidly retreated southwards. After stopping for food and water, Graham ordered the various forces to retire at 1100 hours, the Suakin force stopping en route to burn the miserable huts forming the village of Hashin and to destroy some ammunition found there; they were back at base by 1430 hours. The Handub force camped out that night, returning to Handub next day. It is difficult to see what had actually been accomplished except to allow Graham to see the ground.

The railway was now a mile west of Handub and it was time for the leading troops to move on. Acccordingly, on 19 April, Fremantle occupied Tambuk, five miles ahead of Otao, with the Scots Guards, two guns of 5/1 RA, and some Royal Engineers and Madras Sappers and Miners. Fremantle was appointed Political Officer at the front, with two representatives of the Intelligence Department (Captain Clarke and Mr Brewster) to assist him. Graham had been convinced for some time that Osman's forces were demoralised and disintegrating and he had been negotiating with many of the tribes round Suakin to detach themselves completely from Osman and attach themselves firmly to the British. From the tribes' point of view, the essential condition was that the British must promise to stay and defend them if necessary. Understandably, they were afraid that if the British left again, those who had been friendly would be picked off and destroyed by Osman. Unfortunately, that condition was precisely the one that Graham could not now deliver. On 15 April, while the railway was still short of Handub, the Secretary of State (Hartington) had told Wolseley by telegram that construction of the railway was to be suspended for the time being. The town of Suakin would continue to be held and Wolseley was to advise on what other positions, if any, should be held in the immediate vicinity in order to prevent constant attacks such as had happened prior to the expedition's arrival. Wolseley was also to decide the most convenient place for the railway to terminate; in the meantime, Graham was not to enter into any agreement with the surrounding tribes which was inconsistent with these decisions. Five days later, Hartington warned Wolseley that the Government was about to announce that all troops, including those in the Sudan, were to be made available for service elsewhere. The immediate justification for this was events on the northern frontier of Afghanistan where in March the Russians had occupied the oasis of Pendjeh, well inside the border recognised by the British. The crisis with Russia lasted throughout April.

The Government's announcement was duly made in the House of Commons on 21 April and the news was generally known in Suakin on the 22nd. Among the troops, the news was greeted with relief. There was clearly little chance in the immediate future of any major engagement with the Dervishes; in the meantime, the temperature was steadily rising and the tedious, wearisome work of clearing the ground for the railway and convoying camels to and from Suakin was becoming more and more burdensome. Sickness was on the increase.

Graham, for obvious reasons, was not anxious to see the results of his campaign diminished. He was, no doubt, conscious of the ill-effects of his withdrawal twelve months before. He was keen therefore to push the railway ahead as far as practicable and to consolidate his advantage over Osman. The two objects were, of course, inter-connected. The railway was the visible sign of British power and influence; more important still, it was an earnest of the British intention to stay and was therefore an important determinant in the attitude of the surrounding tribes. Graham was not the only one who believed in the important moral effect of the railway; Wylde, for example, who was perhaps the most experienced observer of the Suakin scene because of his long residence there and his familiarity with the tribes, firmly believed that 'The news of the railway and its engines that could go faster than the quickest horses and camels could gallop had a wonderfully

166

quieting effect . . . many of the Arabs came to see this devil's contrivance and when they found that the English did not want to molest them and did not imprison them, but bought their cattle at a price never heard of before and offered them work, it had a most quieting effect'.[11] He noted that it was now possible to ride across country to Tambuk without escort and although he met many tribesmen with small patches of red or blue on their clothes which was a sure sign that they had been with Osman, he never encountered any unfriendliness. Graham was sure that Osman was on his last legs: 'The dispersion of the main body of Osman Digna's force consequent on the losses suffered in the various encounters which have taken place culminating in the occupation and destruction of Tamai and the apparent difficulties under which he now labours, both as regards the tribes that are wavering in their allegiance and endeavouring to evade the obligations he desires to place them under, and the want of food combine to render it unlikely that he can effect any concentration of followers'.[12] Nevertheless, he expected Osman to continue to harass the advance of the railway and possibly to show some opposition to further reconnaissances.

Graham therefore wanted to push the railway as far as Es Sibil,[13] 32 miles beyond Otao and 50 miles from Suakin, and to station there a substantial body of troops to protect the lines of communication back to Suakin; the main body of mounted troops would be stationed at Otao from whence they could operate up and down the line as well as against any enemy force advancing from the direction of Tamai or Tamanieb to the south.

These were ambitious proposals. Es Sibil was well into the hills, only a few miles from Sinkat, the summer capital of the Red Sea Province. While no proper survey had been possible, it was clear that railway construction through the hills would be a more expensive and slower process than hitherto. Prior to this, the track had been laid in rough and ready fashion with an absolute minimum of grading and without culverts or any other form of civil engineering. In the hills, culverts and even bridges would be required and the actual preparation of the road bed would involve significant labour. The military consequences were also bound to be important. Even allowing for the use of the railway for supply and operational movements, and for the wider use of mounted troops, protection of a line of communication stretching back 50 miles to Suakin was bound to be an expensive business in terms of troops. When Wolseley came to assess the situation early in May, his conclusion was that to hold the railway to Otao only would require the equivalent of two brigades of infantry, a mounted brigade, two batteries of artillery, three Field Companies RE, plus ancillary troops – or nearly three quarters of Graham's present force.

There was one other consideration. Construction of the railway to Es Sibil would have little purpose *unless* it was part of a firm decision to continue to Berber. By itself, a line to Es Sibil was a vulnerable and fragile project of no great military or civil value.

167

Although Graham must have had a shrewd idea of the way matters were likely to go, he was still short of official information. He had not been informed officially of the Government's announcement in Parliament on 21 April; he had learned of it through a Reuters' telegram on the 22nd, at the same time as the rest of the population of Suakin. In any case, he had no orders to stop work, and railway material (and native labourers) were continuing to flood into Suakin; on 22 April there were 20 steamers moored in Suakin harbour, waiting to unload railway material. By 23 April, the head of the railway was three miles west of Handub, by the 25th it was within three miles of Otao. It was time to explore beyond Tambuk and on 23 April, the new Camel Corps made its operational début. A detachment of 105 men, under Major James, left Suakin at 0730 hours and reached Tambuk at 1900 hours. Next day, the detachment, strengthened by 47 Mounted Infantry and 100 Amarar 'friendlies' under Muhammad Ali Bey, reconnoitred towards Es Sibil. Muhammad Ali Bey and his men were extremely reluctant to penetrate as far as Es Sibil itself and the reconnaissance went only some nine to ten miles, arriving back at Tambuk at 1500 hours, having seen only a few of Osman's camel men and capturing one camel. The route followed by the reconnaissance revealed a perfectly practicable line for the railway, without excessive gradients. Nevertheless, it would require a good deal of labour to prepare the necessary road-bed and since the route largely followed a series of watercourses which would flood in the rainy season, culverts would have to be built or damage to the line accepted. The same day (24th) Graham himself went up the line by train to beyond Handub and then rode on to inspect Otao and Tambuk.

Graham had asked Wolseley by telegram on the 24th for instructions about the expedition, and on the 25th Wolseley replied, telling Graham that the expedition was to be wound down and the railway stopped at the first convenient place. Graham was still very keen to strike another, hopefully final, blow at Osman and eliminate his menace, although it is not clear precisely how he intended to do this since Osman could only be winkled out of the hills where he had taken refuge by the use of converging mounted columns which would take time. Meanwhile, there was no alternative to starting the run-down. Orders were issued to stop construction of the four-inch water main alongside the railway and to stop the railway itself at Otao. The first troops – the Royal Marines battalion – moved down from Handub by rail and embarked in the *Australia* for Suez on 28 April. Along with the Berkshires, they had been there the longest and the way in which Graham had used them in all his major actions showed the value he placed on them. Their record had been a distinguished one.

Coincidentally or not, there was now a revival of activity by Osman's men directed against the railway. The camps at Handub and Otao were fired on at night, the telegraph line from Handub to Suakin was cut regularly and on 28 April, rails were removed and the sleepers burned near No 1 Post. The Royal

168

Engineers now produced their masterpiece – an armoured train. It consisted of an engine with its cab and sides protected with ⅜-inch iron plates, and an open truck with its sides similarly protected; two officers and 15 men of the Royal Engineers were carried as guard. It came into service on the night of 30 April, patrolling the line to Otao between 2100 hours and 0400. It was quickly in action. While taking on water at Handub, the train crew spotted fires along the line back to No 1 Post. As the train approached, some 200 Arabs were seen scattering, having placed a pile of sleepers across the track and set fire to them. The rails were already red-hot and as the sappers removed the last of the burning sleepers, so another fire was lit by the Arabs in the rear of the train. Nevertheless, the line was cleared in time for Graham to go by train on the morning of 1 May to Handub, where, escorted by a company of the Shropshires and some Mounted Infantry, he climbed the highest peak of the Waratab range (2000 feet above the sea). The armoured train was now ordered to patrol the line nightly, manned by the East Surreys.

Graham believed that the nightly attacks were partly due to local tribesmen endeavouring to establish their credibility with Osman, against the day when the British withdrew. The material damage was trivial but it served to demonstrate that Osman's opposition had not been eliminated and that holding the line of the railway as far as Otao, let alone Es Sibil, would require constant effort. Indeed, towards the end of April, the expeditionary force was already widely dispersed along the line of the railway. At Otao there were just over 1600 men, comprising mainly the Coldstream Guards and NSW Infantry Battalion, with two guns of 5/1 RA, the Madras Sappers and Miners and detachments of the Camel Corps and Mounted Infantry. A mile or two back, at railhead, there was another 1200 men, consisting of two infantry battalions (Berkshires and Royal Marines) and some Royal Engineers, including some of the Telegraph Company. At Handub, there was the East Surreys and Shropshires, 24 Company RE, 2 guns of the Mountain Battery, 2 squadrons 5th Lancers, 1 squadron 20th Hussars, the NSW Artillery Battery and a mass of transport and other details – in all, some 2200 men. At No 1 Post, there was a detachment of the 17th Bengal Native Infantry. The remainder of the force was located in the main headquarter camp at Suakin close to the railway (3700 men) or on the edge of the harbour, close to Quarantine Island (nearly 2200). When the railway reached Otao on 30 April, some reduction was possible and, as we have seen, the Royal Marines were able to be released. Equally, with the main bulk of stores disembarked and the railway available for transporting men and freight, Graham could expect to reduce his transport and supply organisation considerably. Nevertheless it was obvious that any move beyond Otao was going to require the retention of his fighting troops.

Yet another reconnaissance was made on 29 April, this time towards Hashin, using a mounted column from Suakin and another from Handub.

The two columns met near the site of the old East Surreys' zariba and reconnoitred to beyond Deberet, but saw nothing except two men on camels. Next day (1 May), a small column of Mounted Infantry and Bengal Cavalry reconnoitred as far as M'Neill's zariba at Tofrek. No trace of the Dervishes was found and the column took the precaution of burning what remained of the zariba.

Wolseley had been ordered a fortnight earlier to go to Suakin and report on what should be done there. He arrived at Suakin in the steamship *Queen* on the evening of 2 May. He had never been wildly enthusiastic about the Suakin expedition; he had consistently preferred the Nile route to that from Suakin to Berber and he would have been less than human if he had not begrudged the diversion to Suakin of resources which could have strengthened his own Nile operations. Although Graham was an old friend and Wolseley had been responsible for pushing him, first by giving him a brigade during the Tel-el-Kebir campaign and then by recommending him for the first Suakin expedition, he had by now become somewhat disillusioned by Graham's performance. He had commented in his diary after the action at Hashin on 20 March that 'there seems to have been considerable confusion and greater loss of life than there should have been . . . The fact is that cavalry charges except where the enemy is broken and running away are a mistake with these Arabs'.[14] He was equally unhappy about M'Neill's action at Tofrek: 'although it seems to have taken place within about six miles of Suakin, he seems to have been surprised when making his zariba and to have lost heavily, especially in transport. This is not a good beginning'.[15] Further information only confirmed his view: 'I am disappointed with the beginning that Graham has made. His losses have been inordinate and out of proportion to what he has done: his chief feat has been, as far as I can gather, in shooting his own transport animals when McNeill [sic] was surprised, for surprised he was'.[16]

Characteristically, Wolseley's first observation when he reached Suakin was the absence of enteric (typhoid) fever, from which he drew the immediate (and accurate) conclusion that enteric was due entirely to bad water since all the drinking water at Suakin was distilled and therefore comparatively pure. On the day after his arrival, he had a talk with Chermside, the Governor General of the Red Sea Littoral, who had just been appointed, rather belatedly, Egyptian Commissioner with the Suakin Field Force with effect from 20 March. Although a Royal Engineer like Graham, Chermside was on secondment to the Egyptian Army and clearly saw no particular reason to pull his punches where Graham was concerned. Wolseley noted that 'he [Chermside] did not think much of Graham or of the way in which operations had been conducted here lately. He declares that from the first the truest and most reliable information had been supplied to Graham by the Intelligence Department and that Graham had never consulted him in any way'.[17] This seems to have confirmed Wolseley's own impressions: 'I am afraid that I must give Graham up as incorrigibly stupid. I shall not take him on service any more'.[18] He had also heard criticisms from Greaves, Graham's Chief of Staff, about whom Wolseley now had no illusion either, although he himself had chosen Greaves to accompany Graham: 'Greaves is open-mouthed against him [Graham] but so he would be against any man placed over him in a position that he thought he ought to have. Greaves must have command of a Division and never anything more; he wants discretion and command of temper for an independent command'.[19]

To his wife, Wolseley was even more outspoken and ascribed some of the blame to Greaves himself: 'The force here is all at sixes and sevens. Graham is not exactly brilliant and I don't think Greaves is all he should be to him. Greaves has become too bumptious for the Staff – he should be given a Division under a strong man of decided views'.[20]

A week after he arrived, Wolseley visited the scene of M'Neill's fight at Tofrek, accompanied by Hudson who explained what had happened. As a result of what he heard and saw, Wolseley was even more critical of Graham and Greaves. He could not understand why M'Neill had been sent out with only one squadron of cavalry, instead of the whole available force; too many camels had been sent out in the circumstances; and he thought that M'Neill should not have been surprised (as he thought he had been) because apparently all the spies had warned Graham in advance that Osman meant to attack at the first suitable opportunity while the British were engaged in building their zariba.[21]

Wolseley spent a good deal of time inspecting the troops. He was greatly impressed with the Indian regiments who were all beautifully turned out, 'clean and soldier-like'; the 15th Sikhs, in particular, seemed a splendid body of men, with particularly fine Indian officers. The 5th Lancers, the 20th Hussars, the Berkshires, the Shropshires and the New South Wales Battery were also all beautifully turned out. The villains of the piece were the Coldstream Guards: 'a dirtier, more unsoldierlike set of ragamuffins I never saw on parade; the men were filthily dirty, large numbers of them had no hand guards on their rifles, many of the men had no puggaries and altogether seemed in a very unsatisfactory state'.[22] He was greatly impressed by the *Ganges* which he thought perfectly fitted out although the number of beds (140) seemed small for such a large (4000 tons) ship.

But the main purpose of Wolseley's visit was to assess the future of the railway. Nothing that he saw altered his original lack of enthusiasm for it. Three days after he landed, he telegraphed Hartington, putting the matter bluntly: 'If you have made up your mind to stop railway I propose sending to England ships laden with railway material. Railway should be taken up before troops fall back. We could take it up in a fortnight. Shall I carry out these proposals?'[23] This was going rather faster than Ministers were prepared for. It was going to be hard enough to explain convincingly to the Opposition and to the public the decision which they had just taken to evacuate the Sudan, after all the blood and treasure which had been poured out. To acquiesce in destroying the only thing of tangible value which had been achieved at Suakin was an even more difficult pill to swallow. Accordingly Hartington told Wolseley on 8 May that his proposals were not approved; the line should be held or pushed forward to some convenient, cool spot pending a decision on whether to take it forward to Arriab or even Berber. Could not the local tribes be paid to protect it, he asked?

Wolseley was infuriated. He replied on 11 May, spelling out the facts of life. The railway could not be held if the garrison was to be seriously reduced; it would have to be taken up or simply abandoned. The tribes were in no position to protect the line; they needed protection themselves. If the railway was to be held, then the nearest suitable spot for the troops was six of seven miles beyond Es Sibil, i.e. another 30 miles beyond the present railhead at Otao. Whether any reduction in the number of troops could then be achieved was impossible to say since the country ahead of Es Sibil was not known. If the railway was to be held only as far as Otao it would still need the equivalent of two brigades of infantry, two batteries of artillery, a cavalry regiment and the Mounted Infantry and Camel Corps. Moreover, the Principal Medical Officer's view was that any British unit kept there through the hot weather would need 50 per cent reliefs and would suffer an invaliding rate of 30 per cent. Already, the number of typhoid cases was becoming alarming:[24] 'Unless you have some clearly defined Soudan policy to initiate, any military operations, such as the railway would entail, would be to throw away uselessly valuable lives'.[25] To his wife, Wolseley wrote angrily: 'I won't be a party to the killing of any soldiers to keep a political party in office'.[26]

The Government was in no position to resist Wolseley in the circumstances and on 13 May, Hartington gave Wolseley the go-ahead to take up the railway and send the material back to England. Matters now moved very quickly towards evacuation.

Graham, however, had one last opportunity to strike a blow at Osman Digna's power. Osman himself was inaccessible, in the hills, and it is doubtful if the Intelligence Department actually knew where he was. But it knew where one of his most important subordinates was. Muhammed Adam Sardun was the leader of the Abdurrahmanab clan of the Amarars and a devoted follower of Osman and the Mahdiist cause. When Graham's expedition reached Suakin, Muhammed Adam had been at Hashin with some 2000 men. He had taken little part in the action at Hashin on 20 March and none at all in the attack on M'Neill on 22 March, but he and his men had taken part in the attacks on the convoy to M'Neill on 24 March. Not having taken part in the attack at Tofrek, the Abdurrahmanab had not suffered any very significant casualties and in consequence remained aggressive and cohesive. Since the destruction of Tamai, Muhammed Adam had remained at Therobit, at the western end of the Khor Abent, south-west of Handub. It was

172

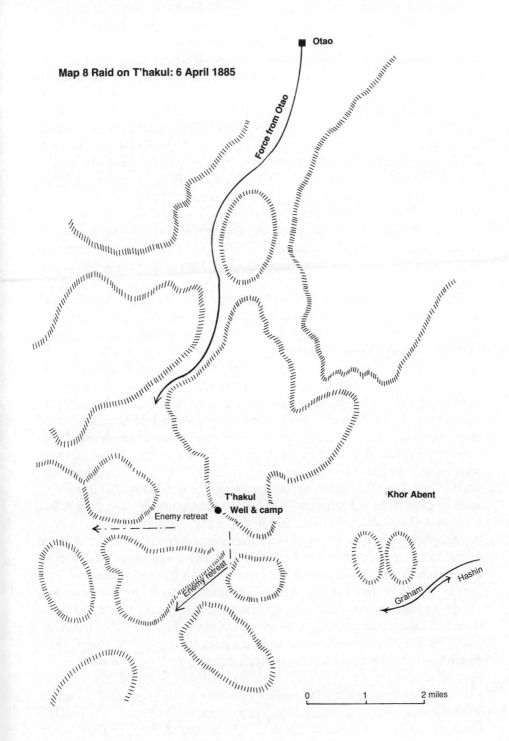

Map 8 Raid on T'hakul: 6 April 1885

Otao

Force from Otao

T'hakul
Well & camp

Enemy retreat

Enemy retreat

Khor Abent

Graham

Hashin

0   1   2 miles

Muhammed Adam's sheep and goats which had been captured by Briggs on 15 April and following that raid, the Abdurrahmanab had moved to T'hakul, 10 miles south of Otao and 18 miles due west, as the crow flies, of Suakin. T'hakul was essentially a side valley of the Khor Abent, containing a large, deep well which enabled Muhammed Adam to maintain substantial flocks of sheep and goats. These enabled him to keep together a force of about 1000 men who had been responsible for the nightly attacks on Otao and Tambuk and the railway generally. He was able to send supplies to Osman in the hills to the west but, above all, his presence at T'hakul with a large, active force acted as a powerful incentive to the other tribes to maintain relations with Osman and not to side with the British. From a military and political point of view, there was a strong case for tackling Muhammed Adam.

The availability of the Camel Corps and the Mounted Infantry, as well as the other cavalry, now gave Graham the opportunity and confidence to undertake a bold operation against T'hakul. Wolseley having given his agreement, the operation was set in hand on 6 May with Graham himself in direct command.

The country was by now fairly well known as a result of the reconnaissances on 15, 18 and 24 April. Graham left Suakin just after midnight on the night of 5/6 May with the 9th Bengal Cavalry, two companies of the Mounted Infantry (Royal Engineers and Guards) and the Camel Corps (877 men in all). It was a sign of the changed times that the force moved at night, in column, with a thin screen of Bengal Cavalry front and rear. It was a very dark night with heavy cloud and movement was initially very slow; Hashin was not reached until nearly 0300 hours. After a short halt, Graham moved on along a relatively easy track through the Khor Abent and with the clouds now dispersing to give a better light. By daybreak (roughly 0530), Graham was within two miles of the entrance to the valley of T'hakul which runs northwards from the Khor Abent for about three miles and is about 1¼ miles wide at its broadest point. The well around which Muhammed Adam was camped was about one mile inside the valley.

Graham moved initially south-westwards across the mouth of the valley to seal it off before turning northwards to attack the encampment; a party of 20 Mounted Infantry was left on the east side of the mouth in case any of the enemy tried to escape that way. The Abdurrahmanab were totally surprised. Small parties endeavoured to escape from the valley mouth and flee westwards and were pursued by a detachment of the Bengal Cavalry. The main body retreated up the valley and took up positions on the west side, from which small lateral valleys running roughly north-westward offered a possibility of escape.

It was now that Graham sprang his surprise. At the same time as he had left Suakin, another column under Major Inglis of the 15th Sikhs, had left Otao, heading south towards T'hakul. It consisted of the 15th Sikhs and a company of Mounted Infantry (673 men in all), with some 200 Sudanese 'friendlies'. The going was easy and by 0530 the Otao column was in position at the north end of the T'hakul valley, effectively sealing it off in that direction. The Mounted Infantry company, which was leading, opened fire on a force of Arabs with camels which was moving up the valley away from Graham's force. Thrown into confusion by the unexpected appearance of the Otao troops from the north, this party of the enemy retreated westwards through one of the small lateral valleys.

In the meantime, Graham's Mounted Infantry, followed by the Guards, Shropshire and Indian Companies of the Camel Corps were moving northwards up the main valley, dislodging Muhammed Adam's men as they clung to the rocks along the west side of the valley. By 0600 the Otao and Suakin columns were in visual communication. Under their combined pressure, the enemy retreated through the lateral valleys to the west, Graham sending a squadron of the Bengal Cavalry in a left flanking move round to the south to try to intercept the flocks of sheep and goat which the enemy was trying to drive off. The rest of the Bengal Cavalry, assisted by the Indian company of the Camel Corps, swept the main valley clear of the flocks which the enemy had failed to get away. By 0700, it was all over. Graham recalled the Otao Mounted Infantry, who had penetrated several miles to the west in pursuit of the enemy, and the united force settled down to water the horses and have breakfast.

Graham had achieved complete surprise. Muhammed Adam and his men had had time only to seize their weapons and flee up the side of the valley; the rest of their property – camel saddles, waterskins, food, clothing and general impedimenta – was left scattered over the site of the encampment. Much more importantly, Graham had captured more than 2000 animals, three standards and three war drums, as well as inflicting an estimated 100 casualties and taking 10 prisoners. One officer and two NCOs had been severely wounded, all from the Suakin column.

At 0900, the Otao column, accompanied by Graham, set off on its return journey and an hour later the Suakin column began its return journey under the command of Colonel A.P. Palmer, 9th Bengal Cavalry, escorting the captured animals. The column was intercepted by small parties of Osman's men, sent from Tamai to help Muhammed Adam, but their fire from the cover of the scrub was desultory and quickly silenced by volleys from the Mounted Infantry and Camel Corps. The Suakin column was back in camp by 1500 hours.

A party of the 28th Bombay Native Infantry, which was protecting a signal party on Dihilbat Hill, was also attacked by parties of the enemy who got to within 300 yards but were driven back by the steady fire of the Indian troops.

Graham's generalship had hitherto been undistinguished and he had come under severe criticism from within his own force and from the newspapers; the *Times* had spoken of Graham and M'Neill having 'committed blunders which would have been unpardonable in a Cadet during his first term at

Sandhurst', a sentiment which Drummond-Hay and his fellow officers had heartily endorsed. But in fairness to Graham, the T'hakul operation had been well planned and remarkably successful. Graham rightly paid tribute to the gallantry, steadiness, discipline and endurance of the troops, some of whom had marched over 40 miles in temperatures of 96°F. The 15th Sikhs, in particular, had marched more than 20 miles on foot. Nevertheless, the coordination between the two columns and the complete surprise achieved were due to good planning and the results were important. Osman's last substantial body of troops had been completely dispersed, in circumstances of some ignominy, and Osman had been deprived of massive supplies. The blow to his prestige and influence was undeniable. Graham was justified in complaining subsequently that the tangible benefits had been thrown away by the decision to evacuate immediately afterwards.

But the operation at T'hakul was remarkable for another reason. Only six weeks after Tofrek, Graham had felt sufficiently confident to take some 1500 men to attack 1000 or more of the enemy, at a distance of 18 miles from his main base at Suakin. That revealed not only a remarkable swing in the psychological balance between the British troops and the Dervishes; it revealed also the value of the Mounted Infantry and Camel Corps. Without their blend of mobility and firepower the operation could not have been undertaken; dismounted cavalry were no substitute, as had been shown at Hashin in March. With his new-found mobility, Graham was now getting into a position where his force could go anywhere – even into the hills to root out Osman. The lesson was clearly not likely to be lost on the surrounding tribes. In that way, also, the prestige of Osman had been severely undermined.

The action at T'hakul was Graham's swan-song. Osman and his supporters were not wholly cowed – the night after Graham's column got back to Suakin, the railway was raided between the West Redoubt and No 1 Post, and telegraph poles removed and taken off to Tamai. But active operations as far as the British were concerned were over and within days the expeditionary force was breaking up. The Grenadier Guards were withdrawn from Otao on 15 May and embarked in the *Jumna* at Suakin the same evening; the Scots Guards followed the next day from Tambuk, while the Coldstream Guards embarked the same day on the *Deccan*. The NSW Contingent left Suakin on the 17th. Rather surprisingly, Graham also left on the 17th in the *Deccan*, leaving Wolseley behind for another two days to take decisions about the disposal of stores and material.

Wolseley had no illusions about the quality or value of the railway so far completed. On 15 May, he had had a long talk with Captain Constable of the Royal Engineers, who had had ten years experience on the Rajputana Railway in India; 'He described this line here as the worst he had ever seen; not even the sidings on a contractor's line are usually so bad. Instead of about 2000 sleepers per mile, there are not he says more than about 1200. The rails are laid level instead of with the usual cant inwards of about 1 in 20, and consequently all the wheels have very little bearing on the rails. The fish plates are not fitted to the rails; the engines cannot drag up more than seven carriages, and yet the gradients are not more than 1 in 100. Altogether a more pitiable attempt to construct a railway, or a more wretched railway when constructed it would be difficult to conceive'.[27] Wolseley had been along the railway to Otao and back, and had seen it all for himself. Nevertheless, he was acutely conscious of the bad political effects, both in England and at Suakin, of taking up the railway which had been so recently and expensively laid. Without much optimism, he had therefore ordered Chermside to try to work out a scheme with the local 'friendly' tribes to protect the railway, in return for arms, ammunition and a regular subsidy of grain. With an armoured train and a little help from 'friendlies' located at Handub and Otao, Wolseley thought that it ought to be just possible to keep the line open. He was not optimistic, not under-rating the power of Osman to threaten and coerce the tribes once the British force had gone. Nevertheless, he had determined not to take up the line even if the 'friendlies' would not agree to protect it. On the afternoon of the 18th, Brewster and Molyneux of the Intelligence Department, who had been conducting the negotiations, came to tell him that despite – or perhaps because of – the British departure, the friendly chiefs had declined to accept any responsibility for the railway; they were, they said, not strong enough to hold Otao and Handub against Osman. Wolseley felt that he had done his duty by the Government in trying to arrange some form of native protection for the railway. Now he was under pressure from the commander at Otao and Handub to remove the troops there in view of the increasing heat. Wolseley had no interest in sacrificing soldiers' lives purely for party political ends and he promptly ordered all work on the railway to cease immediately, and for withdrawal back to Suakin to start at once. There remained the problem of what to do with the mass of railway material which had accumulated on shore and on ships in the harbour. Wolseley had hoped that the Indian Government could be prevailed upon to buy some, if not all, of this material but that Government refused point blank, having been kept accurately informed of its provenance and quality. In the end, some of the material was left to moulder away at Suakin – the sea air quickly reduced it to rust. Some of it was made into spearheads by Osman's men. Some of it went to prop up the houses in Suakin. The Egyptian Government was 'conned' into accepting 500 tons of rolling stock for the 3' 6" gauge railway up the Nile – when the rolling stock arrived, it was found to be standard-gauge. (The ship in which it was sent was called, felicitously, the *Dotterel*.) Finally, the War Office decided to keep 60 miles of rails for possible use at bases in the United Kingdom. It was stored on the remote Thames marshes, at Plumpstead. In due course, when public attention had wandered elsewhere, it was quietly sold off.

Wolseley sailed from Suakin on 18 May for Suez and Cairo, taking with him M'Neill, who was ill, and leaving Greaves behind to superintend the

177

final evacuation and disposal of stores, and Hudson to command the reduced garrison which was to remain.

Disposal of the thousands of transport animals was the major problem in winding up the expedition. Many of the mules went back to Egypt where Stephenson had a use for them; the remainder went back to India. Some of the camels also went back to India and Egypt and some were sold to local buyers. Many camels were in a poor state from disease and overwork, and they were shot. According to Wylde 'some of the camels were sent outside Suakin into the middle of the Red Sea, hauled up from the vessel's hold and swung over the side, shot and dropped into the sea; others, in batches of fifty, were taken down to the ends of the jetties, shot through the head, thrown into the sea, and when the batch was got through, tied to a line and towed out of the harbour'.[28] When Wylde suggested that it might have been more sensible to give the beasts to the local tribes, he was told that strict orders required them all to be destroyed.

As the stations along the railway line were evacuated, they were quickly occupied by Osman's men and the final trains sent on their way with a fusillade of shots. On 25 May, the armoured train ran out towards Handub and found that half a mile of track and sleepers had already been removed.

By the end of May, it was virtually all over and Greaves left Suakin on 6 June, arriving in Cairo on 9 June. Wolseley found him very well and jolly now that he was free from Graham's supervision.

One last bonus was left for Suakin. At its meeting on 27 April 1885, the Mobilisation Committee's Sub-Committee on Water Supply had approved the purchase of two large condensers, each capable of distilling 30,000 gallons a day, for erection on land at Suakin to replace the use of condensing vessels which were very expensive to operate. At the end of May, one condenser was ready for shipment at Liverpool and the other was nearly ready. The decision was taken to send them to Suakin since there would continue to be some British troops there in garrison. They were in due course erected on Quarantine Island, which was re-named Condenser Island, and the citizens of Suakin were able to enjoy the pleasures of pure distilled water as an alternative to the wells at Shata and Gemeiza.

NOTES

1. Hansard, 27 February 1885, Col. 1620.
2. It included a silk necktie, three coloured flannel shirts (but only two pairs of drawers), a spine pad, tropical helmet and a pair of blue goggles.
3. Not to be confused with Brigadier General H.P. ('Croppy') Ewart, commanding the Cavalry Brigade.
4. De Cosson, op cit, p122.
5. Coldstream Guards, New South Wales Battalion, 2 guns 5/1 RA, Mounted Infantry and 17 (Field) Coy. RE.
6. Letter dated 9 April 1885 – NAM 6807-269.
7. Drummond-Hay, op cit, p   .

8. The spelling of these names varies in official returns – for example, *Deb-el-Bahr* appears on occasion as *Deh-el-Babe*, although this may be a simple clerical error.
9. At any given moment one ship was de-scaling and cleaning its boilers.
10. Appendix II to Graham's Final Despatch of 30 May 1885 gives a total of 58 horses, 100 mules and 241 camels died or destroyed. This is certainly an underestimate since more than 500 camels were apparently lost at Tofrek. Even so, the losses were by no means heavy and compare very favourably with other campaigns.
11. Wylde, op cit, Vol II, p115.
12. Graham to Hartington, despatch dated 22 April 1885.
13. Sometimes, and possibly more accurately, rendered as Dissibil.
14. Preston, op cit, p174.
15. Diary for 22 March 1885 – ibid, p174.
16. Diary for 26 March 1885 – ibid, p177.
17. Diary for 3 May 1885 – ibid, p204.
18. Ibid.
19. Ibid.
20. Letter dated 5 May 1885 – quoted in Arthur, op cit, p214.
21. Preston, op cit, p209.
22. Diary 6 May 1885 – Preston, op cit, p206. Drummond-Hay was presumably blissfully ignorant of this devastating criticism – at least, he does not mention it in his diary. The Commander-in-Chief, the Duke of Cambridge, was predictably outraged by this criticism of the Queen's Household troops.
23. Wolseley to Hartington 8 May 1885.
24. This contrasts with Wolseley's earlier reference to the absence of enteric (typhoid) fever at Suakin. But he was now keen to close down the Suakin operation and presumably was prepared to use any lever he could.
25. Wolseley to Hartington 11 May 1885.
26. Arthur, op cit, p215.
27. Diary for 15 May 1885 – Preston, op cit, p211-12.
28. Wylde, op cit, Vol II, p156.

12

Debits and Credits

THE DECISION of the Government to withdraw from the Sudan and to abandon the attempt to smash the Mahdi and avenge Gordon was greeted with deep and widespread dismay in England. The death of Gordon had aroused deep emotions in all classes of society, among Government supporters as well as among the Opposition. The Queen's distress was well known. Once the tardy decision to attempt a relief expedition had been decided upon, huge efforts in terms of resources and personnel had been deployed. Through war correspondents such as Bennet Burleigh and Melton Prior, the British public had been able to follow at close second-hand the progress of the Relief Expedition, to share vicariously in the hardships and progress of the troops, and in the tragic feelings of disappointment over the news of the fall of Khartoum and Gordon's lonely death. Gordon could not be brought back to life but Khartoum could be recaptured and the power of Mahdiism destroyed. The instrument in the form of Wolseley and his expeditionary force was available and even if it needed reinforcement and a period for re-fitting, England expected that in the autumn of 1885 at latest the re-conquest of the Sudan would be set in hand. A significant part in that re-conquest was represented by the Suakin to Berber railway, which many still believed to be the best route to Khartoum, and by Graham's attempt to destroy the Mahdiist power in the Eastern Sudan.

In Gladstone's Cabinet, the decision to abandon the Sudan, and the Suakin-Berber railway was fiercely opposed. In the month after the decision in April at least half of the Cabinet threatened resignation. The Pendjeh crisis, which Gladstone had claimed as the main justification for pulling out Wolseley's and Graham's troops, subsided almost as quickly as it had arisen. Wolseley was bitterly contemptuous of the Government's decision to scuttle: 'Of all the miserable, foolish policies this is the worst. I have protested against it with all earnestness, but party exigencies make it necessary'.[1] He felt, not unreasonably, that he had been the victim of a lack of candour: 'Assuming that we are not to have an Autumn Campaign, it is a cruel absurdity that our silly Cabinet did not in the *first* instance order me to concentrate and fall back at once when they ascertained that Gordon was dead. They made a great splash to save their places'.[2] Baring, no sentimentalist and no profligate with public money, was equally horrified, and pressured the pliant Granville.

The decision to abandon the Suakin railway excited particular criticism. Even if the Sudan and its reconquest had to be abandoned, it seemed sensible not to abandon the railway to Berber, whose extension would be important economically and socially, as well as militarily when the reconquest of the Sudan was taken up again. (Few people expected that the delay would last more than ten years.) Baring again represented to Granville the importance of the railway. He was backed up by Bennett Burleigh in the columns of the *Daily Telegraph*. The redoubtable Baroness Burdett-Coutts, supported by the Anti-Slavery Society, pointed out the moral importance of the railway as an aid to suppressing slavery. In the House of Lords, the Earl of Wemyss initiated a debate on a motion to continue the war against the Mahdi and to complete the Suakin to Berber railway.

It was all to no avail. Gladstone could not be shifted; he had never had his heart in the Sudan enterprise and he was able to manipulate the crisis with Russia to defeat any attempt to re-open the Sudan decision.

Against this background, it was not surprising that Graham received something of a hero's welcome when he finally reached England on 14 June, having stopped off en route to stay with another distinguished Royal Engineer, Sir Lintorn Simmons, now Governor of Malta. Graham not only fitted the popular Victorian image of a general, with his imposing appearance and the VC on his breast; he served as a focus for popular sentiment over the decision to abandon the Sudan and to leave Gordon, his friend, unavenged. He received the Grand Cross of the Order of St Michael and St George and the thanks of both Houses of Parliament. To his already imposing array of medals, he was able to add another clasp ('Suakin 1885') to the three he already possessed on his Egypt Medal ('El Teb', 'Tamai' and 'El Teb-Tamai'); he already had the Khedive's Egyptian Star with two clasps.

Although he was only 54, he was not employed again and in June 1890, he was placed on the Retired List. While it may appear a little surprising that no post was found for him in the Army or War Office, the fact was that his conduct of the 1885 campaign had served merely to strengthen the doubts and criticisms that had followed his earlier campaign in 1884. Given the very large scale of the 1885 expedition, there was bound to be criticism of the apparently meagre results. After the employment of nearly 13,000 men and the expenditure of more than £3,000,000, all there was to show for it was a mere 18½ miles of badly built railway and a long line of graves. Osman Digna remained unsubdued and within weeks of the evacuation of Graham's expeditionary force, Suakin was again in its usual state of intermittent siege.

Graham had come under general criticism within his own force from the beginning and it cannot be said that it was unfair. The remarkably careless and incompetent way in which the unit camps had initially been scattered over the desert outside Suakin, and the almost nightly attacks which had followed, had disturbed morale at the very beginning and aroused doubts as to the higher direction of the enterprise. No doubt Greaves, as Chief of Staff,

181

must bear part of the blame but Graham, as the commander, must bear the ultimate responsibility and the fact that it took him several weeks to correct a situation whose defects were apparent even to the lowliest private is a severe indictment of his capability. It is the more surprising in that, as an Engineer officer, he could have been expected to be more than familiar with the principles of laying out camps.

The expedition to Hashin offered further food for uneasiness. It was by no means clear to those who thought about it that the construction of a post there offered any real value in relation to operations elsewhere, and particularly those along the Tamai line. In any case, if a post at Hashin was desirable, why was it necessary to attack Dihilbat Hill and incur casualties and some risks? The fact that the battalion left to garrison Hashin simply could not be kept supplied once operations developed along the Tamai line and had to be withdrawn after only five days was proof enough to most people that the whole Hashin operation was pointless. The criticisms of the Tofrek operation have already been analysed; again, the fact that when ultimately Tamai was occupied, the bird was found to have flown to a place where he could not be followed added to the general lack of confidence in Graham's direction. It was not helped by the widespread knowledge that Graham did not consult his staff and played his cards so close to his chest that even his closest subordinates did not know what, if anything, he was planning. It was an easy jump from that to believing that the reason for not disclosing his plans was because he had no real plans.

In retrospect, it can be seen that there was a great deal of force in the contention expressed by people like Wylde and Gambier-Perry that Graham's proper strategy should have been to concentrate from the start on pushing forward the railway, rather than seeking a pitched battle with Osman. Graham clearly did not appreciate that Osman had learned from his defeats at El Teb and Tamai the previous year. Osman was too conscious of his losses to risk a head-on collision with a formed British square; hence his decision, known to Graham, to attack only when the British were in process of building a zariba or otherwise not fully in position. By concentrating on construction of the railway, Graham would have forced Osman into a difficult dilemma; he could either attack in an effort to halt construction, in which case he played into Graham's hands or, alternatively, he could hold off, allow the railway to proceed, and see his power and influence slip away. Moreover, as the railway advanced, so it increasingly provided Graham with mobility for men and supplies which further lengthened the odds against Osman. There is no indication that Graham ever analysed the options in this way although one must assume that his staff at least put the arguments to him.

That Graham had not fully learned the real lessons of the 1884 campaign was evident in his slowness to appreciate the importance of mobility. By the time that the Camel Corps was created, the campaign was in effect nearly over. Yet the success of the operation against Muhammed Adam Sardun at

T'hakul showed what could have been achieved if Graham had appreciated fully the value of mounted troops and had equipped himself accordingly from the beginning.

By the end of the campaign, Graham's reputation among his own officers was at a low ebb, and the war correspondents ensured that the criticisms were being echoed in the newspapers. In particular, the near-disaster at Tofrek had aroused a good deal of public unhappiness in England, much of it ill-directed because it was based upon scanty and sometimes highly inaccurate newspaper reports. No doubt, a good deal of criticism had also filtered back in officers' letters; it is unlikely, for example, that the comments made by Drummond-Hay remained restricted to his diary. Hartington had had to answer a number of Parliamentary Questions, pointedly aimed at the performance of Graham and M'Neill. Because of this, Wolseley had been specifically charged with investigating the affair as part of his visit to Suakin. He was extremely loath to undertake it: 'It is hopeless to expect to find a General who does not make mistakes' he wrote frankly to Hartington 'To examine minutely into any faulty dispositions that may have been made, and to publish to the world a condemnation of them, simply takes away from the General implicated all the confidence of his troops without, as far as I can see, any compensating good result whatever'.[3] There was no official action as a result of Wolseley's investigations but the unofficial result was equally disastrous for Graham because Wolseley himself had lost faith in him. 'I have had some talk with McNiell [sic] regarding the late operations near Suakin' Wolseley recorded in his diary. 'He says the Staff sent out were horribly bad. Graham was not equal to the task; he can fight a Brigade, but he can organise nothing. His plans were bad; they were badly designed and misfortune overtook all he attempted. The expedition he sent McNiell on was very badly conceived in every way and from every point of view'.[4] He heard much the same from Greaves later in Cairo. M'Neill was an old and close comrade of Wolseley, having served with him in the Red River Expedition, the Ashanti Expedition and in the 1882 Egyptian Campaign. His views were likely powerfully to influence Wolseley, who must have been conscious that it was his (Wolseley's) advice which had put Graham (and Greaves) in command of the Suakin expedition. In addition to being the dominating figure in the Army, Wolseley was still Adjutant-General, responsible directly to the Secretary of State for War for all matters concerning the promotions and careers of all officers. He was therefore in a position to ensure that Graham was not employed again.

On his showing in the two Suakin campaigns, Graham had no great talents as a general. He clearly had difficulty in conveying his intentions to his subordinates. Thus at El Teb and at Hashin, his cavalry commanders committed blunders which might have been avoided if they had been absolutely clear as to what was and was not required. Ewart, it is true, was probably an indifferent or even incompetent commander, but Stewart was regarded by Wolseley and others as the most brilliant cavalry leader of his day. At Tamai, in March 1884, Graham committed the most elementary mistake in ordering the front face of the square to charge. He was rescued from total disaster only by the accident of Buller's brigade being sufficiently far behind to be able to pour in an enfilading fire to rescue Davis's brigade. A factor in that mistake may have been his dissatisfaction with the conduct of the Black Watch at El Teb which was in turn largely due to his failure to impose his tactical concept on his troops. His responsibility in relation to the near-disaster at Tofrek has already been discussed.

There was indeed no real reason to expect him to be a talented field commander. Although he had seen a good deal of active service as a subaltern (and shown the appropriate gallantry), he had seen no active service during his twenty years as a middle-ranking officer. When he arrived to command a brigade at Tel-el-Kebir in 1882 as a major-general he had never commanded anything larger than a company. While he did well in Egypt in 1882, it was hardly sufficient to demonstrate that he was a natural operational commander. Many men who are competent subordinates are totally lost when placed in independent command.

What was surprising was that Graham showed no great talents in those areas where, as an Engineer officer, he might have been expected to be in his element. We are here face to face with the unhappy saga of the railway. That it was a disaster was apparent to contemporaries. After three months work, a total of 18½ miles of track had been laid across flat desert requiring virtually no engineering work at all. Moreover, this work itself was of the shoddiest kind and the operation of the line remarkable for its incompetence. As the *Times* correspondent pointed out 'only 1100 yards a day were laid over a country much easier than Hyde Park and quite as easy as that in India and the United States where from three to seven miles would be quite possible. Had the expedition gone on and the railway been laid at the same rate . . . Berber would not have been reached until July next year; that is to say, that the protecting army would have had to spend 16 months on a road which has been constantly travelled by camels in 10 days'.[5] That much of this incompetence and delay was due entirely to the civilian contractors is not at issue. Nor should Graham's difficulties under the system of divided responsibility imposed on him from London be underestimated. But from the very beginning, it was clear that the railway could be built only by steadily increasing Army assistance. As the *Times* again put it 'The actual construction work done by Messrs Lucas and Aird's men was the spacing out of the sleepers, placing the rails, spiking them down, screwing up a fish plate here and there . . . and straightening the line when it was being ballasted. The rest of the construction was done by the Army'.[6] It is hard to believe that a Wolseley or a Kitchener would have allowed this situation to persist for even a week. They would have insisted upon taking over complete responsibility for what was, on any sober analysis, the real strategic objective of the campaign.[7] That Graham was slow to grasp this strategic fact and, having grasped it, was unable to exert the necessary initiative to take control of the railway work is harsh proof that he was not really up to command of the expedition in 1885.

His failure could not be ascribed in any way to a shortage of resources. In relation to its task and duration, the Suakin expedition of 1885 was certainly one of the most expensive in resources undertaken by the British Army in the 19th century. At its peak, at the end of April 1885, Graham disposed of nearly 13,000 fighting troops, 10,000 native followers and labourers and more than 15,000 animals – more, in fact, than Wolseley had used in his Nile campaign. When it was over, it had cost almost exactly £3,000,000 of which the railway had cost £865,000 or roughly £47,000 a mile. By contrast, the Second Afghan War, which had finished four years earlier, had cost £19,500,000 although it had lasted ten times longer; the 133 miles of railway from the Indus to the foot of the Bolan Pass, built in 101 days, had cost only some £5,000,000.

Given the scale of the expedition, the staff work in England and in India in assembling the necessary troops, equipping and storing them, and despatching them to Suakin had been of a very high order. Even to a modern logistician, the speed with which the expedition had been prepared and the comprehensive nature of its supplies excites admiration, given the relatively primitive administrative techniques and methods of transport then available. The early and successful attention paid to the question of water supplies, with its concomitant of remarkably low rates of sickness, is particularly noteworthy. The staff work during the campaign, although never bad, was not remarkable for its quality; as we have seen, M'Neill, who was basically a fighting soldier, thought the staff to be horribly bad, and undoubtedly many of the best officers were already with Wolseley on the Nile. Judgement is, however, difficult to pronounce since it is clear that, like most Victorian soldiers, Graham had no real grasp of the way to use a staff and kept his own largely in ignorance of his plans and intentions. Probably the staff was as good as it was allowed to be.

If there was one aspect of the expedition which shone brightly it was the performance of the troops themselves. The conditions in which they marched and fought and rested were by any standards extraordinarily severe – daytime temperatures which hovered constantly in the high 80s and 90s, reaching well over 100°F in the tents, and rarely dropping below 70° at night, with only the occasional breeze to cool; soft sand, rock and prickly scrub to march through; water which was often boiling when it came out of the tanks; and constant dust. Even in camp the ration of two gallons of water a day was little enough to meet the combined demands of cooking, washing and thirst. Nor was the food, especially in the field, particularly appetising – often only hard biscuit and tinned meat which was almost liquid when it emerged from the tin. Yet in these conditions, the troops often marched extraordinary distances, with relatively few men falling out and with very low rates of sickness. During the operations against T'hakul, on 6 May, the 15th Sikhs marched 10 miles out from Otao, fought an action, and then marched back without casualties of any kind. In the same action, the mounted troops from Suakin covered 40 miles, largely in the heat of the day. Moreover, they were fighting an enemy who, in terms of courage, imperviousness to wounds and sheer ferocity, had no equal in British Army history. That few Sudanese prisoners were taken and that Sudanese wounded were habitually killed was less a reflection on the troops than a comment on the fanaticism of Osman's followers. In their own way, the British soldiers admired the 'Fuzzie-Wuzzies' while being under no illusion as to their deadliness.

The Indian Contingent attracted universal praise for its efficiency and adaptability. The sepoys were professionals with longer average service than the British soldiers, and many of them with much active service on the North West Frontier of India. They were hardy, well-disciplined and their camp equipment and transport at regimental level, based upon years of campaigning in India, was superior to that of the British Army. Each regiment brought with it sufficient pack mules or ponies and stretcher bearers to enable it to march out on operations the moment it landed, in marked distinction to the British regiments who arrived with no transport and had to learn painfully how to handle the animals they were issued with at Suakin. The failure of the 17th Bengal Native Infantry at Tofrek was an unfortunate mark against the Indian troops but it did not affect the general perception of the efficiency and steadiness of the remainder, and it is note-worthy that in the latter stages of the campaign Graham came to rely heavily on the Indian units – particularly the 9th Bengal Cavalry and the 15th Sikhs. At T'hakul, for example, the Bengal Cavalry were the only regular cavalry used, while the 15th Sikhs were the only regular infantry present. The Madras Sappers and Miners had always had a high reputation – even Roberts, who was notoriously critical of the quality of Madras troops, had made an exception in their case. In turn, Graham was moved to refer to them as 'first-rate troops, whether for fighting or for work'. Ironically, a year earlier, Wolseley had been dismissive of the possible use of Indian troops. 'It is very doubtful if even the very best of our Indian regiments could stand the charges of the Arabs, such as those which our troops had recently to encounter near Suakin' he wrote to Hartington on 8 April 1884. 'Then, again, Indian regiments take the field encumbered with numerous followers and in operations through desert countries every additional mouth to feed is a matter of consequence, especially when that mouth is not that of a fighting man'.

The British infantry battalions all seem to have performed well once a little jumpiness at night initially had been overcome by experience. Again, whether by coincidence or not, Graham seems to have relied upon the Berk-shires and the Royal Marines more than the other regiments in the early stages but this may have been simply due to the fact that these two regiments had been at Suakin since January 1885 and were therefore more acclimatised. Graham in his final Despatch, referred to the 2nd Brigade as having been 'composed of three remarkably fine battalions' but whereas the Berkshires and East Surreys played a full part in the early actions, the Shropshires were kept mainly at Suakin or on convoy escort, although they played a fuller part along the railway in the later stages.

The Guards Brigade was composed of battalions which had seen no service since the Crimean War or even earlier. Accustomed chiefly to service in London, it was a tribute to them that they could be plucked out of ceremonial duties, transported at short notice to Suakin and pitched into active operations, and yet perform well. So far as one can judge, they were the equal as fighting troops of any of the other regiments present, although none of the British troops equalled the Indian regiments in cleanliness and turn-out! The British cavalry squadrons were, on the whole, less effective than the 9th Bengal Cavalry.

The Royal Engineers played a prominent part throughout – whether in building defences, constructing railways, operating the telegraph system or operating the observation balloon. Very nearly four full companies were present and their work was vital. The Royal Artillery played an unusually small part for the Royal Regiment. Graham might perhaps have made more use of his guns but the opportunities were, in fairness, relatively limited – this was not a gunners' war and potentially the most useful weapons – the Gardners and Gatlings – were largely in the hands of the Royal Navy who had the most experience of them. Of the other departmental corps – all of whom played essential, if not glamorous, roles – a word needs to be said of the Commissariat and Transport Corps. While there was initially at least a certain degree of chaos at the dockside as stores poured in, the fact was that, by dint of huge labour, the Corps succeeded in feeding the whole expedition and providing it with water throughout the duration. There were no cases of the troops not getting their rations or their water allowance.

Of all the troops present, the most remarkable were the New South Wales Contingent if only because it was the first time that Colonial forces had been sent overseas to assist the British Army. They arrived too late to take part in the Hashin operations or Tofrek, and so they saw very little excitement except for the march to Tamai. For the rest, it was tedious garrison duty along the railway line, except for the fortunate few who joined the Camel Corps. Nevertheless, what they did they did efficiently. The infantry battalion was perhaps marginally more effective than the artillery battery which had to struggle with an unfamiliar pattern of gun and unbroken animals. But the whole contingent was warmly regarded by everyone and their physique was equalled only by the Sikhs.[8] There was a hint of things to come in a noticeable informality of dress!

Of the British regiments that took part in the two campaigns, one (the York and Lancasters) elected to be disbanded in 1968 rather than be amalgamated with other Yorkshire regiments. The cavalry regiments had all been amalgamated in 1922. The Black Watch and the three Guards regiments retain their separate existences today but the Gordon Highlanders is merged with the Queen's Own Highlanders. The East Surreys are swallowed up in the amorphous mass of the Princess of Wales's Own Regiment; the Royal Irish Fusiliers are part of the resurrected Royal Irish Regiment; the Shropshires exist as part of the Light Infantry, and the Berkshires form part of the Duke of Edinburgh's Royal Regiment, which is to be amalgamated with the Gloucestershires. Even the King's Royal Rifle Corps now forms part of the Royal Greenjackets.

The Indian regiments had an equally mixed fate. Perhaps not surprisingly, the 17th Bengal Native Infantry did not survive the post-First World War re-organisation of the Indian Army; clearly its failure at Tofrek was never forgotten. The 28th Bombay Native Infantry survived as part of the Bombay Pioneers until 1932 when all Pioneer regiments in the Indian Army were disbanded. Happily, the 15th Sikhs survives today as part of the Sikh Regiment of the modern Indian Army; the 9th Bengal Cavalry (later Lancers) survives as part of the 4th Horse of the same Army. That splendid body of men, the Madras Sappers and Miners, survives as part of the Indian Engineers.

The New South Wales battalion had been an ad-hoc formation and disappeared on its return to Sydney. But it was the forerunner of the magnificent Australian battalions that stormed Gallipoli in 1915 and went on to create an imperishable reputation in France and Flanders. Their splendid physique and notorious informality of dress had, as we have seen, been noticed thirty years earlier.

It had not been a war of any great technological innovation. The single shot, breechloading rifle had been with the British Army for nearly 20 years, and the machine gun had been used in both the Second Afghan and Zulu Wars, six years before, and even earlier in the Ashanti campaign. The electric telegraph and heliograph had also a respectable lineage of service, although the use of a telegraph wagon advancing with the troops and keeping the commander continuously in touch with his base, as at Tofrek, was a new and important tactical innovation. The one noteworthy piece of new technology was the balloon, and it was an enormous pity that it was used only twice. It proved very sensitive to wind conditions but on the one suitable day, when it was flown for some nine hours, it amply fulfilled expectations. For the rest, it was an old-fashioned war in which even artillery played little part and the fighting was determined by the rifle and the bayonet. But if the two expeditions had been unexciting technologically, they had demonstrated a new and important advance in the speed and competence with which the British Army was able to mount an overseas expedition. From the moment that the Cabinet took its decision to send a force to Suakin in February 1885 until Graham made his first advance was only five weeks. The speed with which the troops and their equipment and stores were deployed overseas was impressive by any standard. Moreover it was not only the speed which was remarkable. The quality of the administration was equally impressive. Despite the increasing demands of modern warfare, the needs of the troops had been met with no significant shortages; the standard of medical care, for example, had never been higher and there had been a remarkable absence of disease. From that point of view, the two expeditions had been a distinct success.

For the senior officers, the future held mixed fortunes. Graham was offered the Governorship of Bermuda in 1888 but was forced to decline it for personal reasons. At some stage after 1887 there seems to have been a separation from his wife, for reasons which are not clear, and from 1889 he had no permanent home, only a series of temporary residences. He spent most of his time travelling, showing a highly cultivated interest in pictures. He lost much of his money in a lead-processing company which collapsed. But he was for a time a director of the Maxim-Nordenfeldt Company and thus by chance involved in the development of the first wholly successful and reliable machine gun; it was to be used to great effect when the re-conquest of the Sudan was undertaken in 1897. He died at the end of 1899 while the British Army was suffering disaster in the Second Boer War.

Wolseley served on to become Commander-in-Chief of the British Army in succession to that hitherto immovable figure, the Duke of Cambridge. But the Nile Expedition marked the zenith of his career. Hitherto successful in all he had undertaken, the failure to relieve Gordon marked a point at which Wolseley's brilliant career started to point downhill. By the time he retired in 1900, his capacities and his reputation were both diminished and Roberts had overtaken him. If he had become Commander-in-Chief earlier, he might still have done great things for the Army and conceivably have obviated or prevented much of the catastrophe and confusion which surrounded the early part of the Second Boer War. He died in 1913.

Despite his failure as a cavalry commander, 'Croppy' Ewart continued his career in Court circles and ultimately achieved a knighthood and a major generalship, for largely non-military duties. M'Neill did not serve again nor Lyon Fremantle, who seems to have been a competent officer. Lower down, A.P. Palmer, who had commanded the 9th Bengal Cavalry, went on to become a full general and Commander-in-Chief in India in 1900. E.P. Leach, who had commanded 24 Field Company, also rose to be a full general. Hudson, who seems to have been a most competent officer, went on to become Commander-in-Chief of the Bombay Army in 1893 but died the same year as a result of a riding accident.

Of those officers who had served in the 1884 expedition, only two rose to the heights. Despite an ambiguous performance as Wolseley's Chief of Staff during the Gordon Relief Expedition, Buller rose steadily under Wolseley's patronage. By 1887, he was Quarter-Master-General of the British Army, succeeding Wolseley as Adjutant General in 1890. In 1899, he was sent out to South Africa as Commander-in-Chief against the Boers but after a disastrous series of defeats, was replaced by Roberts. He returned home to resume command of the Aldershot Command but was forced to retire prematurely in 1903 as a result of criticising the Government publicly. Plumer, of the Yorks and Lancasters, commanded the 2nd Army in France 1915-18. Stewart, who had commanded the cavalry of El Teb and Tamai, also went up the Nile with Wolseley. He was killed commanding the Desert Column which reached Khartoum two days after it had fallen; it fell to Buller to conduct the retreat of the Column. Valentine Baker, that tragic figure, never fully recovered from the face wound he had received at El Teb; he died in Cairo in 1887 at the relatively early age of 60. If he had ever been guilty of the charge of indecent assault in 1875 – which seems highly improbable – his subsequent career and service had amply made up for it; the loss was entirely the British Army's. Percy Barrow, who had been so severely wounded at El Teb, commanded a squadron of the 19th Hussars with great distinction in Wolseley's Relief Expedition; like Baker, he never recovered from his wounds and died in Cairo in 1886 at the very early age of 38. Fred Burnaby, that extraordinary figure, was also killed with the Desert Column, at Abu Klea. A.K. Wilson ('Old 'Ard 'Eart', as he was called by the sailors) – he who had knocked over his Dervish attackers at El Teb with his enormous fists – rose to become an Admiral of the Fleet and First Sea Lord in 1910. He made a surprising, if ultimately disappointing, reappearance as an adviser to Winston Churchill at the Admiralty in 1914.

Chermside, who spent most of his life in diplomatic rather than military posts, became Military Attaché in Constantinople in 1889 and from there went on to be Military Commissioner and Commander of the British troops in Crete from 1897-9, in the aftermath of the Greco-Turkish War. He commanded the 3rd Division in South Africa in 1900, without great success; his last post was as Governor of Queensland from 1902-1904.

Among the politicians, Gladstone, whose Government was defeated by the Conservatives in June 1885, largely as a result of the failure to relieve Gordon, resumed office as Prime Minister in February 1886 but held it only for a few months. He formed his fourth and last Government in 1892. He died at the age of 89 in 1898. Hartington split with Gladstone over Home Rule for Ireland; when the Conservatives won the election in June 1886, he was offered the premiership by Salisbury but refused it. He refused it again at the end of 1886. Nine years later, having succeeded to the title as Duke of Devonshire, he joined Salisbury's third Conservative government as Lord Privy Seal. He resigned in September in 1903 over the issue of free trade and died in 1908. But in 1888, he had performed one service which might have had the most profound benefits for the British Army – he had chaired a Royal Commission which had recommended sweeping reforms to the higher organisation of the War Office, including the abolition of the office of Commander-in-Chief and the formation of a General Staff headed by a Chief of General Staff, with a War Office Council identical with the later Army

Council. The recommendations were thwarted by Campbell-Bannerman and the ageing Commander-in-Chief, the Duke of Cambridge. If the recommendations had been properly implemented, much of the confusion and waste of the Second Boer War might have been avoided. Granville was Colonial Secretary in Gladstone's short-lived government of 1886 but held no further office, dying in 1891 while the Conservatives were still in power.

When Graham sailed from Suakin on 17 May 1885, one fact was indisputable; despite two large-scale expeditions against him, Osman Digna was still in the field. Both in 1884 and 1885, Osman was able to say that the British had come, fought and been forced to sail away again. Suakin in the summer of 1885 was superficially what it had been for three years – a besieged town in which the garrison ruled only as far as the range of their guns. Graham was correct in warning (and implicitly criticising) the Government in his final Despatch as to the poor effects of the evacuation: 'At the period at which the evacuation of the advanced posts commenced, the political question was practically solved. A large number of the Amarars had placed themselves unconditionally at my disposal, and a movement in our favour, which even embraced some of the Hadendowa clans, was on foot. It will be a matter of regret if the evacuation of the advanced posts prevents any advantage being derived from this movement and the more so since the dissolution of the Amarar League in its infancy may serve to restore Osman Digna's prestige and to throw increased power into his hands.'[9] As for the railway, poorly constructed as it was and devoid of any immediate economic impact, it was clearly destined to disappear and thus remove the only tangible monument to the two expeditions.

It is not surprising therefore that the judgement of history so far has been that both of the Suakin expeditions were unnecessary and expensive failures, the difference between them being that one had cost nearly nine times as much as the other.[10] Royle summed it up thus: 'Its departure [the 1885 expedition] left Osman Digna still uncrushed and the Souakin-Berber route still unopened; and Osman was enabled to claim in 1885, as he had done in 1884, that he had driven the British out of the country'.[11] Of course, the original intention had never been to attempt to force the railway through to Berber in the spring of 1885. Wolseley had always been clear that the reconquest of the Sudan, including the capture of Berber, could only begin in the autumn of 1885, afterthe hot weather was over. But he had clearly counted on Osman Digna being out of the way by then and the railway from Suakin having got at least as far as Arriab, i.e. nearly half way to Berber.

It is however worth asking if the conventional judgement on Graham's two expeditions is the correct one. While the position in June 1885 appeared superficially to show that nothing of any permanent significance had been achieved, it is possible to argue that the position had changed fundamentally in three ways. In the first place, there was now in practice a permanent British presence on the Red Sea littoral. In 1884, Hewett had taken over

Suakin as a temporary measure to keep it from falling into Osman's hands; there had been no suggestion that the British might accept a permanent role – quite the contrary. But the hard fact of history was that after 1885 the British remained in permanent control of Suakin, with a permanent and gradually growing dominance over its hinterland. That presence was further solidified by the political relations into which Britain was inevitably drawn, as a result of its presence on the Red Sea coast, with the Abyssinians, the Italians and the French. By staying in Suakin, the British had become a Red Sea 'Power'. After 1885, there was never any real prospect of the British abandoning responsibilty for Suakin. The evacuation in 1885 of the rest of the Sudan, left Suakin as the only Anglo-Egyptian bridgehead in the Sudan. Suakin became in effect the symbol of a British determination at some stage to come back and re-conquer the rest of the Sudan. That in turn had a powerful effect on the tribes, creating in its turn a moral commitment not to abandon them.

Secondly, while it is true that Osman had not been completely crushed in 1885 – and indeed was to live to mount further attacks on Suakin – the Hadendowa who formed the core of his force had suffered enormous losses which it would take years to replace.[12] For the forseeable future he would be in no position to take on the British in pitched battle. By skilful guerilla warfare, he could hope to restrict the British to the area between the Red Sea Hills and the sea, although the attack on T'hakul, properly analysed, had demonstrated a new mobility on the part of the British. The overwhelming superiority in defensive firepower shown by the British troops at El Teb, Tamai and Tofrek was likely to increase, rather than diminish, as machine guns and rifles became more reliable on the one hand and the stocks of Remingtons continued to dwindle on the other. Osman would find it difficult to recruit allies to stand up against the British; only a successful guerilla-type war offered a long-term solution to Osman's manpower difficulties if the British stayed. And in the shorter term, the increased tranquility and prosperity brought by a continuing British presence in and around Suakin was likely to make the non-Hadendowa tribes more reluctant to throw up everything to join Osman.

All these things could only be dimly perceived at the time. As Graham sailed away, grieving that the apparent results of his expeditions were being thrown away, and Osman was left to point out to the tribes that twice the British had come, twice fought against him and twice sailed away again, it was indeed possible to believe that Osman remained master of the field and the true victor of the bloody encounters.

NOTES

1. Diary for 21 April 1885 – Preston, op cit, p196.
2. Diary for 24 April 1885 – ibid, p198.
3. Galloway, op cit, p362.
4. Diary for 20 May 1885 – Preston, op cit, p216.

192

5. *Times* 15 May 1885.
6. Ibid.
7. Contrast Kitchener's handling of the construction of the Desert Railway from Wadi Halfa to Abu Hamed in 1897. Hartington's formal instruction to Graham of 27 February 1885 specified that 'direction of the works will be entirely under your orders and control'.
8. According to Inglis (op cit, p126), the average height of the Australian contingent was about five feet seven inches which says something about the physique of the British working class at this time.
9. Final Despatch dated 30 May 1885, paragraph 27.
10. The cost of the 1884 expedition, over and above the normal peacetime cost of the troops and services used, was put at £352,352. On a comparable basis, the cost of the 1885 expedition was £2,127,762, plus £865,369 for the railway.
11. Royle, op cit, p436.
12. A precise calculation of the Dervish losses is impossible. At El Teb, Tamai and Tofrek, Osman's losses in killed must have exceeded 5,000. Not all were fighting men although clearly the great majority were; similarly, not all were Hadendowa although the majority probably were. These losses have to be set against an original estimated strength of some 15,000 fighting men.

13

The Decline and Fall of Osman

SUAKIN WAS left in the hands of a garrison consisting of the Shropshires, the Indian Contingent, and 6/1 RA (re-equipped with 5/1's guns), under the command of Hudson. Chermside continued as Govenor General of the Red Sea Littoral – reduced in practice to Suakin. Concurrently with the departure of the bulk of Graham's force from Suakin, Wolseley's Relief Expedition was evacuating the Sudan. By the end of July, 1885 the troops at Suakin constituted the only British presence in the Sudan.

The Shropshires settled into a new, permanent camp at Graham's Point, on the southern side of the narrow entrance to the Harbour. The camp was protected by a ditch and earth parapet, strengthened by wire entanglements, running round in a wide half-circle from the harbour channel in the north to the sea coast to the south-east. As Wylde noted, the sea coast end of the line was easily outflanked since shallow water, nowhere exceeding four feet, ran out for nearly a quarter of a mile. In practice, the Dervishes never appeared there. Of the Indian Contingent, one battalion occupied the Sandbag Redoubt, to the north-west of the town, protecting the approaches from Handub; a second battalion held the western face of the defences and Suakin town itself, while the third battalion linked up along the southern face of the defences with the Shropshires. H Redoubt, in the gap between Sandbag Redoubt and the harbour was held by the artillery battery and the mounted infantry company of the Shropshires. Two companies of Indian infantry held Quarantine Island which still contained the static distillation plant, the Ordnance Depot and the Officers' Hospital.

The garrison and the English community soon settled into a comfortable routine. The bands of the various regiments played every evening, and several times a week the officers' messes of the various regiments held open house for the British residents. There was horse racing once a month, a regatta in the harbour nearly every week, together with cricket, athletics and even lawn tennis (where is not quite clear!). For the troops, there was capital fishing in the harbour for gray mullet, bream, bonita, gar fish, rock cod, wrass and cavalha, all of which provided not only entertainment but a welcome variety to the standard rations. For the officers and sometimes the NCOs, there was shooting in the surrounding plain – quail, sand grouse, pigeon and even the occasional bustard, although the latter was said to be more prevalent at Tokar.

The great prize was gazelle, and extraordinary risks were sometimes taken to shoot it because the unpalatable fact was that Suakin had been invested by Osman's men at virtually the same moment as the last troopship carrying the remnants of Graham's expedition left the harbour. Every morning, camel pickets of the Dervishes would arrive from Hashin and Tamai, returning in the evening. Beyond a thousand yards from the fortifications, the country was not safe for anyone from the garrison. A scouting picket of cavalry or mounted infantry would patrol around the town, morning and evening, frequently exchanging shots with Osman's men, usually without casualties. The danger did not prevent officers venturing out to shoot, and Wylde records a number of narrow escapes as officers had to ride for their lives to avoid being cut off by the Dervish camel men. On one occasion, the Dervishes set a trap for the daily picket, baiting it with a live gazelle tied to a bush. Luckily, the trap was spotted and the only casualties were to the Dervishes.

But the basic situation could not be hidden and while the presence of the garrison produced a certain amount of prosperity for some of the traders in Suakin, for many of the population there was only deprivation and disease since Osman was able to limit the amount of local produce entering the town. In the meantime, New Tamai had been rebuilt and was growing in size daily, as was the Mahdiist ascendancy. Indeed, while maintaining a cordon of investment round Suakin, Osman was pursuing a bigger immediate objective. Apart from Suakin, the only Egyptian garrison which still held out in the Sudan by the late summer of 1885 was at Kassala, roughly 260 miles to the south, on the border with Abyssinia. There was no possibility of the British relieving it since it was also some 230 miles inland, and the Italians who had occupied Massawa by agreement were in no position to venture a large expedition inland. Only the Abyssinian emperor, John, was in a position to help but his offers had been rejected. In the autumn of 1885, John was finally asked to relieve Kassala but it was too late. Osman brought off perhaps the biggest *coup* of his career by forcing Kassala to surrender, with its Egyptian garrison, towards the end of August 1885. Osman and Mahdiism were now supreme in the Eastern Sudan, although it would be erroneous to assume that all the tribes were his fervent supporters. Many, such as the Amarar, were now enemies of the Hadendowa who formed the core of Osman's supporters, and as time went on, others were alienated by the harsh nature of the Mahdiist rule. Nevertheless, until the final defeat of the Mahdiist state at Omdurman in 1898, there was never a native party able and ready to challenge Osman's domination. Significantly, the slave trade to Jedda and Arabia continued to flourish. By the spring of 1886, New Tamai had grown to such an extent that some of its huts could be seen with a telescope from Suakin.

Osman's absence at Kassala between August 1885 and January 1886 nevertheless allowed dissension to creep in, even among the Hadendowa. Osman

Osman had left his nephew, Fai Digna, in command and Fai was forced to levy taxes, at the rate of three dollars per camel or 25 sheep, to meet the cost of keeping his forces in being. This taxation aroused great opposition, including that of Shaykh Mussa Gidif of Harndab, hitherto one of Osman's staunchest supporters. The Amarar, never wholly in sympathy with Osman, now transferred their allegiance wholly to the British; henceforth the Amarar were lost to Osman. Fundamentally, the weakness of Osman's position lay in his inability to create the necessary machinery of government to enable him to administer the Eastern Sudan. His difficulty was not helped by news of the death of the Mahdi himself in June 1885. The latter's successor, the Khalifa, was able, after an intense struggle, to create a true Mahdiist state, based on Omdurman, but he was aided by a number of factors, including possession of a body of trained Egyptian and Sudanese administrators and the remnants of an Egyptian administrative structure. Such resources were never available to Osman, who lacked the necessary administrative talents himself. Thus, despite the growth of New Tamai, the containment of the garrison of Suakin and the capture of Kassala, Osman's power remained evanescent.

Towards the end of 1885, Tokar, the main granary of Osman's forces, was reported to be lightly held since Osman had taken many warriors with him to Kassala. Chermside was approached by a deputation of friendly tribal leaders to authorise an attack on Tokar before the wheat crop could be gathered. The British authorities were not prepared to embark on a potentially dangerous expedition, given the strength available. Osman reacted swiftly, by reinforcing his troops in the area and mounting a series of raids round Suakin, capturing some camels and killing a Mounted Infantryman.

The onset of the hot weather in June 1885 had an immediate effect on the health of the troops, particularly the British. At the end of July, 133 men were sick out of a total British contingent of 930 (or nearly 14 per cent); the Indians were in better shape with 161 sick out of 2400 but even their health was described as only fair. As a temporary expedient, half of the Shropshires were relieved by a detachment of the 2nd Battalion Royal Sussex Regiment from Egypt but it was clear that all the troops needed relief. Temperatures in August had reached 120°F in the tents during the day and even at night did not fall below 100°. The British soldiers in particular were described as exhausted and depressed by the heat. At the end of August, plans were made to relieve the Indian contingent and to dispense with the British battalion.[1] The main changeover took place in October and November, 1885 with the 16th Bombay Infantry, the 8th and 20th Madras Infantry, a squadron of the 4th Madras Light Cavalry and B Company of the Madras Sappers and Miners taking over from the Shropshires and Hudson's original Indian units. Hudson himself remained in command.

The result was a debâcle. In January 1886, the Viceroy signalled the Secretary of State in London, pressing for the Indian troops to be brought home as quickly as possible; as the Viceroy put it, service at Suakin was extremely trying, beyond the sphere of the legitimate duties of the Indian troops and caused great discontent. From January onwards the sickness rate increased dramatically. Within four months, a medical report concluded, the 20th Madras Infantry had been rendered totally ineffective as a unit through a combination of arduous work, poor food and the effects of the climate; the Sappers and Miners were in a similar condition. No doubt, morale had played a part in it; the Indians were a long way from home, carrying out duties in miserable conditions, for purposes which seemed to have no direct connection with India or the Indian Army. That the duties were heavy, in terms of escorting convoys and providing guards twenty-four hours a day, was a tribute to Osman's continuing threat. But perhaps the major cause of the trouble was under-nourishment again. The Second Afghan War five years before had demonstrated clearly that the Indian troops were not being fed properly while on active service. In part, it was a problem of inadequate rations and efforts were hastily made at Suakin to increase supplies of meat, fresh vegetables and lime juice to overcome clear symptoms of scurvy. But the real problem almost certainly lay in the cooking arrangements. Unlike the British Army where cooking was done on a unit basis (usually by companies), the Indian Army persisted in a system of individual cooking. The result was that men coming off an exhausting spell of convoy or guard duty were too tired to grapple with the problem of preparing and cooking their own food; there might not even be enough time to do so before the next duty or fatigue party. Rations were being consumed raw or even not at all.

The Indian contingent was accordingly withdrawn at the beginning of May 1886 and replaced by units of the new Egyptian Army.

Chermside was succeeded by Colonel Sir Charles Warren who pursued an active and enlightened policy of conciliating the local tribes and gaining their confidence and support. Wylde, who was an admirer of Warren's methods, believed that if Warren had been given sufficient time, there would have been a settlement once and for all of the Eastern Sudan problem. But Warren was replaced in May 1886 by Major C.M. Watson. Watson too was an intelligent and enlightened officer and had no hesitation in continuing Warren's policy: 'If Government were to declare that the war was at an end, and to re-open trade, it is possible that, after a time, the country would settle down' he wrote. But he went further and actively encouraged the leaders of the friendly tribes to attack Osman's supporters up and down the coast, and even to blockade Tamai. All this was strong meat for the authorities in Cairo and London to digest, and Watson had made himself unpopular in some quarters by his strongly expressed opinions in favour of the Suakin-Berber route to Khartoum, as opposed to the Nile. Fearful of being sucked into another expedition, the Government in August 1886 appointed Lieutenant Colonel Herbert Kitchener to succeed Watson.

Kitchener had made his name as Head of Intelligence for Wolseley's Nile expedition, and was to remain continuously in Egypt and the Sudan until 1900, by which time he was a Field Marshal. Kitchener was sensitive about the way in which he had been appointed to succeed Watson, a fellow Engineer, who had had no idea that he had been replaced. But, in fact, the authorities were determined to replace him and if Kitchener had not accepted the post, another officer would have been appointed.

The situation which Kitchener inherited when he took up office in September 1886 remained ambiguous. The majority of the tribes north of Suakin had been persuaded, largely by Wylde, with the active encouragement of Watson, to turn against Osman, and a force of Dervishes under Muhammad Medani, a nephew of Osman's, was attacked and slaughtered near Shaykh Barghut (the modern Port Sudan). Osman's forward post was now Hashin, which was commanded by Muhammad Adam Sardun, Graham's old adversary at T'hakul. The centre of Osman's power remained at Tamai, which had reached a population of 15,000, and at Tokar, the source of much of his food. Osman had however committed a major blunder in executing Hamed Mahmud, the leader of the Amarar tribes. No tribal leader could now feel entirely safe and in the summer of 1886, Osman's immediate strength in fighting men had begun to dwindle. Worse still for Osman, doubts had been aroused in Omdurman about his policies and he was summoned to see the Khalifa. In his absence, and under strong pressure from Kitchener, Tamai was attacked and taken by a confederation of tribes led by Muhammad Ali, of the Fadlab branch of the Amarar who had been fighting against Osman since 1884. Wylde, who visited Tamai a day or so after it had been occupied and looted, was impressed by the size of the place. It stretched from the site of the 1884 battle nearly to Tamanieb, some two and a half miles. Each cluster of huts was surrounded by a zariba, and there was a circular fortification of sandbags in the centre of the town, with a stone magazine, fortified, on a ridge overlooking the Khor Ghob. There was a market on each side of the town and a huge, hutted mosque, nearly 200 feet long.

If the Government had been prepared at that stage to pursue a modest 'Forward Policy' and occupy Tamai and Tamanieb, it is conceivable that Osman, whose power in the autumn of 1886 was at a low ebb, might have been permanently defeated. But there was to be no change in the defensive policy towards the Sudan. Kitchener had to content himself with building a stone wall round El Geif and strengthening the fortifications. Suakin was impregnable to Osman but equally Kitchener could only stand by and watch as Osman returned from the Khalifa, re-occupied Tamai and began to re-establish Mahdiist rule. Significantly, Osman was accompanied by an emissary of the Khalifa, Abu Qarja, who was in effect to act as political officer.

By the end of 1887, Osman had regained a large measure of his original strength. Some of the tribes who had hitherto supported the British at Suakin now transferred their allegiance, and Osman, encouraged, occupied

Handub, his old base for attacks on Suakin, and then attacked the Water Forts. The fixed defences of Suakin were not susceptible to occupation by Osman's troops who had no cannon or siege apparatus of any kind but the menace was too obvious to ignore. Kitchener was forbidden by the Government in Cairo to take out the garrison of Suakin on offensive operations but he was authorised to reconnoitre. Interpreting this largely, he took out a small force of regular mounted troops in support of a force of friendly tribesmen. This mixed gathering succeeded in capturing Handub on 17 January 1888 but then dispersed to loot. It was counter-attacked by Osman and the tribesmen fled towards Suakin, covered by Kitchener and his small regular force. Kitchener himself received a bullet in the jaw and was forced to return to Cairo for treatment.[2] He was succeeded as Governor General by Lieutenant Colonel Charles Holled-Smith, of the King's Royal Rifle Corps.

Holled-Smith inherited a dangerous situation. Strengthened by reinforcements sent by the Khalifa and encouraged by the success at Handub, Osman closed in on Suakin in March 1888 and proceeded to blockade it, firing into it heavily each night. By September 1888, the Dervishes were showing every sign of mounting a serious attack to take the town. A disaster of that magnitude was too much even for the authorities in Cairo to contemplate and by the middle of December a striking force of 750 British and 4000 Egyptian and Sudanese soldiers had been concentrated at Suakin, under the direct command of Major General F.W. Grenfell, the Sirdar (or Commander-in-Chief) of the Egyptian Army: Kitchener and Holled-Smith acted as brigade commanders. Osman was totally defeated outside Suakin, on 20 December 1888, in what was subsequently known as the battle of Gemaizeh. But the success was not followed up in any decisive fashion and when the British troops re-embarked the situation in the Red Sea Littoral returned to its usual uneasy state.

Osman was in difficulties on his own home front however. At the Khalifa's behest, he had reluctantly transferred his headquarters to Tokar, nearly 50 miles further away from Suakin than Tamai. At the same time, disputes between Osman and Abu Qarja, and between Osman and his own followers, led the Khalifa to send four commissioners to investigate the situation and to look into charges that Osman had misappropriated money and grain. The commissioners held a public enquiry in front of all of Osman's men in March 1889. It was brought to a hasty conclusion in face of threats from the armed Beja tribesmen but it had shown that while Osman himself was free from corruption, his own bad administration and the fact that some of the financial officials were members of his own family had caused legitimate grievance.

The Khalifa was now forced to act. In April 1889, he ruled that while Osman was to remain as commander of the troops, Abu Qarja was to be his deputy in charge of the Treasury, and, while nominally under Osman, would send monthly accounts direct to Omdurman. Osman and Abu Qarja staged a public reconciliation a month later. Whatever his shortcomings as an administrator, Osman's value as a fighting commander and his loyalty to the Mahdiist cause were of enormous value to the Kalifa, surrounded as he was in Omdurman by a network of rivalries and intrigues. The Khalifa's army suffered a major defeat on the Egyptian frontier, at Toski (near Wadi Halfa) in August 1889. It marked the end of the Mahdiist advance on Egypt but it also caused the Khalifa to fear that it marked the beginning of an Anglo-Egyptian re-conquest of the Sudan. He therefore summoned Osman to Omdurman. The latter returned in December 1889 with instructions to recruit intensively among the Red Sea tribes for a new Holy War (jihad) in order to distract the British and Egyptians from any invasion of the Northern Sudan.

Unknown to Osman or the Khalifa, Holled-Smith and Grenfell had pressed hard in the aftermath of Toski for an advance round Suakin, arguing that the Mahdiist power in the Eastern Sudan had declined, that many of the tribes wanted Anglo-Egyptian rule but that they could not throw off the Mahdiist yoke unless they had direct assistance. These arguments fell for the moment on deaf ears but Osman's advance was stopped dead by a combination of bad harvests and Kitchener's insistence on stopping grain imports via Suakin and Trinkitat in August 1890. Famine raged throughout the Eastern Sudan until the end of 1890 and this was the decisive factor in Osman's decline. Sensing the weakening of his position, Baring in Cairo, aided and abetted by Grenfell and Holled-Smith, pressed the British Government for permission to attack and occupy Tokar, on the somewhat specious grounds that the Italians from Massawa were planning to seize Kassala and needed to be headed off. Salisbury, the Prime Minister, agreed in February 1891.

In anticipation, Holled-Smith, on his own initiative, had seized Handub on 27 January 1891. On 15 February, he concentrated 2000 Egyptian troops at Trinkitat and occupied Tokar on the 19th. Osman and a force of some 6000 was at Afafit and advanced to attack. Holled-Smith formed his infantry in a semi-circular formation and under the steady fire Osman's troops melted away. A cavalry charge completed their dissolution. The obvious decline in the fighting power of Osman's Dervishes, as compared with the savage battles against Graham only a few years before, is very striking and clear evidence of the loosening grip of Mahdiism.

The capture of Tokar was a decisive blow. It put an end to the trade with Arabia in which Osman exported ivory in return for munitions and food. Osman himself retreated to Adarama on the Atbara river far to the west but continued to foment attacks round Suakin. In 1895, he raided Tokar from the Erkowit Hills and in retaliation a small force was despatched from Suakin which drove him back into the hills. His power in the Eastern Sudan was finished but with some followers he retreated to Adarama again where he managed to collect some 5000 men.[3] The occupation of Berber by the Egyptians in September 1897 threatened his position on the Atbara and accordingly at the end of September 1897 he moved across the Atbara north-westwards to join the Amir Mahmud with the main Dervish army at Metemmeh on the Nile. The move removed any threat to the Suakin-Berber route and so after a delay of 13 years, the route was at last open. Ironically, it was Osman who had opened it.

Osman was with Mahmud at the bloody defeat of the Atbara on 8 April 1898 but, true to form, was virtually the only Dervish leader to escape and join the Khalifa's forces further south. As the senior amir since the death of al Majurni at Toski in 1889, he commanded a division of the Mahdiist army at the final battle at Omdurman in September 1898, being responsible for the famous ambush of the 21st Lancers in which Winston Churchill was involved. Osman escaped south with the Khalifa and when the latter and most of his surviving Emirs were killed at the battle of Umm Debeikerat in November 1899, Osman was the only major leader to survive. There was now nowhere for him to go except back to the Red Sea Hills which had been his hunting ground for so long.

In considering the Sudan in the Mahdiist period between 1883 and 1898, British military historians have tended to regard it as a straightforward struggle between the Anglo-Egyptian forces and the Mahdiists. But through-out the period there was a third major protagonist which posed a constant threat to the Mahdi and his successor, the Khalifa Abdullah – the kingdom of Abyssinia, lying along the south-eastern border of the Sudan.

Abyssinia, the legendary land of Prester John, had been a Christian kingdom long before Islam had been born. It was the source of the Blue Nile and its peoples were proud, savage and warlike. The northern boundary of the Abyssinia kingdom where it abutted on to the Sudan had never been de-limited and for centuries there had been fighting between the local Sudanese tribes and the Abyssinians in the border areas where the mountains of northern Abyssinia came down to the desert plains of south-eastern Sudan. The Egyptians had been involved in a war with the Emperor of Abyssinia in the 1860s but the British expedition to Abyssinia in 1867-8 to rescue hostages, which had resulted in the defeat and death of the half-mad Emperor Theodore, had caused Abyssinia to draw in on itself for more than a decade.

The rise of the Mahdi changed that. Between the fiercely Christian Abyssinians and the fanatically Muslim followers of the Mahdi there could never be friendship or peace. The British were quick to spot the possibilities and, in the spring of 1884, Admiral Hewett, accompanied by John Wylde, was despatched to negotiate a treaty of mutual friendship and support with the Emperor John. Under the Treaty, signed at Adowa on 3 June 1884, the Abyssinians and the Egyptian and British Governments agreed to permanent peace. For his part, the Emperor John undertook to assist in the evacuation of the Egyptian garrisons besieged by the Mahdi at Kassala and other towns; in return, the areas of what is now Eritrea (described in the

201

Treaty as the Bogos country) which had been occupied by the Egyptians earlier were returned to the Emperor. There would be free transit for all goods, including arms and ammunition, through the Egyptian part of Massawa and criminals fleeing across the borders would be automatically delivered up. Any disputes between the Abyssinians and Egyptian Governments would be referred to the British Government for arbitration. A subsidiary anti-slavery treaty was signed at the same time.

The Emperor was as good as his word. Abyssinian armies evacuated the Egyptian garrisons at Gallabat and Jira in February and July 1885, but Kassala, after a long siege, fell to the Mahdiist army at the end of July 1885.

As we have seen, Wylde recruited a number of Abyssinians to act as scouts during Graham's 1884 campaign. Wylde had the highest opinion of the Abyssinians as fighting men and had no doubt that they were more than a match for the Mahdi's followers. He regretted bitterly that the opportunity was not taken in 1885 to recruit a really substantial body of Abyssinians to fight against Osman Digna; they would have been invaluable, he thought, in harrying Osman when he returned into the hills.

With the detailed events on the south-eastern border after 1885 we are not directly concerned. Fighting continued between the Dervishes and the Abyssinians, culminating in an overwhelming victory for the Khalifa's forces outside Gallabat in March 1889, in which the Emperor John was killed and his head carried off in triumph to Omdurman. By that time, yet another player had appeared on the Sudan stage. Italy, keen to play a part on the international stage and seeing itself shut out of the scramble for Africa, had been allowed to occupy Massawa in 1885; the Egyptian Government did not have the resources to defend and develop it, while the British were still determined to abandon the Sudan. With the death of John in 1889, the Italians seized the opportunity to expand inland at Abyssinia's expense and to create the colony of Eritrea; in 1894, they even occupied Kassala temporarily.

All the events had an indirect effect on Suakin. For one thing, Osman was responsible for Kassala and the hinterland of Massawa and he took a prominent part in the siege and occupation of Kassala in the summer of 1885. His absences from the Suakin area produced friction and arguments among his followers and undoubtedly reduced his influence in the long term; certainly they militated against the establishment of a solid administrative structure for the area. When the crunch came in the 1890s, Osman's power melted away because it was built on no solid, permanent basis. In the second place, the war against the Abyssinians ate up the Khalifa's resources in both men and money, and increased the burden on the rest of the Sudan. While it could not be described as a fatal running sore, there can be no doubt that the conflicts with Abyssinia distracted attention and resources from the basic task of creating a stable Mahdiist state.

NOTES

1. Already in July 1885, the HQ and two squadrons of the 9th Bengal Cavalry had returned to India, leaving just one squadron at Suakin.
2. There is a good story in Colonel E.W.C. Sandes *The Royal Engineers in Egypt and the Sudan* (Chatham, 1937). Kitchener, having dislodged and swallowed the bullet accidentally, was given a purgative. In reply to an enquiry from the Queen, the doctor replied, 'Kitchener passed good night and bullet.'
3. In the spring of 1896, in face of an expected Mahdiist advance on Egypt, the Indian Government was again asked to garrison Suakin. Between June and November 1896, Suakin was held by a force under Brigadier General C.C. Egerton, consisting of the 1st Bombay Lancers, the 26th and 35th Bengal Infantry, No 5 (Bombay) Mountain Battery and No 1 Company Madras Sappers and Miners. Each battalion had been hastily given a Maxim gun which they learned to operate in the ships bringing them from Bombay.

The Madras Sappers and Miners were the last to leave Suakin on 8 December 1896.

Epilogue

IN THE SECOND week of January 1900 a messenger arrived in Suakin to see the Governor. He came from Muhammad Ali al Amir Or, the head of the Gemilab branch of the Hadendowa, hitherto among the staunchest supporters of Osman Digna. The message he brought was a surprising one. It said that Osman had sought refuge with the tribe and was hidden in a cave in the Waribba Hills, some sixty miles south of Suakin. He had been given a servant and a dog to protect him but the Gemilab were tired of fighting and they wished to surrender him to the authorities.

There had been rumours for months that Osman had returned to the Red Sea coast after the death of the Khalifa and small parties of police and soldiers were scattered over the whole area looking for him. Indeed, a small party under Captain Burges was somewhere in the Waribba Hills at that very moment. The temptation to dismiss the message from Muhammad Ali as yet another rumour was therefore strong. But the messenger insisted that it was true and that, as the nephew of the shaykh, he was not there only for some petty reward. Persuaded, the commandant of the police at Suakin, Muhammad Ahmad Bey, collected a small party of police mounted on camels and set out on the morning of 11 January.

For fifty miles, the route lay over the flat desert, bare and dusty, with only the odd mimosa bush to break the monotony of the view. In the evening, the party reached the foothills of the Waribba; beyond them lay the steep cliffs of the Hills proper, rising some 3000 feet above the desert.

Next morning, the party climbed up through the hills, on to the main plateau and made its way towards the peak of Beredima where Osman was alleged to be hiding; 'Ridges of shining basalt rocks and granitic outcrops, sparkling with mica, here and there star the plain' wrote a subsequent witness, 'In every direction appear ranges of mountains, in some places as many as fifty miles away. The general effect one gets is of being in a rather shallow saucer with the mountain tops for the rim'.

In the course of the day, the party met Captain Burges and his patrol, the combined party now numbering about twenty-five. At sunset on the 12th, they set off to find Osman.

Towards dawn on the 13th the party heard a dog bark and knew that they were close to their quarry. Osman's dog had picked up the sound of the police when they were still a considerable way off but Osman's suspicions had been lulled by the servant, acting on the instructions of Muhammad Ali, who had assured him that it was only a passing party of tribesmen. Osman, reassured, settled down to read the Koran while the servant prepared the morning meal. As dawn broke, the police rushed the mouth of the cave.

Years of being hunted had given the great Hadendowa leader a sixth sense of preservation and, as the police stumbled and crashed their way up the boulder-strewn slope to the cave mouth, Osman was already escaping through the rear entrance. Captain Burges, encumbered by his sword, stopped to take it off. As he did so, he caught a glimpse of a shadowy figure in a white tunic some thirty feet above him on the hillside. Summoned by his shout, the rest of the party closed in and found themselves holding a tall Sudanese with a hawk face and deep set, burning eyes. Even then they could not be sure that this was the man that they were looking for because none of them had ever seen Osman. Muhammad Ahmad Bey, however, remembered that Osman had been wounded in the head, wrist and back seventeen years before, at Sinkat. The scars were there and the party knew that the man before them was indeed the legendary Uthman ibn Abu Bakr Dignai. He had, according to his own testimony, been planning to escape to Arabia.

He was heavily shackled and taken back to Suakin. From there he was hastily despatched to the prison at Rosetta, in the Egyptian Delta, where the other remaining Mahdiist leaders were confined. When that prison blew down in a hurricane in 1901, Osman was transferred to Damietta and then, in 1908, after agitation from the Sudanese tribes, he was moved to Wadi Halfa, just inside the Sudan, where he remained for the rest of his life, except for a pilgrimage to Mecca in 1924. He died two years later from an enlarged prostate, at the age of approximately 86. He had outlived everyone – the Mahdi, the Khalifa, Graham, Kitchener, and all his fellow amirs. He never wavered in his devotion to the cause of the Mahdi and while he lived the torch of Mahdiism still burned.

Even in death he contrived to cause maximum embarrassment. In 1964, the construction of the Aswan High Dam threatened his grave in the cemetery of Sidi Ibrahim at Wadi Halfa and the Sudanese Government decided to move his body to a grave outside the Kitchener Gate at the entrance to Suakin. But fearful of the emotions that this might stir, it had second thoughts and in the end he was buried in the Erkowit Hills from whence he had so often sallied forth to cause fear and destruction.[1]

Apart from the Mad Mullah in Somaliland and perhaps the Fakir of Ipi on the North West Frontier, no single man ever caused the British Army so much difficulty and embarrassment over so long a time as Uthman ibn Abu Bakr Dignai, known to history as Osman Digna. His fame has indeed hampered any searching analysis of his qualities and achievements.

His military achievements are clear. Between 1883 and 1884, he destroyed the Egyptian Army in the Eastern Sudan. From 1884 until 1900, he managed to wage a continuous campaign against the Anglo-Egyptian forces, in the course of which he came very close on two occasions (at Tamai in 1884 and at Tofrek in 1885) to annihilating a British brigade. In between times, he defeated the Abyssinians and inflicted a defeat on Kitchener, wounding him in the process. The record therefore is impressive. Two questions however remain. How far were these achievements due to Osman himself? Could he have achieved more?

On the first question, the evidence is by no means clear-cut. There is little doubt that in the early, small scale attacks on the Egyptian garrisons and relief forces, Osman was both present and active – indeed, as we have seen, he was severely wounded at Sinkat in 1883. There is, however, no real evidence that he was present, in active command, at any of the subsequent major actions in 1884 and 1885, starting with Baker's defeat at El Teb. On the contrary, the evidence is that he invariably delegated tactical command to his subordinates, many of whom were killed in the process. That in no way implies any suggestion of cowardice. It is far more likely to have been linked to the Beja belief that when the commander was killed the battle was automatically lost.

The fact that Osman was not himself present at the major engagements does not, of itself, prove that he was not involved in their tactical and strategic planning. On the tactical side, as we have seen, there is clear evidence from the events surrounding Tofrek that Osman himself was responsible for the decision to attack British squares only when they were on the move or when they were constructing zaribas; no doubt that decision was reached in discussions with his lieutenants. Equally, it showed that he had learned from his defeats at El Teb and Tamai. Those battles had resulted in enormous losses for Osman's troops and it is tempting therefore to criticise him for allowing his men to destroy themselves in blindly battering against impregnable British squares. That would be an injustice. Just as the British had been totally unprepared for the devastating nature of the Dervish attack, so Osman and his men were totally unprepared for the fighting power of the British in square. In 1884, no Dervish had ever encountered British troops and their experiences against Egyptian troops armed with breechloaders and in square, as at Shaykan and Second El Teb, provided ample evidence that European-style troops, whether in square or not, could easily be broken; Osman had no evidence that British troops were so different in quality from the Egyptians as to render all previous experience suspect. Hashin and Tofrek showed an advance in tactical thinking for which Osman, as the overall leader of the Mahdiist forces in the Eastern Sudan, must deserve some credit.

It has been argued by some British writers that the Dervishes under Osman had evolved a clear tactical principle of attacking the rear corners of a square since these were undoubtedly the most vulnerable points while the square was on the move or just halted. There is no evidence to support such a belief. At El Teb and Tamai Osman's men attacked the front face of the square; at Tofrek, they attacked what was in effect the front corner and side of the square. At Hashin, the squares were not attacked at all, the Dervishes contenting themselves with firing at the squares from cover.

To talk of a strategic level to Osman's campaigns is perhaps to elevate matters to an unreal, theoretical plane. Of course, he had a strategic objective which was to destroy the Anglo-Egyptian forces, expel the Egyptian administration and occupy the Eastern Sudan for the Mahdi. It is doubtful, whether those aims were ever embodied in any real form of strategic plan or whether Osman's strategy ever went much beyond a decision to attack the Anglo-Egyptian enemy whenever a suitable opportunity arose. There are perhaps two pieces of evidence for concluding that the latter was the case. In the first place, a coherent strategy would surely have involved a greater effort to engage the support of all the tribes, and particularly the Amarar. Not only did Osman singularly fail to do this but he went out of his way on occasion to alienate potential allies – for example, by the execution of the Amarar shaykh, Hamed Mahmud, in 1886. In the second place, there is the curious reluctance to attack Suakin itself. On at least three occasions – after First and Second El Teb in 1884 and after Graham's departure in April 1884 – Osman had very clear chances of occupying Suakin; indeed after First and Second El Teb, he could almost certainly have occupied the city at the drop of a hat and observers such as Wylde fully expected him to do so. Had he done so, the whole complexion of subsequent Sudanese history might have been changed since it is unlikely that, with Suakin in Dervish hands, the British Government would have been prepared to launch an expedition to re-occupy it. It was one thing to land troops to shore up a weak defence; it was quite another to attack an occupied city. With Suakin occupied and its trade in Mahdiist hands, it is probable that the other tribes, such as the Amarar and the Beni Amir, would have been prepared, however reluctantly, to come to terms with Osman. Why Osman failed to attack Suakin in any meaningful way will be discussed later but the failure to do so argues at the very least for an absence of clear strategic thinking. If one goes outside the theatre of the Eastern Sudan, there is one aspect of Osman's military career which deserves consideration and that is his role at the battle of Omdurman in September 1898. That he achieved a clear tactical surprise in ambushing the 21st Lancers is beyond dispute. It was not an accident – British observers in the gunboats on the Nile had seen the ambush being carefully prepared. Whose idea the ambush was is not clear. In 1898, Osman was the senior amir in the Dervish army and his fighting, if not his administrative, record gave his opinion weight among his peers and with the Khalifa. It is unlikely that his contingent would have been allotted a role to which Osman seriously objected. Equally, the nature of the ambush itself echoed to some extent the sort of fighting to which he was accustomed in the Eastern Sudan. We may therefore assume that Osman's ambush was largely his own idea, and it clearly sheds new and intriguing light on his military capacity.

Even so, Osman's precise place as a general is difficult to pin-point. In 1884-5, he delegated his tactical leadership to others and was almost certainly not present at the major actions. But the clear change in Dervish tactics between Graham's first and second campaigns must have owed something to him. Of wider, strategic thinking, there is really no evidence at all. One is left with the conclusion that Osman's fame as a fighting man derives partly from the sheer length of his fighting career and, perhaps overwhelmingly, from the unique quality of his individual soldiers. Without the legend of the 'Fuzzie-Wuzzies', there would have been little of an Osman Digna legend.

The answers to the second question – could he have achieved more in the military field? – tends to reinforce that conclusion. It is, of course, important not to underestimate the difficulties of keeping a Dervish force in the field. At best, the tribesmen of the Eastern Sudan managed to achieve little more than a subsistence level of existence. Apart from the area round Tokar, the land grew little food and provided only limited supplies of water. Food and much else of the requirements of life had to be imported through Suakin, and paid for largely in camel-driving and trading with the interior. If the tribesmen were fighting, they could not be earning. Hunger therefore put a brake on the period of time for which a Dervish force could be assembled. That in turn limited the amount of time that could be used for training. Nor were the tribesmen natural subjects for discipline since their whole life was one of natural independence in fighting the hostile quality of the land. Nevertheless, Osman can be fairly criticised in retrospect on three counts. In 1884, against Graham, he started with a considerable armament of breech-loading rifles and large stores of ammunition. Those assets were gradually frittered away to no real purpose. If the tribesmen had been trained to fire accurately and effectively, Graham's task might well have been impossible. The British square was excessively vulnerable to musketry, and other opponents, such as the Maoris and Pathans, had shown that so-called 'savage' tribes could learn to shoot accurately and exercise a degree of fire discipline. Osman's men never learned either.

In the second place, Osman failed in 1885 to develop an effective strategy of guerrilla warfare. It was clear after Tamai that he could not hope realistically to triumph on an open, stand-up fight; British discipline and fire-power were too much for that. It was equally obvious that the Dervishes possessed a clear superiority in mobility, they could travel faster and on less than their opponents, even including the British cavalry. A guerrilla strategy was therefore the obvious strategy to follow. Properly applied in 1885, the results could have been far-reaching. Such a strategy would have left the British with only two realistic options – to withdraw or to adopt a system of garrisoned posts to enable convoys and troops to move safely. The failure of the attempt to maintain a garrison at Hashin and the slow and expensive progress of the railway both indicated what would have been involved if the British had decided on the second option. In the event, Osman failed to develop a proper guerrilla strategy; he failed most noticeably to realise the importance of the railway development, probably through total ignorance of what the railway actually meant in military and economic terms. For their part, the British did gradually learn the importance of mobility. The replacement of the cumbersome infantry with the more mobile Mounted Infantry and Camel Corps, as exemplified in the attack on T'hakul, is striking.

In the third place, as we have seen, Osman failed signally to mobilise the full tribal strength. Only the Hadendowa supported him fully, probably because he was a Hadendowa himself. Perhaps half of the Amarar supported him at any given moment. The other tribes – notably the Beni Amir and the remainder of the Amarar – actively opposed him. The consequences of this failure were important. Osman deprived himself of much more than half of the available fighting men.[2] Equally important as time went on, the British were able to use the tribes to acquire intelligence and as guides, and active auxiliaries with the same mobility as Osman's men.

Finally, there is the unresolved question as to why Osman made no serious attempt to seize Suakin even when it lay open to him as in February 1884. Since he had suffered opposition and banishment at the hands of the ruling factions there, it might have been expected that he would have been keen to avenge himself by seizing the city. It has been argued already that if that had happened, the British would have been unlikely to send an expedition to recapture it. With the valuable Jeddah trade in his hands, Osman would have been able to build up his military power and might then have ruled unchallenged until after Omdurman. Why, then, did he fail to attempt to seize it? There are two possibilities. He may have been frightened of attacking the fortifications. He had no siege equipment, including artillery, and he possessed no real experience of siege warfare. Tokar and Sinkat had fallen through starvation and disease; Suakin as a port could not easily be starved out and could, in theory, be easily reinforced. Most of his supporters were desert tribesmen, unused to cities, and they may well have been reluctant to become involved in a thoroughly unfamiliar milieu. But equally Osman himself may have been reluctant to become involved in the complexities of civil government of a (relatively) sophisticated society for which he had no training and no pool of experience to draw upon. This is speculation because we have no evidence of Osman's thinking. What is beyond doubt is that the failure to occupy Suakin was a fatal blunder. In the hands of the British, Suakin constituted a rival centre of power encouraging the continued split among the tribes. As the years went by, the economic prosperity and the peace and stability provided under the auspices of the British in and around Suakin exercised a growing attraction for tribesmen becoming tired of ceaseless campaigning. Peace and justice, even under the auspices of an alien rule, began to appear an attractive alternative to the tyrannical and arbitrary rule of Osman and the Khalifa. Suakin became a tumour which gradually invaded and ultimately destroyed Osman's body politic.

This brings us on to the second leg of any assessment of Osman's achievements and stature. Even without Suakin, Osman was, by the middle of 1885, in possession of a considerable territory, stretching from Kassala in the south to Shaykh Bargut in the north, and from the Red Sea inland for at least 50 miles. Whether he liked it or not, he had perforce to become an administrator, collecting taxes and dispensing justice. Again, there is very little direct evidence as to how he set about it and how well he succeeded. But from time to time isolated pieces of evidence shed some light. The very fact that he was able to keep a force in the field over so long a period indicates that he had established at least a rudimentary system of supply. The ability of his nephew, Fai Digna, in Osman's absence at Kassala at the end of 1885, to levy taxes indicates that some form of tax-gathering, however elementary, already existed. We know that the Mahdi and his successor, the Khalifa, had succeeded in establishing a reasonably effective and comprehensive civil administration covering nothern and central Sudan, based upon the use of written records – cruel, arbitrary, but incontestably a genuine administration. Thus, when in 1889, Osman found himself at odds with his supporters in a way which endangered the Mahdiist cause in the Eastern Sudan, the Khalifa was quick to despatch officials to bring Osman under the financial control of the Treasury in Omdurman. Finally, there is the phenomenon of the growth of New Tamai, to a population of some 15000 and with a municipal apparatus of mosques, stores, forts and assembly halls. Unlike the Mahdi and Khalifa, Osman had not acquired a staff of captured Egyptian clerks to assist in running his administration, and he himself brought only the elementary administrative skills of a trader. It is not surprising therefore that Osman's administration appears in retrospect a shadowy and elusive thing, glimpsed only occasionally and then only by implication and not in its actual operations. What is reasonably clear is that just as he was no general of genius, so Osman was no administrator of great talents. The failure to pursue a coherent policy of reconciliation with the estranged tribes such as the Beni Amir is ample proof of that.

One is left therefore to speculate upon the nature of Osman's real talents. That he made serious errors of judgement and omission is not in dispute. But it is equally indisputable that virtually to the end, in 1900, he was able to maintain an army amidst the shifting sand of tribal rivalries. That cannot be put down simply to the power of Mahdiism or religious fanaticism. Nor, I believe, can it be put down to the use of violence and fear although it is clear that Osman practised the one and inspired the other. The character of the Beja tribesmen made it highly unlikely that they could be led by coercion. It argues for leadership and charisma, and that is indeed the nub of the matter. He was quite simply a leader of genius. Unfortunately for the historian, no European met Osman in the days of his ascendancy. His Sudanese contem-

poraries were agreed that he shared all of the basic qualities of the Hadendowa – truculence, fearlessness, independence, vindictiveness and pride.
Like other Hadendowa, he possessed great physical endurance; he had
apparently a tendency to over-eat but this was balanced by a self-discipline
which enabled him to fast for long periods when required. But he was
possessed of two other qualities which distinguished him and formed the
basis of his success as a leader. He was, in the first instance, an orator of
genius – passionate, fiery, full of conviction. In a tribal society largely based
upon oral communication, that talent was of great importance. Secondly, he
was totally and unreservedly loyal to the Mahdi and to the Mahdiist cause.
He had, as we have seen, studied Islamic law and theology as a youth and
there is no reason to doubt the intensity of his religious faith. He had been
conquered by the force of the Mahdi's own personality and belief in his
divine mission when he had first met him at El Obeid in 1883. Osman never
wavered in his support for Mahdiism and although he was often at logger-
heads with his fellow Amirs, he was with the Khalifa to the bitter end and he
was still fighting years after the rest of the Mahdiist leaders were dead or in
prison. If he was the great survivor, it was in part because he was also the
great believer. To the end of his life he remained totally dedicated to the
Mahdi and his cause, never changing. Leadership, ultimately, is not to be
defined by lists of characteristics but by the ability to retain the hearts and
minds of men. By that test, Osman Diga was a leader of genius.

Today there is little or no trace of those far-distant campaigns. The Suakin
to Berber railway disappeared long ago. Even in 1935 only a small stretch of
earthwork and some rusty scrap on Condenser (Quarantine) Island was all
that remained. Some of the fortifications round Suakin can still be traced but
the rest of the town is now derelict and disused. There is a railway still but it
is a branch line connecting Suakin with the main railway to Berber which
starts at Port Sudan, the old Shaykh Barghut.

Shaykh Barghut had been selected in 1904 to replace Suakin as Sudan's
main port and the new harbour was opened, as Port Sudan, in 1909. Thereafter, the decline of Suakin, with its narrow, winding entrance channel and
encroaching coral reefs, was rapid. The final blow came in 1937 when Port
Sudan officially replaced Suakin as the capital of the Red Sea Littoral. Thereafter, Suakin was quickly abandoned.

NOTES

1. See D.H. Johnson, *The imprisonment, death and re-burial of Osman Digna*, in *Soldiers of the Queen*, No 44 (March 1986), pp17-19.
2. Accurate numbers are not available but Chermside estimated in July 1884 that the Beni Amir numbered some 15000 males, the Amarar some 6500 and the Hadendowa nearly 9500. Report entitled *Tribes inhabiting the Eastern Sudan*. Suakin, 3 July 1884.

Appendix 1
Major Units Taking Part

1884 Campaign

Cavalry

10th Hussars (now the King's Royal Hussars)
19th Hussars (now the Light Dragoons)

Infantry

1st Battalion The Royal Highlanders (Black Watch) (42nd Foot)
3rd Battalion The King's Royal Rifle Corps (60th) (now The Royal Green-jackets)
1st Battalion The York and Lancaster Regiment (65th) (disbanded 1968)
1st Battalion The Gordon Highlanders (75th) (merged with The Queen's Own Highlanders)
2nd Battalion The Royal Irish Fusiliers (89th) (now The Royal Irish Regiment)
Royal Marine Light Infantry (now The Royal Marines)

Artillery

6 Battery, 1 Brigade, Scottish Division (Garrison)
M Battery, 1 Brigade, Royal Artillery
Royal Marine Artillery

Engineers

26th (Field) Company, RE

1885 Campaign

Cavalry

5th Lancers (now The 16th/5th Lancers)
19th Hussars (now The Light Dragoons)
20th Hussars (now The King's Royal Hussars)
9th Bengal Cavalry (now the 4th (Hodson's) Horse, Indian Army)

Infantry

3rd Battalion Grenadier Guards
1st Battalion Coldstream Guards
2nd Battalion Scots Guards
1st Battalion Berkshire Regiment (49th) (now The Duke of Edinburgh's Royal Regiment)
1st Battalion The King's Shropshire Light Infantry (53rd) (now The Light Infantry)
2nd Battalion The East Surrey Regiment (70th) (now the Princess of Wales's Own Regiment)
Royal Marine Light Infantry (now The Royal Marines)
15th Bengal Native Infantry (Loodhiana Sikhs) (now 2nd Battalion , The Sikh Regiment, Indian Army)
17th Bengal Native Infantry (Loyal Purbeah) (disbanded 1922)
28th Bombay Native Infantry (2nd Baluch) (disbanded 1933)
New South Wales Infantry Battalion (disbanded 1885)

Artillery

G Battery B Brigade, Royal Horse Artillery
5 Battery 1 Brigade, Scottish Division (Garrison)
6 Battery 1 Brigade, Scottish Division (Garrison)
Royal Marines Artillery (now the Royal Marines)
New South Wales Artillery Battery

Engineers

10th (Railway) Company RE
17th (Field) Company RE
24th (Field) Company RE
F Company, Queen's Own Madras Sappers and Miners (now the Indian Engineers, Indian Army)

Appendix 2
Campaign Medals and Victoria Crosses 1884-5

Campaign Medals

British and Indian troops taking part in the campaigns were awarded the EGYPTIAN MEDAL 1882-89. The medal is of silver and the obverse bears the familiar head of Queen Victoria; the reverse, the Sphinx with 'EGYPT' above (and the date '1882' for the medals awarded for that year only; there is no date for later awards). The ribbon consists of three bright blue and two white stripes, of equal width. There are bars for 'El Teb', 'Tamai', 'El Teb-Tamai', 'Suakin 1884', 'Suakin 1885' and 'Tofrek'.

The Khedive also issued a bronze star – the Khedive's Egyptian Star – for which British and Indian troops were also eligible. The obverse bears a representation of the Sphinx, with three pyramids behind, all within a circle bearing 'Egypt' and the appropriate date, in English and Arabic; the reverse bears the Khedive's monogram 'TM', also within a circle. The ribbon is dark blue. There is a bar 'Tokar', for the action on 19 February 1891, but otherwise the relevant star is simply dated '1884' (for the period 19 February to 26 March 1884) and '1884-86' (for the period 26 March 1884 to 7 October 1886).

Victoria Crosses

Four VCs were awarded specifically for actions in the Eastern Sudan, all during the 1884 campaign:

EDWARDS, THOMAS, Private, Black Watch
For defending a Gardner gun at Tamai 13 March 1884, while attached to the Naval Brigade as a mule driver.

MARLING, PERCIVAL SCROPE, Lieutenant, KRRC
For saving the life of Private Morley, Royal Sussex Regiment, at Tamai, 13 March 1884.

MARSHALL, WILLIAM THOMAS, Quartermaster Sergeant, 19th Hussars
For rescuing Lieutenant Colonel Barrow, 19th Hussars, at El Teb on 29 February 1884.

WILSON, ARTHUR KNYVET, Lieutenant, RN
For defending a Gardner gun at El Teb on 29 February 1884.

214

Appendix 3
Uniform

1884 Campaign

Cavalry: the 10th Hussars (from India) wore khaki drill frocks, blue pantaloons, blue puttees, with ankle boots. They appear to have worn the white Foreign Service helmet stained brown although they might have been expected to wear the white helmet with a khaki cover, as in India. Officers wore the same except for knee boots in place of puttees and ankle boots.

The 19th Hussars (from Egypt) wore grey frocks, Bedford cord pantaloons and knee boots, and brown-stained Foreign Service helmets; officers the same.

The Mounted Infantry detachment appear to have worn grey frocks, Bedford cord pantaloons, blue puttees and ankle boots, with helmets stained brown; officers the same.

Infantry: the two Highland regiments wore grey, cut-away frocks (or jackets) with the regimental kilt, coloured hose, white spats and ankle boots, with brown-stained Foreign Service helmet. The two regiments from India wore khaki drill frocks and trousers, with khaki puttees and ankle boots and the white Foreign Service helmet with khaki cover. The KRRC (from Egypt) wore grey frocks and trousers.

Officers wore virtually the same except that mounted officers would normally wear blue puttees and ankle boots. The brown Sam Browne belt was almost universal except in the KRRC.

The Royal Marines appear to have worn grey frocks and trousers with unstained white helmets. The Royal Navy contingent wore their normal blue jumpers and trousers, with canvas leggings and their ordinary caps with white covers. Officers wore white tunics, trousers and leggings, with white Army Foreign Service helmets.

1885 Campaign

Khaki was the prescribed colour for all units; no grey uniforms were ordered or sent out but there were some stocks of grey frocks and trousers in Egypt and these may have been worn by some men prior to khaki being issued.

Cavalry: The British regiments work khaki frocks, Bedford cord pantaloons and brown-stained Foreign Service helmets; the troopers wore puttees and ankle boots, the officers knee boots. The 9th Bengal Cavalry wore khaki frocks (or kurtas), khaki pantaloons, blue puttees and ankle boots (officers knee boots). The men wore the regimental turban, the officers khaki helmets.

The Mounted Infantry and the Camel Corps wore the same as the cavalry, except that the Camel Corps wore large, mushroom-shaped solar topis made up and sent from India; officers of both corps wore puttees and ankle boots.

Infantry: The British regiments (and the NSW battalion) wore khaki frocks and trousers, with ankle boots. (The Berkshires and Shropshires may have worn grey until it was replaced with two suits of khaki). The khaki coloured Foreign Service helmet was universal. Officers wore the same as the men except when mounted when they wore Bedford cord pantaloons, blue puttees and ankle boots.

The Indian regiments wore khaki blouses and knickerbockers; the 28th Bombay Native Infantry wore canvas leggings and ankle boots, the other two regiments khaki puttees and ankle boots. All wore the regimental turban. Officers wore khaki frocks, Bedford cord pantaloons and knee boots, with khaki Foreign Service helmets.

Artillery and Engineers: the Horse Artillery followed the cavalry. Royal Engineer and other Artillery officers followed the cavalry; their men wore the same as the infantry.

The Royal Navy contingent wore their normal blue jumpers, with white trousers, canvas gaiters and ankle boots, with straw sennet hats. Officers again wore white tunics and trousers, gaiters and ankle boots, with white helmets.

The Madras Sappers and Miners were described at Hashin as wearing their scarlet tunics with blue trousers and black turbans (or 'duptas') but they are likely to have worn khaki in the later stages of the campaign.

General: The brown Sam Browne belt, with single strap worn over the right shoulder, was almost universal for officers except in the Guards where twin braces (one over each shoulder) were worn.

All ranks were issued with blue goggles (often worn looped round the helmet for convenience), neck covers for attachment to the helmet, veils against flies, and padded spine pads worn outside the frock against the heat.

Officers took with them, for undress wear, red or blue serge frocks or patrol jackets, and blue trousers, with undress forage caps or pill-boxes.

Cloth pagris were worn round the helmets, different coloured pagris denoting the different arms as follows:

Cavalry – khaki with green twisted through it
Infantry – khaki with colouring determined by Commanding officers
Artillery – all blue
Engineers – red and blue
Commissariat and Transport – khaki
Divisional staff – khaki, with dark blue
Brigade staff – khaki, with red
Cavalry staff – red
Other administrative staff – khaki

Appendix 4

Biographical Notes

Baker, Valentine (1827-87). Commissioned Ceylon Rifles 1848. Dismissed British Army 1875, joined Turkish Army and fought in Russo-Turkish War 1877-78. Transferred to Egyptian Gendarmerie 1882.

Baring, Evelyn, 1st Earl of Cromer (1841-1917). Commissioned Royal Artillery 1861. Private Secretary to Viceroy of India 1872-76, Financial Member of Viceroy's Council 1880-83, Agent, Consul General and Minister Plenipotentiary in Egypt 1883-1907. Baron 1892, Viscount 1898, Earl 1901.

Barrow, Percy Henry Stanley (1848-86). Commissioned 19th Hussars 1868. Service in Zulu War 1879, First Boer War 1881, Sudan 1884, Nile Expedition 1884-85. Lieutenant Colonel 1883. Died of after effects of wounds received at El Teb in 1886.

Buller, Redvers Stanley (1839-1908). Commissioned King's Royal Rifle Corps 1858. Service in Second China War 1860, Red River Expedition 1870, Ashanti Expedition 1873-74, Sixth Kaffir War 1878, Zulu War (VC) 1879, First Boer War 1881, Egypt 1882, Nile Expedition 1884-85, Second Boer War 1899-1900. Major General 1884, KCMG 1882. QMG War Office 1887-90, Adjutant General 1890-97, Commanded troops in South Africa 1899, Aldershot Command 1901-07. General 1896, retired 1906.

Burnaby, Frederick Gustavus (1842-85). Commissioned Royal Horse Guards 1859. Service in Russo-Turkish War 1877, Sudan 1884, Nile Expedition 1884-85. Lieutenant Colonel 1880. Killed at Abu Klea 1885.

Chermside, Herbert Charles (1850-1929). Commissioned Royal Engineers 1868. Service in Russo-Turkish War 1877-78, Egypt 1882, Sudan 1884-85, Second Boer War 1900-01. Military Consul Asia Minor 1878-80, Egyptian Army 1880, Governor General Red Sea Littoral 1884-86, Military Attaché Constantinople 1889-96, Military Commissioner and Commander Crete 1897-99, Governor of Queensland 1901-05. Major General 1898, KCMG 1897. Lieutenant General 1901.

Clarke, Andrew (1822-1902). Commissioned Royal Engineers 1844. Service in New Zealand 1847-48. Surveyor General Victoria 1853-57, Director of Engineering Works Admiralty 1864-73, Governor, Straits Settlements 1873-75, Public Works Member of Viceroy's Council, India 1875-80, Inspector of Works, War Office 1882-85. KCMG 1873, Major General 1885, Lieutenant General 1886.

Davis, John (1832-1901). Commissioned 35th Foot 1852. Service in Mutiny 1858-59, Sudan 1884-85. Major General 1883, KCB 1885.

Ewart, Henry Peter (1838-1928). Commissioned Life Guards 1858. Service in Egypt 1882, Sudan 1885. Major General and KCB 1885, baronet 1910.

Fremantle, Arthur James Lyon (1835-1901). Commissioned 70th Foot 1852, transferred to Coldstream Guards 1853. Service in Sudan 1884-85. Major General 1882, KCMG 1894. Scottish District 1893-94, Governor of Malta 1894-99. General 1894.

Graham, Gerald (1831-99). Commissioned Royal Engineers 1850. Service in Crimea (VC) 1854-56, Second China War 1860, Egypt 1882, Sudan 1884-85. Major General 1881, KCB 1882, Lieutenant General 1884, retired 1890.

Granville, George Leveson Gower, 2nd Earl (1815-91). Under Secretary, Foreign Affairs 1840-41, Secretary of State for Foreign Affairs 1851-52, Lord President 1852-54, Secretary of State for Colonies 1868-70, for Foreign Affairs 1870-74, 80-85, for Colonies 1891.

Greaves, George Richards (1831-1922). Commissioned 70th Foot 1852. Service in Mutiny 1857-58, New Zealand 1862-66, Ashanti Expedition 1873-74, Sudan 1885. Adjutant General India 1879-85, commanded division of Bengal Army 1886-90, Commander-in-Chief Bombay 1890-93. KCMG 1881, Major General 1882, General and retired 1896.

Hartington, Spencer Compton Cavendish, Marquess of, and later Duke of Devonshire (1833-1908). Under Secretary, War Office 1863-66, Secretary of State for India 1880-82, for War 1882-85, Lord Privy Seal 1895-1903.

Hewett, William Nathan Wright (1834-88). Joined Navy 1847. Service in Second Burma War 1852, Crimea (VC) 1854-56, Ashanti Expedition 1873-74, Egypt 1882, Sudan 1884. KCB 1874, Rear Admiral 1878. Commander-in-Chief, East Indies 1882-84, Channel Fleet 1886-88. Vice Admiral 1884.

Hicks, William (1830-83). Commissioned Bombay Fusiliers 1849. Service in Mutiny 1857-58, Abyssinian Expedition 1867. Lieutenant Colonel 1874. Assistant Adjutant General, Bombay Army 1877-80.

Hudson, John (1833-93). Commissioned 97th Foot 1853. Service in Persian War 1856-57, Mutiny 1857-58, Abyssinian Expedition 1868, Second Afghan War 1878-80. Major General 1886, KCB 1886, Lieutenant General 1892. Commander-in-Chief Bombay Army 1893.

M'Neill, John Carstairs (1831-1904). Commissioned Bengal Infantry 1850. Service in Mutiny 1857-58, New Zealand (VC) 1861-65, Red River Expedition 1870, Ashanti 1873-74, Egypt 1882, Sudan 1885. KCMG 1880, Major General 1882.

Stephenson, Frederick Charles Arthur (1821-1911). Commissioned Scots Fusilier Guards 1837. Service in Crimea 1854-56, Second China War 1860. Major General 1868, KCB 1884, General 1885. Commander-in-Chief Egyptian Army 1883-87.

Stewart, Herbert (1843-85). Commissioned 37th Foot 1863. Service in Zulu War, First Boer War 1881, Egypt 1882, Sudan 1884, Nile Expedition 1884-85. KCB 1884, Major General 1885. Mortally wounded at Metemmeh 1885.

Wilson, Arthur Knyvet (1842-1921). Joined Royal Navy 1855. Service in Crimea 1855-56, Second China War 1860, Egypt 1882, Sudan (VC) 1884. Rear Admiral 1895, KCB 1901, Vice Admiral 1901, Admiral of Fleet 1907. Commander-in-Chief, Channel Fleet 1901-07, First Sea Lord 1910-12.

Wolseley, Garnet Joseph, 1st Viscount (1833-1913). Commissioned 12th Foot 1852. Service in Second Burma War 1852-53, Crimea 1854-56, Mutiny 1857-58, Second China War 1860, Red River Expedition 1870, Ashanti 1873-74, Zulu War 1879, Egypt 1882, Nile Expedition 1884-85. KCMG 1870, Major General 1874. QMG War Office 1881-82, Adjutant General 1882-90, Commander-in-Chief Ireland 1890-95, Commander-in-Chief British Army 1895-1900. Field Marshal and Viscount 1885.

Select Bibliography
(All books published in London except where otherwise stated)

A. **Official Papers (published)**

C-4280 Egypt No 2 *Correspondence respecting British military operations in the Soudan*. HMSO 1885.

C-4324 (1885) *Correspondence respecting offer by the Colonies of troops for service in the Soudan*. HMSO 1885.

C-4325 *Agreement between the Secretary of State for War and Messieurs Lucas and Aird for the construction of a line of railway from Suakin towards Berber*. HMSO 1885.

C-4345 Egypt No 9 *Further correspondence respecting British military operations in the Soudan*. HMSO 1885.

C-4437 (1885) *Correspondence respecting offers by the Colonies of troops for service in the Soudan*. HMSO 1885.

C-5014 *Report of the Committee on Cutlasses and Cutlass Sword Bayonets supplied to the Royal Navy*. HMSO 1887.

Special Committee on Small Arms: report on the jamming of cartridges in Martini-Henry rifles and complaints with regard to bayonets in Egypt. War Office 1886.

Suakin (Cost of military expedition): Return by the War Office, 19 November 1885. HMSO 1885.

B. **Official Papers (unpublished)**

The Insurrection of the False Prophet (4 parts, 1881-1884). Intelligence Branch, War Office.

Diary of principal events at Suakin (5 parts, April 1884-March 1885). Intelligence Branch, War Office.

Report to accompany sketch map of routes between Suakin and Berber (compiled by Lieutenant J.J. Leverson). Intelligence Branch, War Office, 4 January 1884.

Précis of information regarding the water supply on the Suakin-Berber route (compiled by Major Talbot Cole). Intelligence Branch, War Office, 21 January 1885.

Report on the principal caravan routes from Egypt and the Red Sea to Berber and Khartoum (compiled by Captain Leverson). Intelligence Branch, War Office, 23 May 1884.

Correspondence relative to the expedition to Suakin 1884 (Reference 0959). War Office 1884.

Proceedings of the Confidential Mobilisation Committee (1884).

Proceedings of the Confidential Mobilisation Committee (117th-121st, 124th days, 1885).

Proceedings of a Sub-Committee of the Confidential Mobilisation Committee on water supply at and from Suakin (1885).

Staff, Special Service Officers and Officers of the various Departments; and also a return showing the strength of the Force detailed for the Suakin Expedition. Horse Guards, War Office, 7 March 1885.

Despatches from Lieutenant General Sir G. Graham to the Secretary of State for War (21st March to 30th May 1885). War Office 1885.

Diary of the Suakin Expedition 1885, compiled in the QMG's Department. HMSO 1885.

Action at To-Frik, 22nd March 1885. Intelligence Branch, War Office, 5 October 1885.

P/2565 Government of India Military Department Proceedings: Suakin 1885. India Office Records.

L/Mil/7/6926-6948 (Collection 152) Military Department Records – Loan of Indian troops to the Sudan. India Office Records.

P/5251 Government of India Military Department Proceedings: Indian Military and Marine: Suakin 1896-1897. India Office Records.

Remarks on the working of machine guns on shore by naval brigades. Admiralty (G Branch) (No 18) 1884.

PRO WO 32/8380 Parliamentary Questions on Sudan.

C. Private unpublished sources

NAM 7003-2 *Letters of Sergeant Danby, 10th Hussars* 1884.

NAM 6807-269 *Letters of Private Fergusson , 20th Hussars* 1885.

NAM 8111-30 *Papers of the Edwards family.*

NAM 8107-16 *Memoirs of Private Starr, 10th Hussars.*

Diary of Lieutenant James Drummond-Hay, Coldstream Guards (in the private possession of Brigadier P.N.R. Stewart-Richardson).

DRL3/2783 *Letter of Private Thomas Mulready.* Australian War Memorial.

DRL3/1936 *Letter of Sergeant A. Butler.* Australian War Memorial.

Wolseley Papers, Hove Library.

D. General Background

Colborne, Colonel J. *With Hicks Pasha in the Soudan* 1884.

Hill, Richard *Egypt in the Sudan 1820-1881* 1959.

Holt, P.M. *The Mahdiist State in the Sudan 1881-1898.* Second edition, Oxford 1976.

Jackson, H.C. *Osman Digna* 1926.

MacMichael, H.A. *A History of the Arabs in the Sudan* 2 vols. Cambridge 1922.

Warner, Philip *Dervish: the rise and fall of an African empire* 1973.

Wingate, F.R. *Mahdiism and the Egyptian Sudan.* Second edition, 1968.

Zulfo, Ismat Hasan *Karari: The Sudanese account of the battle of Omdurman* 1980.

E. Military Operations

Arthur, Sir George *The Life and Letters of Lord and Lady Wolseley* 1922.
Burleigh, Bennett *Desert Warfare* 1884.
Colville, Colonel E.H. *History of the Sudan Campaign* 2 vols. HMSO 1889.
De Cosson, Captain E.A. *Days and Nights of Service with Sir Gerald Graham's Field Force at Suakin* 1886.
Galloway, William *The Battle of Tofrek* 1887.
(Gambier-Parry, Captain E.) *Suakin 1885* 1885.
Gordon, John *My Six Years with the Black Watch 1881-1887* Boston, 1929.
Keown-Boyd, Henry *A Good Dusting* 1986.
Preston, Adrian *In Relief of Gordon: Lord Wolseley's Campaign Journal of the Khartoum Relief Expedition 1884-1885* 1967.
Royle, Charles *The Egyptian Campaigns 1882-1885*. Revised edition 1900.
Sartorious, Ernestine *Three months in the Soudan* 1885.
Symonds, Julian *England's Pride* 1965.
Vetch, Colonel R.H. *Life, Letters and Diary of Lieutenant General Sir Gerald Graham* 1901.
Wylde, A.B. *'83 to '87 in the Soudan* 2 vols. 1888.

F. Regimental Histories

Biddulph, John *The Nineteenth and their times* 1879.
Marling, Colonel Sir P. *Rifleman and Hussar* 1931.
Liddell, R.S. *The Memoirs of the Tenth Royal Hussars* 1891.
Petre, E. Lorraine *The Royal Berkshire Regiment* Vol 1, Reading, 1925.
Sandes, Lieutenant Colonel E.W.C. *The Royal Engineers in Egypt and the Sudan* Chatham, 1937.
Wylly, Colonel H.C. *The York and Lancaster Regiment 1758-1910* 2 vols. Privately printed, 1930.

G. Articles

Army Quarterly
Clark, Peter 'The Hicks Pasha Expedition' October 1978, pp470-78.
Journal of Imperial and Commonwealth History
Preston, Adrian 'Wolseley, the Khartoum Relief Expedition and the Defence of India 1885-1900' May 1978, pp254-80.
Journal of the Royal United Services Institution
Wingate, Sir R. 'Two African Battles. Sheikan, 4th and 5th November 1883' February 1964.
Military Chest
Priest, Graham 'The Inferior English Bayonet?' Vol 5, No 3, pp30-32.
Myatt, Major F. 'The Battle of Tofrek, 22 March 1885' Vol 4, No 2, pp27-29.
Royal Engineers Journal
Green, Captain A.O. 'From Cairo to Trinkitat with the Suakin Field Force' Vol XIV, pp75-76, 99-102.

Times Correspondent 'Balloon Work in the Sudan' Vol XV, p114.

Kundhardt, Captain H.G. 'Notes on the Suakin-Berber Railway' Vol XV, pp97-100.

Templer, Major J.F.B. 'Balloon work on active service' Vol XV, p119.

Cavendish, Anne. 'Nile' Vol 98, pp243-56.

Journal of Society for Army Historical Research

Barthorp, Michael 'The Battle of Tofrek' Vol LXIII (1985), pp1-10.

Sudan Notes and Records

Hill, R.L. 'The Suakin-Berber Railway' Vol XX, pp107-25.

Montagu-Stuart-Wortley, Major General, 'My reminiscences of Egypt and the Sudan' Vol XXXIV.

Bloss, J.F.E. 'The Story of Suakin' Vol XX, pp247-80.

Soldiers of the Queen

Johnson, D.M. 'The imprisonment, death and re-burial of Osman Digna' Vol 44, pp17-19.

H. Miscellaneous

Report of the operations of the British National Society for Aid to the Sick and Wounded in War during the Egyptian Campaign 1884-1885 1886.

Gordon, Major L.L. *British Battles and Medals* 5th edition, 1979.

Inglis, K.S. *The Rehearsal* Sydney, 1985.

Stanley, Peter (ed). But little glory: The New South Wales contingent in the Sudan, 1885 Canberra, 1985.

Temple, B.A. and Skennerton, I.D. *A Treatise on the British Military Martini: the Martini-Henry 1869-c.1900* Burbank, Australia, 1983.

Spiers, E.M. *The Late Victorian Army* Manchester, 1992.

Index

(ranks are those held at the time)

227

228